Monsters and Monarchs

Monsters and Monarchs

Serial Killers in Classical
Myth and History

DEBBIE FELTON

University of Texas Press ⟡ *Austin*

Requests for permission to reproduce material from this work should be sent to:
    Permissions
    University of Texas Press
    P.O. Box 7819
    Austin, TX 78713–7819
    utpress.utexas.edu/rp-form

♾ The paper used in this book meets the minimum requirements of
ANSI/NISO Z39.48–1992 (R1997) (Permanence of Paper).

Library of Congress Cataloging-in-Publication Data
Names: Felton, Debbie, author.
Title: Monsters and monarchs : serial killers in classical myth and history / Debbie
    Felton.
Description: First edition. | Austin : University of Texas Press, 2021. | Includes
    bibliographical references and index.
Identifiers: LCCN 2020056879
    ISBN 978-1-4773-0379-5 (cloth)
    ISBN 978-1-4773-2357-1 (paperback)
    ISBN 978-1-4773-2305-2 (library ebook)
    ISBN 978-1-4773-2306-9 (non-library ebook)
Subjects: LCSH: Serial murderers—History. | Serial murders—History.
Classification: LCC HV6507 .F45 2021 | DDC 364.152/32—dc23
LC record available at https://lccn.loc.gov/2020056879

doi:10.7560/303795

Contents

Theseus attacking Procrustes with the killer's own ax. Greek red-figure vase, 470–460 BCE, by the Alkimachos Painter.

Monsters and Monarchs

Serial Killers in the Ancient World

When I first suggested a book about serial killers in classical antiquity, the typical (and understandable) response was, "You can't be serious!" The general sentiment was that serial killers did not exist back then, that serial murder was a problem arising from the ills of modern society. But I had read stories in Greek and Roman literature describing characters and behaviors that sounded startlingly similar to modern accounts of serial murder: men, and occasionally women, who killed a number of people over a period of time, usually with a consistent method, and often targeting specific victim types, such as young men or young women. Sometimes the murders also included a sexual component and/or mutilation of the victims' bodies. Sometimes the killers took "trophies," such as body parts. The ancient authors recounted tales of serial ax murder, serial poisoning, and collections of decapitated heads. And I was not the only one who had noticed the similarities between modern serial killers and various mytho-historical characters described by Greek and Roman writers. Many modern, general-audience compilations of serial killers (such as Michael Newton's *The Encyclopedia of Serial Killers* and Harold Schechter's *The Serial Killer Files*), besides pointing out instances of mutilation murder going back as early as medieval Europe, have also given a nod to ancient Rome by listing serial poisoners, such as Locusta of Gaul, or various bloodthirsty emperors, such as Caligula and Nero, as prototypes for the modern serial killer. In short, the dozens of cases from classical antiquity seemed well worth investigating. Why were the Greeks and Romans telling stories like this, and how might such stories inform modern conceptions about serial murder?

The sources for these stories ranged over a thousand years, from Homer in Archaic Greece down through the Roman Empire. And they ranged across genres and styles: myth, history, biography, drama—whether poetry or prose, the same types of character and behavior turned up repeatedly, in different forms, but still consistent over the centuries. The question then became one of approach. Modern criminology has a vast advantage: behavioral profilers can interview convicted serial killers in an attempt to understand their psychology. Profilers can investigate whether a serial killer had an unusually difficult childhood, suffered any physical trauma (such as a blow to the head), heard voices telling them to kill, got sexual gratification from killing, and many other similarly relevant questions. The Greek and Roman authors rarely went into this level of detail, and the fields of psychology and criminology as we know them did not exist back then. But some ancient authors nevertheless provide surprising psychological insights into the motivations of murderers, enough to show that the Greeks and Romans were well aware of serial murder as an unusually deviant behavior. They took the killing of (most) fellow humans very seriously, had laws addressing different kinds of homicide, and recognized serial murder when they saw it, even if they did not have a specific expression, such as "serial killing," to describe it. In fact, our phrase "serial killer" and related terminology did not exist until the 1980s, and before then criminologists struggled to come up with an appropriate term for multiple murders that presented specific patterns and suggested a certain type of perpetrator.

The widespread and ongoing modern interest in serial killing (even without that useful phrase at hand) apparently started with Jack the Ripper back in 1880s London and the sensationalistic newspaper reports about the ghastly mutilation murders of prostitutes in Whitechapel. The fact that authorities never apprehended the killer turned the crimes into a gruesomely appealing unsolved mystery that spawned all sorts of theories about who Jack really was. An accomplished but insane doctor? A psychopathically misogynistic member of the aristocracy? His identity remains unknown to this day. But since the time of the Whitechapel murders, as evidenced by the number of books, slasher films, TV shows, and podcasts about serial killing, public interest in the phenomenon has scarcely waned, partially because several new cases of serial murder come to light nearly every single year. The Museum of Death, with branches in Hollywood, California (closed for relocation as of this writing) and New Orleans, Louisiana, showcases serial killers and their artwork and has proved terribly popular despite (or perhaps because of) visitors reportedly fainting at the graphic nature of many displays, such as the alleged head of modern French "Bluebeard" Henri Landru.

But the public's fascination with serial killers probably goes back even further. In recent years, a number of criminologists and other scholars have theorized that various legends and folktales of early modern Europe may obliquely refer to serial killers, centuries before Jack the Ripper prowled the East End. Retired FBI criminal profiler John Douglas neatly summarizes this theory in his book *Mindhunter*: "Serial murder may, in fact, be a much older phenomenon than we realize. The stories and legends that have filtered down about witches and werewolves and vampires may have been a way of explaining outrages so hideous that no one in the small and close-knit towns of Europe and early America could comprehend the perversities we now take for granted. Monsters had to be supernatural creatures. They couldn't be just like us."[1] Yet because so many people still consider serial killing to be an ailment or symptom of the decadent modern world, no one has taken a close look at the stories from classical antiquity and considered the possibility that two and three thousand years ago or more serial killers roamed the world, and that such discernible conditions as sociopathy, with its lack of moral compass, or other conditions causing a similar lack of empathy existed back then just as now.[2] This book aims to fill that void by examining evidence from ancient Greece and Rome that hints at or outright describes what would now be called serial killing. Some of the stories describe historical figures, such as Greek tyrants and Roman emperors, who, filtered through the biased perceptions of disgruntled citizens, strongly match our understanding of serial killers. Other stories, told as myths to children and adults to help shape their roles as productive members of society, present heroic characters who face and vanquish monstrous creatures hardly distinguishable from modern-day mutilation murderers.

The first three chapters provide necessary background information about the general nature of serial killing, starting in chapter 1 with sources for our evidence from classical antiquity and an explanation of why and how the ancient evidence remains relevant and significant. Chapter 2 then takes a look at what might define a "serial killer" according to modern law enforcement agencies such as the FBI. That is, how do authorities know when they are dealing with a serial killer? How many victims do these killers need to have, and over what length of time? And what marks the difference between a serial killer and someone who kills more than a hundred people en masse? As it turns out, many serial killer characteristics listed by criminal profilers, such as a specific modus operandi, appear in the stories from ancient Greece and Rome, hardly changed over the millennia, providing a clear enough picture of who is or is not a serial killer. Chapter 3 considers the motivations of serial killers: Why do they do what they do? Are they motivated by revenge, greed, sexual compulsion, or something else entirely? Are they all psychopaths or sociopaths? And how can anyone know what motivated the killers from classical antiquity when the writers who recorded their stories were not trained as criminologists or psychologists? Here, too, there is more evidence than expected regarding the inner thoughts of the killers. Even if the ancient authors did not realize it, they noted a pattern common among serial killers that includes movement from lesser crimes in childhood (such as theft) to bolder crimes in teen years (such as assault and battery) to incredibly violent crimes in adulthood (such as rape and murder). In some cases, the authors even provide clues as to motivation; the emperor Nero, for example, most likely had what Freudians would consider extraordinarily serious mother issues.

Chapter 4 delves more deeply into ancient Greek attitudes toward homicide and into the evidence for serial killing in ancient Greece. The Athenians, for example, developed several distinctions among types of homicide, and had no fewer than five different courts to deal with the various issues involved. They recognized that some killers committed multiple offences, and they even described the devastating effects that such serial murder had on the community. The penalty for intentionally killing a fellow Athenian citizen, depending on the circumstances and intent, was usually death, and then as now the perpetrator could be put to death only once. "Citizen" is the operative word here: the Greeks and Romans valued human life, but much more so when that life belonged to one of their own. They were far less concerned when the victims were foreigners or slaves. In fact, the latter instances were at various points in history legally considered "loss of property" rather than homicide. But whereas the Athenians took homicide seriously enough to create five separate courts to prosecute the crime, and other Greek city-states had detailed law codes of their own, the Romans demonstrated a high level of indifference toward homicide except in exceedingly prominent cases. Chapter 5 shows how the Romans concerned themselves primarily with citizens and even more so with the safety of the state as a whole, as serial and mass murder bothered them mainly when it posed a threat to public and political order. Also, as chapter 6 explains, unlike Greece, Rome experienced an unusually high number of serial and mass poisonings, reflecting not only the growing availability of many different poisons but also the popularity, especially within the Roman imperial family, of using a difficult-to-trace method to get rid of undesirable relatives as well as personal and political enemies.

After considering these cultural and social contexts, the discussion turns from historical sources to myths, legends, and folktales. Chapters 7 and 8 focus on two prominent Greek heroes: Heracles and Theseus. Although famous for his Twelve Labors, which involved fighting a number of monstrous animals, plus the Amazons (apparently the patriarchal society of ancient

Greece considered a foreign tribe of self-governing warrior women to be something monstrous), Heracles had a number of unusual side adventures in which he encountered extremely menacing human opponents. These monstrous men took pleasure in exerting their power over others, in torturing their victims, and in killing them. Several of them showed a predilection for taking their victims' heads as trophies. Heracles's younger cousin Theseus, before becoming celebrated for slaying the Minotaur in the Cretan labyrinth, encountered and defeated half a dozen unusually dangerous criminals who had methodically killed and mutilated untold numbers of unsuspecting travelers before Theseus came along. In the myth cycles of Heracles and Theseus, these sinister opponents could represent various real-life concerns, such as the tension between nature and encroaching civilization, the dangers of traveling alone in wildernesses where bandits prowled, and the political enmity between early Greek city-states. At the same time, the specific details present in these stories show a disconcerting awareness of serial mutilation murder as an identifiable, real, and terrifying phenomenon.

Moving from general myths to local legends, the next two chapters look at stories confined to specific locations in the ancient Greek world. Chapter 9, in considering how the Olympic sport of boxing might have provided a productive outlet for otherwise hostile impulses, focuses on two stories that present their antagonists in serial killer form. In the first, a foreign king shows his fondness for beating visitors to a bloody pulp until one of Jason's Argonauts finally defeats him. In the second, boxing proves useful in defeating a revenant—a "solid" ghost or walking corpse, literally one who has "come back" from the dead—that exhibits many behaviors also found in serial killers. Chapter 10 discusses several creatures, such as dragons and the Theban Sphinx, that fit into the theory explained by John Douglas: the possibility that monsters of legend had some basis in serial mutilation murders that affected entire communities.

Chapter 11 examines more explicit examples of serial killing in classical myth and history, focusing on serial slaying of suitors and spouses. Looking first at the folktale motif group known as "tests connected with marriage," we find evidence that many such tales from around the world and especially from ancient Greece involve the systematic killing of unwanted or unworthy suitors who are executed when they fail either to solve a riddle or to meet another type of challenge posed to them.[3] The chapter also includes stories from antiquity about "Black Widows" and "Bluebeards," serial killers who target their husbands and wives, respectively, often getting away with murders for years before authorities catch up with them. Aside from indicating an awareness that serial murder occurs in actuality, these stories also tend to reflect anxieties about common rites of passage, such as marriage and childbirth. Fathers have difficulty letting daughters go, mothers warn daughters about the dangers of pregnancy and bearing children, young women fear loveless unions and domestic abuse, and men feel resentment when scorned by women. Such concerns also provide the motivation for many real-life serial murders.

Chapter 12 turns to an exceptionally disturbing kind of serial killing: the murder of children. Modern history has recorded many appalling cases of serial child-murder, including those perpetrated by grandfatherly rapist and cannibal Albert Fish, notorious couple Ian Brady and Myra Hindley, and the Atlanta child-murderer. And serial child mutilation murder appears to have occurred in antiquity, too. The Greeks and Romans usually attributed such deaths to witches and similarly malevolent but clearly supernatural creatures. So, on the one hand, stories about witches and child-killing demons provided an explanation and outlet for grief for infants who died in utero or in the cradle from natural causes, such as SIDS (Sudden Infant Death Syndrome). On the other hand, bits and pieces of material evidence, such as tombstone inscriptions (epitaphs), indicate that slightly older children—from toddlers through early teens—were mysteriously snatched away, only to be found dead and mutilated under suspicious circumstances that in reality point more toward pederastic serial killers than to so-called witches.

The last chapter provides a broad overview of where the Greek and Roman cases fit into the chronological and global history of serial killing. For a very long time, criminologists and psychologists believed serial killing to be a modern phenomenon particularly symptomatic of Western culture. But with the increasing availability of various media, such as newspapers, radio, television, and the internet, and as countries around the world, such as China and Russia, allowed increasing journalistic freedom, wider dissemination of information has proved serial killing to be a global and long-standing phenomenon going back not just centuries but millennia. Despite having no forensic (i.e., scientific) evidence of serial murder from classical antiquity, literary, historical, and material evidence from Greece and Rome shows that people back then experienced and understood serial murder. Even if it is impossible to scientifically prove one solid, real case after two or three thousand years, literary and historical accounts clearly show that the Greeks' and Romans' familiarity with this type of crime allowed them to describe it in their stories as an outlet for various cultural anxieties.

Although this study includes a lot of material from classical antiquity, this book is not intended specifically for classical scholars or other hardcore academics. I have no background in criminology or psychology; anyone expecting a nuanced study of the criminal mind will be disappointed. Rather, this discussion is intended for anyone in the general public interested in the history of serial killing as a cultural phenomenon. To this end, ancient examples are compared and contrasted with modern cases throughout. Additionally, certain academic aspects of this research have been kept to a minimum, such as excessive footnotes, exhaustive lists of ancient and modern sources, and technical jargon.

All translations from Greek and Latin are my own, except where otherwise noted.

CHAPTER 1

Identifying Serial Killers Then and Now

A man lurked in the night shadows by the roadside, contemplating potential victims, intent on robbing the next vulnerable traveler to pass by. But
this highway bandit differed from most. Although typical brigands of his
day occasionally resorted to killing, they usually did so only if their victims put up a serious fight. This man, however, did not murder his prey for
their wealth; he enjoyed torturing them much more than he enjoyed stealing their money. When he finished, he cut their bodies to pieces. Yet by
day no one ever considered this man capable of such crimes; his friends and
neighbors thought him polite and mild mannered, and so his objectionable
nocturnal activities evaded detection for a very long time.

This story comes to us from a fourth-century CE fictionalized court case
called "Against a Murderer," presented to Greek schoolboys as a rhetorical exercise and intended as a model of both persuasive argument and good
writing. The story's author, Libanius, was widely admired for his excellent
prose. But the speech's sensationalistic contents, including references to torture and mutilation, probably interested the students more than the virtuoso
writing style did. Libanius invented the criminal described in this speech,
but must have based him on a real-life criminal type recognizable across the
Roman Empire; otherwise, the exercise would have served no purpose. And
this type of criminal may sound surprisingly familiar to a modern audience:
without knowing that Libanius wrote the speech more than 1,500 years
ago, you might think it took place yesterday, given the similarities between
Libanius's fictional murderer and modern serial killers. People considered Ted Bundy attractive and charming, and no one would have guessed
that he took great pleasure in torturing and killing young women—more
than a dozen, back in the mid-1970s. In 2005, a man of similarly innocuous demeanor, Dennis Rader, turned out to be the (somewhat redundantly

named) "BTK Killer" ("Bind, Torture, Kill") who had terrorized the Wichita, Kansas, area in the 1970s and 1980s. Rader murdered at least ten people, mostly female, but outwardly behaved like such an upstanding citizen that he never fell under suspicion. Though neighbors described him as occasionally arrogant, Rader was a highly respected family man who served as president of his church and led his son's Cub Scout troop. If he had not continued to taunt the police by sending eleven letters to them over the course of several months in 2004–2005, they might never have caught him. Describing a serial killer as a "polite neighbor" is now so common as to be cliché, but the cliché points to one especially frightening aspect of serial killers: how normal so many of them can seem, at least superficially. In contrast to the isolated, angry, disturbed young person or adult who attacks multiple people at once in a school, movie theater, or mall, serial killers often blend into society very well rather than coming across as the sort of "social misfit" who is known to commit mass murder. The most widely accepted definition of a serial killer is oddly brief and broad: someone who unlawfully kills at least two individuals on separate occasions over a certain time period, usually by the same method. This definition involves various nuances, such as the difference between serial mutilation murder and serial poisoning, and certainly there are differences between a hired assassin and a secret murderer, though both can be characterized as carrying out killings on a regular basis. So, for now, here is a description that may provide the best general indicator of a serial murderer at work: at least two people killed over a period of time by methods similar enough to suggest the same actor (or actors) committed them, outside of any legal context (such as warfare), with the killings often accompanied by a sexual element and/or bodily mutilation (which usually distinguishes them from assassinations).[1] All the more significant, then, that Libanius's account and others like it have been around for thousands of years.

Recognizing that serial killing is a much older phenomenon than originally thought is important inasmuch as such acknowledgment can help counteract the widespread misconception that the ills of modern society have not only created the "serial killer" type of criminal but also caused serial killings to proliferate. A discussion about serial murder in the ancient world allows us to reexamine these assumptions and their underlying reasons. Such reflection can also help us reassess why modern society has an ongoing fascination with serial killers. For a long time, news coverage of these crimes received an inordinate amount of attention compared to other homicides, but in the 2010s increasingly frequent mass shootings drew attention away from serial murder.[2] Yet the odd gruesomeness of such murders, the disturbing psychology behind them, the media's sensationalistic reporting, and movies portraying both fictional and real-life serial killers all continue to galvanize our attention. It is therefore worth continuing to ask not only why serial killers have apparently existed throughout recorded human history (and probably prehistory) but also why people have been interested in them for just as long. At the same time, the questions of why people commit serial murders and why so many people eagerly read about such violence remain extremely complicated and lack any single answer or explanation. Serial killers come from various backgrounds and have varying motivations, and so do the people interested in reading about them. And audiences have mixed responses: revulsion, fear, curiosity, fascination.

We even have a tendency to turn some serial killers into sympathetic antiheroes, occasionally rooting for these killers and even admiring them. Audiences felt considerable sympathy for the good-looking, terribly conflicted, Mother-obsessed Norman Bates as portrayed by Anthony Perkins in Alfred Hitchcock's *Psycho* (1960),[3] and perhaps even more regarding the characterization of the younger Norman by actor Freddie Highmore in the A&E television series *Bates Motel* (2013–2017). In the original 1959 novel *Psycho*, author Robert Bloch described Norman Bates as physically repellent, extremely creepy, and interested in pornography—an intentionally unsympathetic characterization. Hitchcock innovatively and controversially changed the character to an attractive young man so that audiences would sympathize with the character. Similarly, serial killer Hannibal Lecter as played by Anthony Hopkins in 1991's *Silence of the Lambs* was so charismatic that, despite his cannibalistic murders, audiences rooted for him not only to escape his captors but even to kill the film's most annoying character, the incompetent and patronizing Dr. Frederick Chilton (played by character actor Anthony Heald). Similarly popular was Dexter Morgan, a serial killer who targeted only other criminals, as depicted in a series of novels by author Jeff Lindsay and in the television series *Dexter* (Showtime, 2006–2013). The highly successful show, which hinged on Michael C. Hall's portrayal of Dexter, is as of this writing scheduled for a reboot (planned for a fall 2021 release). These are only a few examples of *fictional* serial killers who became audience favorites. Real-life serial killers often receive similarly rapt attention when their stories make news headlines, as Ted Bundy and Dennis Rader did in their day and as ex-cop Joseph James DeAngelo ("The Golden State Killer") did in the late 2010s. Some people truly idolize these real-life killers, feeling sympathy for their alleged "causes" and admiration for their cleverness, and collecting memorabilia in the form of serial killer trading cards or artwork produced by the killers, such as John Wayne Gacy's clown self-portraits. True crime collectibles can fetch high prices, sometimes in the tens of thousands of dollars.[4] Psychologists also note an increasing awareness of *hybristophilia*, a sexual fetishism or fanaticism in which people—often, but not exclusively females—become sexually attracted to violent offenders such as serial killers, send them fan mail in prison, and even marry them. Ted Bundy had many female admirers and married one while he was still on trial. Charles Manson—who directed the 1969 Tate–LaBianca murders, killed at least two people himself on other occasions, and spent from 1971 until his death in 2017 imprisoned in maximum security—received thousands of fan letters during his nearly five decades in prison. The current interest in serial killers (unfortunately) shows no signs of slowing.[5] This is just one of many reasons to investigate the earliest recognizable accounts of such crimes, including those from ancient Greece and Rome.

Two important questions frequently come up when trying to make arguments about what motivated people in antiquity, and these questions apply both to the serial killers and to the people who told stories about them. First, how can we discuss anything about the psychology of long-dead people whose minds we cannot examine through direct physical evidence and interviews? In other words, how can we apply modern psychological constructs to the ancient Greeks and Romans? Most current knowledge about how serial killers' minds work comes from painstaking interviews with dozens of incarcerated serial murderers and from detailed crime scene examinations. No such evidence survives from two- and three-thousand-year-old murders. Second, how can we even begin to guess at the psychology of individuals in a society not only from a different time but from a different culture? Didn't the Greeks and Romans value life differently than we do? And what about the tens of thousands of Romans who enthusiastically watched arena games in which animals and people underwent cruel torments and were encouraged to wound and even kill each other in various imaginatively gruesome combats?

Although these objections might seem reasonable, they indicate a skewed view of both antiquity and modern times. The fact that our evidence comes from a different time and different cultural context, making certain types of methodological examination impossible, does not automatically invalidate psychological considerations. It is too easy to make the dismissive argument that stories from antiquity cannot possibly be relevant to any discussion of serial killers because we cannot conduct modern psychological studies. On the contrary, we can indeed consider what people were thinking and feeling in the ancient Mediterranean world; the human mind, human behavior, and human emotions have remained very much the same across time and cultures, even if they vary in the details. If this were not true, ancient Greek and Roman literature would not resonate with us the way it still does. Rather, modern minds can understand, analyze, and empathize with the actions and motivations of people in other historical eras. Odysseus in Homer's *Odyssey* and Medea in Euripides's *Medea* behave in ways we can understand and relate to, and they exhibit behaviors we still see today.[6] As Garrett G. Fagan has noted, this is the basis for "the celebrated timelessness of great literary works, the reason they are hailed for their deep humanity, psychological insight, and elucidation of the human condition. . . . The ability to identify with the behavior of people far removed from us chronologically, geographically and culturally is fundamental to the entire business of history."[7] It also explains why authors and artists so easily adapt such works to modern contexts: their themes and complex psychology remain relevant. And yes, the Greeks and Romans did value human life differently—but mainly in terms of "Greek" or "Roman" versus "Other" (non-Greek, non-Roman). The Roman games involved torture and execution of criminals and noncitizens, such as slaves, and arena audiences cheered for justice (as they perceived it) to be done. When taking cultural differences such as these into account, we can see that the ancient Greeks and Romans recognized the phenomenon we now call "serial killing," and we can also, to a certain extent, analyze the criminals as well as the reactions to the crimes. Evidently, we have more in common with the ancient Greeks and Romans than expected—and that is without remarking upon the similarities between the ancient gladiatorial games and modern sports that are dangerous and sometimes fatal, such as American football, car and motorcycle racing, Mixed Martial Arts (MMA), and many other spectator sports.

Stories of serial killings in antiquity come from two main sources. The first and larger source consists of classical myths, legends, and local folklore. The second consists of nonfiction works, such as rhetoric and biography, purporting to give factually accurate accounts of historical figures. But whether dealing with myth or history, it is crucial that we consider our evidence with a skeptical eye: many sources contain political and other biases, and stories take certain shapes for different reasons. Yet beneath the authors' motivations and no matter what their biases, the stories unquestionably describe what modern society recognizes as serial killers, and these stories sound unsettlingly familiar because of their similarity to real and fictional murderous characters we hear and read about on an increasingly frequent basis.

Myths, Monsters, and Monstrous Behavior

The town of Thebes, a stronghold in central Greece, had a serious problem. As the largest settlement for many miles, Thebes had heavily fortified walls and seven strong city gates. Anyone attacking Thebes for its wealth would have difficulty breaching such defenses. What the Thebans had not counted on was someone or some*thing* besides the Thebans themselves watching the main road leading into the town. Travelers trying to reach the town—merchants, tourists, relatives of townsfolk—encountered a frightening creature blocking their path. This monster had the head of a woman, the body of a lion, and the wings of a giant bird. She would not let travelers pass unless they could first solve a riddle she posed: "What goes on four legs in the morning, two legs at noon, and three legs in the evening?" For a long time, no one could answer the riddle, and the creature killed them all. It was said that her victims were mainly young men and that she disposed of every single one by the same method: strangulation.

This monstrous hybrid creature was the Sphinx, whose riddle was finally solved by the Greek hero Oedipus, who replied, "Man: As an infant, he crawls on four limbs; as an adult, he walks upright; and in his old age he walks with a cane." The monster, enraged and humiliated that a mere mortal had solved her riddle, killed herself, and Thebes was saved. The Sphinx, whose name means "Strangler" in Greek, potentially represents many different things, given that monsters in myths from around the world often allegorize the chaos of the natural world, for example, as opposed to the order and restraint that man tries to impose on nature.[8] But a different, less symbolic interpretation is possible, one related to the quote from John Douglas's *Mindhunter* in the introduction. As theorized by Douglas and others, many stories of monsters from around the world may reflect an awareness or recognition of serial murder as a phenomenon. Stories associated the Theban Sphinx with a series of similar victims, killed by similar methods, within a particular geographical area at various intervals over a period of time. Some versions of her story even suggest she raped the young men. All of these elements, including the sexual aspect, describe the essence of a serial killer.

Dozens of similar stories have come down to us from ancient Greek and Roman literature—stories of local monsters terrorizing and killing the residents of nearby towns, leaving gruesome mutilation murders in their wake. This is certainly not to say that stories featuring monsters must necessarily have originated in specific, real-life incidents of serial killing. Rather, the point is that some such stories were inspired by or reveal a recognition of real crimes, a recognition that these fictions might reflect what people sometimes encountered in reality. The idea that mythical monsters such as werewolves and vampires may represent serial mutilation murderers has been gaining traction, and such a theory helps explain the unusually large number of such stories that survive from ancient times. In the Greece of three thousand years ago, people had no means of mass communication other than orally transmitted stories that were passed down from generation to generation and that, thanks to this unreliable method, changed over time. The same thing happened to stories in antiquity passed down orally for hundreds of years, until the original version mutated (often beyond recognition) or became forgotten entirely.

But the theory that mythical monsters reflect an understanding of real-life serial killing is nothing new. Many ancient Greeks themselves "rationalized" monster stories in this same way. One of them even suggested in passing that the story of the Theban Sphinx arose as a way to explain a series of local ritualized killings of young men. In the fourth century BCE, about two hundred years after the Sphinx became closely tied to Thebes and the Oedipus myth, the Greek writer Palaephatus suggested in his *Peri Apiston* (*On Unbelievable Things*) that the Sphinx was in reality a robber woman who preyed on travelers to and from Thebes. According to Palaephatus, the king of Thebes offered a reward to anyone who caught this bandit. When Oedipus—taken as a historical figure in this ancient interpretation—heard this, he organized some Theban troops, went out during the night, and ambushed her. Palaephatus says that the rest of the Oedipus myth grew up around these events.[9]

Although Palaephatus intentionally wrote down myths as a way to preserve them, many fellow Greeks criticized his rationalized interpretations. The Greeks probably preferred to think that their myths had deeper meanings and may not have enjoyed what they considered trivialization of their culturally important stories. But Palaephatus was not alone in his rather reasonable (if unimaginative) wish to point out that a creature like the Sphinx could not possibly have existed in the real world. A similar account appears in the work of the second-century CE Greek geographer and travel writer Pausanias (*Description of Greece*). His writing method included gathering oral histories, and he concluded from his interviews with local inhabitants that the legend of the Theban Sphinx was based on the true story of a female bandit who had terrorized Thebes for an extended period of time, regularly emerging from her hideout in the surrounding mountains.[10] Evidently, like Palaephatus centuries earlier, a good number of the local people in Pausanias's time were not convinced that a fantastical hybrid monster such as the Sphinx had ever really existed.

Such rationalizations of famous mythological monsters occasionally still show up in pop culture versions of the myths.[11] But even if these rationalizations have not been widely accepted, it is worth considering the possibility that a logical basis exists for them. Adrienne Mayor used this approach to great effect in her 2000 study of fossilized remains from the Mediterranean area, *The First Fossil Hunters: Paleontology in Greek and Roman Times*. Observing that clusters of dinosaur and Ice Age mammal fossils corresponded geographically with certain myths, she speculated that such creatures as griffins might have been based on fossil finds of *Protoceratops* remains, and that mammoths and mastodon fossils, with the huge nasal cavities in their skulls, could have inspired myths of the gigantic, one-eyed Cyclopes. A similarly rational explanation would oversimplify the Sphinx's story yet still provide a basis for parts of it. Sphinxes existed as fabulous creatures of the imagination in many cultures (including Egypt and the Near East), with their own meanings. The story of the Theban Sphinx, though, could have coalesced as a conflation of an already established creature from myth combined with an awareness that mutilation murder occurs in real life. As mentioned above, the theory that some monstrous creatures of myth originated from a societal recognition of real-life murders has been floated occasionally since Palaephatus's time, even if it has not received much publicity. For example, in a 1994 paper, scholar Brian Meehan suggested that the murderous monster Grendel from the Old English epic poem *Beowulf* was modeled after serial killers. Again, this is not to state definitively, as Palaephatus overtly did, that in reality a specific instance of serial murder occurred in the vicinity of Thebes, or, for that matter, in the Heorot mead hall in *Beowulf*'s sixth-century Scandinavia. Rather, the theory allows us to speculate that such murders may have occurred at various times and places in the ancient and medieval worlds, and that they were consequently—however consciously or unconsciously—incorporated into stories passed down over the years, decades, centuries, and millennia.

Classical myths and legends describe not only monsters but also human beings who commit horrendous crimes. Theseus had a series of adventures prior to his encounter with the Minotaur. On his way from southern Greece to Athens, he met several men whose behavior is best described as that of serial killers. Each of the men had his own specific method of murdering unwary travelers. In these cases, the Greeks did not depict the men themselves physically as monsters in literature and art; only their actions were monstrous. Theseus also nearly died at the hands of Medea, the princess-witch who exhibited several serial-killer characteristics. Her motives centered not on material or political gain but on the men in her life, primar-

Corrado Giaquinto (1703–1766), *Medea*. The sorceress is pictured with her wand and other paraphernalia for magic spells. At her feet lie her two murdered children.

ily the Greek hero Jason, whose quest was to fetch the Golden Fleece from Colchis, a land on the eastern edge of the Black Sea. Medea fell so in love with Jason that, after defying her father to aid Jason's theft of the fleece, she cut her own brother into pieces to facilitate Jason's escape from Colchis, dropping pieces of the body into the sea because she knew that her father would slow his naval pursuit in order to gather the body parts and give the boy a decent funeral. But when Jason brought his foreign bride back to Greece, he slowly grew disenchanted with her, despite her having borne him two sons. Whereas Medea had previously committed murder out of misguided and obsessive love for Jason, she now killed out of hatred, wanting revenge for Jason's cold rejection of her. She sent a poisonous robe to his new fiancée, the princess of Corinth, and the girl died horribly, engulfed in flame, as did her father, the king of Corinth, when he tried to help her. According to the tragedian Euripides, Medea also killed her own two sons to spite Jason and later, after fleeing to Athens, unsuccessfully tried to poison Theseus with a deadly dose of aconite when his presence threatened her relationship with Aegeus, the king of Athens, who also happened to be Theseus's father. Once again she escaped, although her ultimate fate was a matter of debate among ancient authors.

Fictional characters, such as the homicidal highwaymen Theseus meets, along with Medea and many other well-known mythological figures, were sometimes portrayed as killers for political reasons. Often they were foreigners, and depicting them in a highly negative manner served to contrast the "civilized" Greeks (as they saw themselves) with their unseemly neighbors. Sometimes these characters were fellow Greeks but enemies of Athens, the city-state from which we have inherited much surviving Greek literature. Such murderous fictional characters rest on the border between mythical monsters and historical figures intentionally depicted as serial killers.

History, Monarchs, and Murders

A number of infamous rulers, among them several Roman emperors, may well have been genuine psychopaths or sociopaths, or were at least intentionally portrayed by their various biographers as mentally unstable. According to various contemporaneous sources, Caligula exhibited sadistic behavior even as a child, sexual deviancy and cruelty as an adult, and as emperor of Rome (r. 37–41 CE) sometimes invited parents to witness the executions of their own children. He enjoyed killing people himself on occasion rather than ordering his soldiers to do it for him. But his psychological problems went far beyond mere murder. He considered himself to be a god, and his odd behavior included (supposedly) committing incest with his sisters and appointing his horse to the priesthood, with plans to promote the animal to the rank of consul. Caligula showed megalomaniacal tendencies and characteristics of narcissistic personality disorder, but he also exhibited a psychopathy considerably beyond that of most serial killers. The various political rulers in antiquity and beyond—Greek, Roman, or other (such as Julius Caesar, Genghis Khan, and Joseph Stalin)—who killed dozens, hundreds, thousands, or even millions of political rivals, disobedient citizens, and foreigners through direct or indirect means (such as disease and famine), did not necessarily act out of sadistic pleasure so much as paranoid and/or power-hungry concerns for the security of their political positions and territory. Thus, a Greek tyrant such as Periander of Corinth, who ordered his political rivals killed, or a Greek king such as Cleomenes of Sparta, regarded by his contemporaries as insane, does not exhibit serial-killer behavior. Neither does the Roman emperor Tiberius. Though notorious for the excessive number of executions he ordered over his long reign, Tiberius did not enjoy what he perceived as political necessity. Kings and emperors over the millennia have frequently ordered the (often indiscriminant) execution of anyone who, in their opinion, posed a threat, but such action constitutes abuse of power rather than epitomizing the psychology of a serial killer.

On the other hand, Nero, who, like Caligula, became emperor (r. 54–68 CE), resembles the textbook serial killer in many ways. According to his unofficial biographers, the Roman historians Tacitus and Suetonius, he demonstrated deviant behavior even in childhood. Although at first he indulged his repulsive vices secretly, later he became less concerned about hiding his behavior. As a youth he exhibited excessive cruelty, and his actions grew increasingly disturbing as he approached adulthood. He regularly started bar fights. He would throw stones and bits of broken benches during brawls, and once even cracked a man's skull during a fight. He smashed his way into shuttered shops and robbed them. He raped an unknown number of women. As he grew older, he prowled the streets in disguise at night, looking to savagely beat men as they went home after enjoying a dinner out. If they resisted, he stabbed them and threw their bodies into the sewer. He enjoyed dressing up in the skin of a wild animal and torturing both men and women by binding them naked to stakes and attacking their genitals, as if they were his prey.

Unfortunately for the Romans, even when Nero's incredibly disturbing crimes became quite well known, they could not bring him to justice. He was a member of the imperial family of Rome, a grandnephew of the emperor Claudius (r. 41–54 CE). He may even have had a hand in Claudius's death. The infirm emperor died from poisoning, and Nero liked to drop hints about the wonderful benefits of mushrooms, the food with which Claudius was poisoned. When Claudius died, Nero became emperor and had even less need to hide his depravities. For years he continued to kill people with impunity, and his victims included a large number of Roman politicians along with several more of his own family members—various cousins, his aunt, and his own mother. But the Romans eventually grew tired of Nero's appalling behavior. He became so universally hated that, finally, facing a widespread rebellion, he fled Rome, and after trying unsuccessfully to kill himself ordered one of his underlings to stab him to death. (The fellow obliged without hesitation.) Nero was thirty-one years old.

In the cases of Nero and other homicidal rulers who abused their power, much more specific information survives about their methods of killing and about their victims than survives for less infamous individuals or for mythical monsters whose behavior resembles that of serial killers. Oral transmission of stories prevailed for hundreds of years, but by the fifth century BCE written records had become more common. At this point, instead of only traditional stories of murderous monsters and the heroes who slew them, we start to see legends and historical accounts of kings, tyrants, and aristocrats, many of whom abused their power and used it to kill their enemies indiscriminately. Similarly, several lengthy histories of Rome were written between the first century BCE and the second century CE, and because of political biases they tended to depict a number of Roman emperors and members of the imperial families as unusually murderous.

One might argue that such accounts do not necessarily describe serial killing, which we tend to think of as a more secretive and less public endeavor, and one that follows particular patterns. Similarly, one could argue that it strains the point to compare the psychology of individuals such as Nero, raised in highly dysfunctional households full of political tensions, rivalries, and murders, to that of a person raised in a less complicated environment but who later emerges as a psychopath. But those who raise these objections forget that, whereas Caligula and Nero were almost certainly not serial killers in actuality, historians of ancient Rome had a vested interest in portraying them as such—whether to ruin their legacies, to make subsequent rulers look better by comparison, or for other, more personal, reasons.[12] Also, the suggestion that a "less complicated" environment—that is, an upbringing in a less well-known household—is unlikely to produce a serial killer is not supported by what psychologists know of modern serial killers, many of whom grew up in highly dysfunctional home environments where they suffered abusive or absent parents, were bullied at school, had few material advantages, or experienced other serious difficulties. And some serial killers emerge from uneventful households with kind families, financial advantages, no abusive relationships, and so on. Their minds simply turned out differently despite their environments.[13]

Yet even exaggerated and biased accounts from antiquity, such as those of Caligula and Nero, can help us understand the ancient attitudes toward homicide. To a larger extent, they allow us to see that the Greeks and Romans recognized characteristics of serial killing, even if the Greeks and Romans did not specifically identify "serial killing" as a phenomenon separate from other types of homicide. Nero, for example, progressed from relatively minor crimes (drunken fights) to more serious crimes (robbery), to utterly reprehensible ones (rape, murder). This progression typifies the behavior pattern of many serial killers. The problem lies in thinking that the concept of "serial killing" by modern standards cannot possibly apply to a culture so far removed from us in time and space. But our ancient sources tell us that although the Greeks and Romans did not value the lives of certain classes of people, such as slaves, they did not tolerate the homicide of fellow citizens. And they considered serial murder absolutely horrendous. The attitude toward those most heinous crimes was no different in Greece and Rome than it is now.

Some ancient historical accounts—which, again, should be taken with a grain of salt, given the authors' biases—delve into the motives of these murderous rulers. The written records provide recognizable psychological information similar to what we might find in modern psychoanalytic analysis. There is little doubt, for example, that Nero had mother issues. And classical myth and history are notoriously full of gruesome killings, cannibalistic feasts, and mass murders, which may to some extent have mirrored real-life events or at least real-life concerns. Later legends and folktales, such as those compiled by the Brothers Grimm, reflected social realities of their times, and modern scholars note that the grisly content of the Grimms' folktales strongly suggests that people in premodern Europe recognized serial killing as its own phenomenon, even if the real stories behind the crimes became generalized to the extent that the original murderers went unidentified.[14] These so-called fairy tales, though now commonly considered stories for children, were originally intended for adults. Before Jacob and Wilhelm Grimm, faced with negative reviews, watered down the stories for a younger audience, and before Disney diluted them even further, these tales contained disturbingly explicit sex and violence. The French tale of a serial wife-killer—along with its variants "Mr. Fox" and "The Robber Bridegroom"—provides just one potent example: the bridegroom makes a habit of bringing home young women, getting them drunk, killing them, chopping them up, and eating the pieces. The existence of such stories implies that their audiences were depressingly familiar with serial murder. Accounts of mutilation killings in the small towns of early Europe spread by word of mouth, just as they would have done in ancient Greece and Rome, and over time such accounts easily took on the guise of legend rather than fact, particularly when the crimes so horrified people that they did not want to believe fellow humans capable of such acts, as John Douglas notes.

Many of the Grimms' fairy tales are folktale "types," meaning that variants of these stories exist in other times and places, including the ancient world. Greek myths make clear that humans have long exhibited extraordinarily barbaric behavior: Atreus, for example, killed the children of his brother Thyestes and served them up to him in a stew, in just one of the many revenge-via-cannibalism stories from classical antiquity. Unsurprisingly, then, various myths and local legends from the ancient world sound as though they might have been inspired by a cultural understanding of mutilation murders. To see how old the phenomenon of serial killing really is and to demonstrate why this earlier dating matters, the following chapters present stories like the ones above and many others in a search for clues to the existence and behavior of serial killers in those societies of two and three thousand years ago. The stories show that serial killers were a known quantity and as geographically widespread in the ancient Mediterranean world as they are in the modern one, and that such psychologically aberrant behavior has been around for much longer than many people realize. This affects not only how we view society in ancient Greece and Rome but also how modern assumptions about serial killers must be modified. It is no longer reasonable to conclude that various problems unique to modern society, such as increased population, lax sentencing for criminals, and lack of available and effective mental health care, have caused what superficially appears to be a drastic increase in sociopathic behavior and serial murder. Rather, antisocial behavior, even in its worst manifestations, has been around for an extremely long time, and then as now has attracted a high level of unseemly interest.

CHAPTER 2

Methods to the Madness

Along the lonely, dusty stretch of road, rest stops were few. With nearly fourteen miles to the next town, a traveler on foot carrying provisions needed more than a day for the tiring journey. By dusk, the traveler would be glad to see a friendly stranger by the roadside offering food and lodging at his nearby home—the closest thing to an inn available in such a desolate area. But this stranger's idea of hospitality was unusual. A traveler who accepted the man's offer of a room for the night soon found himself a prisoner, tied down to the bed. Imagine the poor traveler's growing terror as he watched his seemingly congenial host take out a set of tools: a hammer, a saw, and an ax! Unfortunately for the traveler, his legs were slightly too long for the bed. Without even administering anesthesia (not that it would have mattered much), his grinning host calmly picked up the saw and began amputating the horrified man's legs just below his knees. Before long, the traveler bled to death.

This unfortunate man was hardly the first passerby to disappear along this stretch of country road. But for whatever reason, a long time elapsed before anyone became suspicious. Maybe the host, who could outwardly seem quite friendly, did not kill every lodger he took in, so no one noticed a pattern of people vanishing in the proximity. Maybe his house was set far enough back from the road that it was not easily visible, especially since he himself came out to the main road to look for lone, exhausted travelers who would not put up a struggle. But eventually rumors of these ritualistic torture-murders spread. Finally, in the absence of any law enforcement, a vigilante took it upon himself to rid the countryside of this menace. Intentionally traveling alone and appearing vulnerable after a long journey, he presented an easy target for the killer, who led him back to the house. There, however, the vigilante beat the murderer at his own game: he tied the surprised killer to the bed—the same one in which the man had previously dispatched so many unsuspecting houseguests—and chopped off his limbs. This stretch of road, at least, was now safe for travelers.

In a very different time and place, a similar event occurred. Out in the wilderness, on a rough road between towns set far apart, stood a ramshackle little inn run by a family of four: an elderly father, a middle-aged mother, and their son and daughter, both in their twenties. The shabby little "inn," as it was advertised, was really just half of the small house, divided by a curtain from the family's living quarters. For a small price, the family offered food, drink, and lodging to anyone passing by. But over time at least a dozen travelers disappeared after stopping there. Considerable time elapsed before the sparse local law enforcement realized this, and when a group of men finally went to investigate the disappearances, the family who had run the inn was long gone. The men found the bodies of the vanished travelers buried in an orchard out back. Most of the victims' heads had been bashed in, as if by a large hammer.

A reader familiar with Greek myth might already have recognized the murderer in the first story as Procrustes and the "vigilante" as the Greek hero Theseus. Some stories about Procrustes also say that if one of his houseguests was too short for the bed, he hammered out the poor fellow's limbs until they were long enough to fit. Either way, Procrustes's victims would have experienced lingering, extraordinarily painful deaths, through the sort of torture we might more readily associate with the Spanish Inquisition. The story of Procrustes dates back to at least the early fifth century BCE, nearly 2,500 years ago. But few if any of the story's details, apart from the names, allow us to understand that this story was not set more recently, in the nineteenth or twentieth century, for example. The myth of Theseus may be fiction, but parts of it, such as this story, reflect real-life concerns common among the ancient Greeks, such as the dangers of traveling alone. Notably, a number of characteristics common to many real serial killings appear here: luring in an unsuspecting victim by being friendly; the ritual nature of the murders, including a "murder kit" with tools; and even the emphasis on the bed, which hints at the sexual nature of many serial killings.

Procrustes shares a large number of significant characteristics with modern serial murderers, including the family described in the second story. This family of four, consisting of John Bender, his wife, "Ma," son, John Jr., and daughter, Kate, became known as the "Bloody Benders," who ran a run-down "hotel" on the sparsely populated Kansas frontier in the early 1870s. The posse that investigated the Bender home in 1873 deduced that the family targeted wealthier travelers. The Benders sat an unsuspecting guest at a table with his back toward the curtain, and during the meal one of the family members, standing behind the curtain, smashed the man's head in with a sledgehammer. The family then robbed the body of any money and objects of value, stripped it, and dumped it in the cellar, later dragging the rotting corpse out for burial in the orchard. Unlike Procrustes, the Benders were never caught. Real-life stories do not always end as neatly as many fictional ones do.

What Is a Serial Killer?

Most serial killers are decidedly not delightful, dotty, well-meaning homicidal maniacs like Abby and Martha, the elderly Brewster sisters in *Arsenic and Old Lace* (a 1939 play and a 1944 film), who murder lonely old men by offering them poisoned elderberry wine, thinking they are doing the poor men a favor. Most resemble Procrustes and the Benders. Given the media attention paid to serial murder in the past few decades, many people probably already have a good idea of what characterizes a serial killer without having to resort to formal definitions. A serial killer is usually someone who murders several people over a period of time, usually by the same recognizable method. The concept of "serial killer," though, and the specific expression itself, did not come into common use until the 1980s, and there existed no word or phrase in the ancient world to describe this type of criminal phenomenon. Yet the Greeks and Romans, even without specialized terms, noticed patterns of criminal behavior and described them both in fictional stories, such as the myth of Theseus, and in other sources, such as historical records and political speeches, telling us that most behavioral characteristics now associated with modern serial killers were also present and recognized as abnormal even in antiquity.

In recent decades the media has inundated the public with information about serial killers. Sometimes it seems as though one appears in the news nearly every week, alongside dozens of movies and TV shows with serial killers as their central characters. Anywhere from 100 to 2,000 serial killers remain at large in the world every year, according to the most conservative and most liberal recent estimates, respectively. But the definition of "serial murder" can still vary considerably. For example, there exists no consensus as to how many victims define someone as a serial killer. The FBI used to state that serial murder "generally involves three or more victims," preferably in separate events in three or more separate locations with an emotional cooling-off period between homicides. But the FBI recently refined its criteria to identify serial murder as "the killing of two or more victims over an extended time period and at various locations."[1] Other agencies similarly look for a series of two or more murders, committed as separate events, usually (but not always) by one offender acting alone. The crimes may occur over a period of time ranging from days to years.

Nevertheless, state and federal agencies understand that these specific definitions can present serious problems. Trying to pin down a set number of victims to "qualify" an offender as a serial killer is difficult. What if an incipient serial killer manages to murder one victim, but authorities catch him before he has a chance to commit a second crime? What if a killer leaves two victims at one scene and a third victim elsewhere, as the Zodiac Killer did in his first known attacks—does this count as two killing "events" or three? And why suggest that the killings need to be at various locations? Many murderers whom criminologists and psychologists diagnose as serial killers have used their own homes as the murder site and have garnered the nonclinical nickname "homebodies" for that reason. In the 1970s, John Wayne Gacy brought young men back to his home in the Chicago suburb of Des Plaines and murdered them there. He buried several of them in the crawlspace, and police eventually found on the premises more than two dozen bodies in various states of decomposition. Dennis Nilsen, who killed fifteen young men between 1978 and 1983, was nicknamed the "Muswell Hill Murderer" after his capture because he committed all the murders in his own home in the Muswell Hill section of north London. He also disposed of the bodies on the premises, either by burning them or cutting them up and flushing them down the toilet. (Perhaps not surprisingly, it was the plumbing difficulties caused by this rather inefficient disposal method that tipped off the police.) Nilsen was even retroactively referred to as "the British Jeffrey Dahmer" because, like Wisconsin's Dahmer (active 1978–1991), he enticed young men back to his home and killed them there, mutilating their bodies both before and after death.

And what about the vague and highly variable "cooling-off" period of anywhere from days to weeks to months to years and even, in some cases, to decades? Given such loose parameters, law enforcement authorities look for many other characteristics when trying to determine whether a serial killer is at work. At a bare minimum, a "serial killer" is someone who kills more than one person over a period of time. The ability of a serial killer to wait between murders, even if only for a matter of days, indicates a person with a certain amount of self-control, clearly not someone who panics at having committed a murder. Also, this ability to control oneself generally distinguishes a serial killer from a mass murderer, someone who kills many people at once or in a very short space of time, such as over several hours, often targeting a specific group. Mass murders usually involve shooters with semiautomatic handguns, AR-15s, or other similar weapons, and the people who carry out mass murders tend to be loners who have already exhibited behavior noticeably different from that of most people around them until something—often unknown—sets them off. When this type of killer uses a gun, law enforcement authorities refer to such incidents as "active shooter events," so defined when one or more people with mass murder as their primary motive attack in a confined or highly populated area (a definition that does not include gang- and family-related shootings). Unlike serial killings, the number of active shooter events rose dramatically in the 2010s. Acts of terrorism in which many people are killed make up yet another separate category of homicide, usually politically and/or religiously motivated.[2]

Given the level of self-control necessary to commit serial murder, it is not entirely surprising that, especially between murders, the serial killer may appear to live a mundane life, often holding down a steady job, possibly maintaining a stable family with a spouse and children, and socializing within his—or, much less frequently, her or their—community. Ted Bundy, who murdered at least seventeen young women in the 1970s, decapitating many of them, was a charismatic, good-looking law student, social and overall quite popular. He even worked for the Republican Party, attending a number of meetings and events. Few who encountered him (and lived to tell about it) thought there was anything amiss, as Bundy was outwardly friendly and "normal."[3] Not all serial killers appear outwardly stable, but many do appear functional and friendly upon first acquaintance, particularly the so-called homebodies.

These characteristics help explain why so many people are willing to go home with serial killers, who often have no relationship to their victims. Although some target their own family members, usually the victims are strangers and often chosen at random: the killer may spot someone and then obsess about that person for a while before formulating a plan for abduction and murder. Many serial killers fixate on a certain type of victim, a group with characteristics in common, such as men who remind the killer of his abusive father or (more likely) women who remind him of his controlling mother. Jack the Ripper preyed on prostitutes. Dennis Nilsen preferred young men. Some serial killers target children. But not all of them focus on a consistent type; sometimes the perpetrator kills based simply on available opportunities, exhibiting impulsiveness that contrasts with their self-control.

Procrustes exhibited most of these characteristics. Travelers unfamiliar with local rumors would not have heard of him. The story does not give

FEMALE VICTIMS IN ANTIQUITY

Starting with Jack the Ripper's evisceration of multiple prostitutes in the seamy East End of 1880s London, the victims of most recorded serial murders have been women. Henri Désiré Landru killed nearly a dozen women in France in the early twentieth century, attracting them via lonely-hearts ads, and earning himself the description of "real-life Bluebeard." Gary Ridgway, the "Green River Killer," strangled forty-nine women that we know of. Samuel Little, considered (at the time of this writing) to be the worst known serial killer in U.S. history, claimed to have killed ninety-three women; the FBI has confirmed at least fifty of these. The reasons why serial killers so often focus on women vary considerably. Psychologically, many of these killers resent their mothers for perceived or actual abuse, whereas others feel a more generalized misogyny, taking feelings of inadequacy and rejection to extremes. Physically, women make easier targets than men. Although some serial killers target entirely different demographics—young men, for example, or children—women remain overwhelmingly the typical victims. But in ancient Greece and Rome, females were far less likely than males to be the victims of murder, most likely because they were not expected (and often not allowed) to leave the house alone. When they did venture out, male family members such as a father, brother, or husband, or a number of servants, accompanied them. In short, female victims were less readily available.

us any information about his family life, but he was evidently personable enough that people trusted his offer of hospitality, and he preferred to kill them in his own home. The myths imply that he victimized males traveling alone, all strangers who had never met him before. Procrustes also exhibits specific characteristics attributed to serial killers by law enforcement authorities and criminal psychologists. For example, authorities acknowledge that although most serial killers do not kill for profit, some are indeed motivated by desire for material gain.[4] Specific types of murderer, such as "Black Widows," women who kill fiancés and spouses for their money, frequently appear on lists of serial killers, as do "Bluebeards," men who kill their wives for their property or life insurance. Notably, modern literature often refers to Procrustes as a highwayman, a person who waylays travelers to steal their money and other valuables, but though some Greek and Roman myths call Procrustes a robber, they focus almost exclusively on his torture-murder of travelers and his comeuppance at the hands of Theseus. Profit hardly seems to have been his main motivation.

Also, apart from serial poisoners, most serial murderers become physically violent during the commission of their crimes, subjecting their victims to excessive brutality, including torture. Frequently, but not always, the violence exhibits a sexual component, such as rape, penetration with an object, or another kind of sexually violent humiliation. Many serial killers need to dominate their victims sexually, but even when they do not, they may still have an urge for control in other respects, possibly to compensate for feelings of inadequacy.[5] John Wayne Gacy had such issues. He needed to feel important and liked to think of himself as in charge. Homosexual from an early age but evidently not at ease with his sexuality, he got married and fathered two children. This first marriage broke up when his wife divorced him after he was arrested and imprisoned for sodomizing an underage employee. Gacy married again, but slowly became impotent with his wife, and eventually abusive. She, too, divorced him. He had already been killing carefully for several years, keeping her unaware, but now he had free rein at home. When he brought an unsuspecting young man to his house, he first incapacitated the fellow with drugs and alcohol, then handcuffed and sodomized him. Next, Gacy covered the victim's head with a plastic bag and held him down in a bathtub full of water until the victim almost drowned. Then Gacy repeated the process. If his victims did not eventually die from the water torture, Gacy strangled them with a rope.

This sexual dominance aspect lurks in the story of Procrustes: the bed in the story allows the inference that he had sexual issues, though I should stress that the myths about Procrustes absolutely do not provide enough details to definitively attribute this kind of psychological motivation to him. One characteristic of serial killers that more clearly relates to Procrustes is their need for a particular, repeated method or pattern of killing, a modus operandi (MO). The MO can include the victim type, the place where the killer commits the crime, and how the killer approaches and subdues his victim. Procrustes's MO included prowling along the highway, approaching vulnerable individual travelers, and inviting them back to his lodging. Many serial killers also have a "signature," an aspect of the crime unique to the specific offender, sometimes referred to as the killer's psychological "calling card."[6] Procrustes's signature consisted of the unique torture he inflicted on his victims, driven by his need to make them fit his guest bed. And the stories emphasize that Procrustes tortured his victims brutally before they died (presumably of shock, internal injuries, or blood loss).

A serial killer's ritualistic MO and signature often involve what crimi-

SERIAL KILLERS AND THEIR WEAPONS

More than half of murders in the United States are committed with firearms, but only a quarter of murders result from what we might call "personal" violence—beatings, strangulation, stabbings, and other types of hands-on violence. With serial killers, however, the statistics are reversed. More than half of them kill their victims manually. Fewer than one quarter of serial murders involve guns. David Berkowitz, whose crimes set New York City on edge from 1975 to 1977 and who was more familiarly known as the "Son of Sam," was thus relatively unusual in his use of a gun for serial murder. Hence his other nickname, the ".44-Caliber Killer."

Ted Bundy's murder kit, including ski mask, gloves, belt, rope, and trash bags.

nologists refer to as a "murder kit," a group of items the killer uses regularly in the commission of his crimes. Peter Sutcliffe, Britain's "Yorkshire Ripper," who was convicted in 1981 of murdering thirteen women between 1975 and 1980, used a hacksaw, various knives, a screwdriver, and several hammers. Ted Bundy kept a set of specific articles in the trunk of his VW Beetle, found by the police after they arrested him in 1978. Bundy's kit included a ski mask, stockings, handcuffs, a length of rope, and trash bags, among other things. "BTK Killer" Dennis Rader created what he called a "hit kit" consisting of his bowling bag packed with paraphernalia he used in his murders. This kit variously included one or more pistols, tape, rope, a hunting knife, plastic gloves, a mask, stockings, and handcuffs. The fictional Dexter had an entire chest full of murder implements, including knives, scalpels, latex gloves, trash bags, a syringe, plastic wrap, and duct tape, among other things. Procrustes's kit consisted of a hammer, ax, and saw.

The rituals that form a serial killer's MO may be traced to his younger days. Many serial killers progress to murder after experimenting with less heinous crimes, often beginning in childhood or adolescence. During those early years they might steal, set fires, and/or torture small animals. As they enter their teenage years and early twenties, they tend to continue such activities and add heavy drinking and drug use to the list of problems. As a child, Jeffrey Dahmer experimented with dead animals, dissecting them and mutilating them in various ways; he decapitated rodents, poured acid on squirrels, and put a dog's head on a stake. He drank heavily as a teen. He committed his first murder shortly after graduating from high school. Such background details are often lacking for characters from classical mythology and history, such as Procrustes, but descriptions of Nero's youth demonstrate such a pattern, and Libanius describes his fictional killer in "Against a Murderer" specifically as having moved from minor offences to murder: "He seems to me," says Libanius, "to have arrived at this point by progressing from lesser crimes. He got away with stealing many items, he broke through a few walls . . . he committed violent acts. By not paying the penalty for each of these crimes, he was taught to shrink from nothing, and by remaining unpunished for his other crimes, he has come down to us as a murderer."[7]

After dispatching their victims, many serial killers complete the ritual by keeping a trophy or souvenir. Psychologically, this may provide necessary proof to themselves that they completed their fantasy of killing. Alternatively, a trophy may remind them of the pleasure, excitement, and triumph they felt during the murder. They might keep an item of clothing or piece of jewelry that belonged to the victim. Sometimes they keep a body part. Ed Gein, the inspiration for Norman Bates in Robert Bloch's novel *Psycho*, saved body parts from female corpses and displayed them in his home. His "souvenirs" included a lampshade he made from human skin in (mistaken) emulation of the Nazis, who allegedly made lampshades of human skin— a now debunked rumor, though some Nazis did keep pieces of tattooed human skin. Jeffrey Dahmer amassed a collection of severed heads, hands, and other body parts from his victims. Oliver Thredson, aka "Bloody Face," the fictional serial murderer from the FX channel's miniseries *American Horror Story: Asylum* (2012–2013), owned a lampshade he had fashioned from the skin of one of his victims and an ashtray he had carved from a human skull. There is no evidence, literary or otherwise, that Procrustes collected such souvenirs, but Greek myths about other serial murderers indicate an awareness of trophy-taking. Antaeus, who appears in the myth of Heracles (Hercules to the Romans), was one such character. Like Procrustes, Antaeus killed travelers passing by his territory, but his MO and signature were very different. He decapitated his victims, kept their skulls, and used them to build a shrine to his father (we are not told what his father thought of this). Such trophy-taking may relate to wartime practices known around the world. According to the fifth-century BCE Greek historian Herodotus, for example, the ancient Scythians collected the scalps and skulls of their enemies, hanging the scalps from their horse reins and drinking from the hollowed-out skulls.[8] The Scythians did this only in wartime, however, or in the case of a family feud. When one person, outside of group custom and outside of a context such as war, repeatedly kills others and takes souvenirs, he is exhibiting the pathology of a serial murderer.

The locations of serial homicides also form part of a killer's pattern, and killers generally have two main preferences. Some are homebodies, like John Wayne Gacy, Dennis Nilsen, and Jeffrey Dahmer. Other serial killers do not leave home to acquire their victims, instead allowing the victims to come to them. In early twentieth-century Germany, for example, Karl Denke, a friendly fellow well liked in his community, ran a local inn catering to poor travelers and the homeless. In 1924, police found that Denke had murdered at least thirty of his guests over the course of three years and kept meticulous records of their body weights. He also kept body parts in pickling jars in his kitchen and admitted not only to eating bits of them himself but also to serving them to other guests. For his victims Denke had chosen beggars and other travelers unknown around the neighborhood and unlikely to be missed, just as Procrustes did.

But even more serial killers travel away from home to commit their crimes, calculating (correctly) that distance reduces the likelihood of any incriminating evidence. Because of this, a large number of serial murders occur on highways, which allow anonymity for both killer and victim. For example, until he was identified and convicted, Gary Ridgway was called the "Green River Killer" because he had picked up his victims along Pacific Highway South near Seattle and Tacoma in Washington state, and dumped most of the bodies in or along the nearby Green River. The still unidentified "New Bedford Highway Killer" picked up his(?) nine known victims, all prostitutes or drug addicts, in random spots and then dumped most of the bodies along Massachusetts Route 140 and parts of I-95 in the southeastern section of the state. Some serial killers combine both highways and homes, preying on anonymous travelers, like the "Bloody Benders" with their flea-bag roadside inn in Kansas. What we know from ancient Greece and Rome provides similar information about serial killers' preferred locations. As evidenced in the stories of Heracles and Theseus (see chapters 7 and 8), the several murderers these heroes encountered during their travels prowled the roadways, watching for unsuspecting, unprotected travelers. Procrustes, for one, gives us a combination of both highway killer and homebody: he chose travelers for his victims, unwary passersby on a sparsely populated stretch of road, but killed them in his own home after convincing them to stay for the night. The stories do not say how or where he disposed of the bodies. Other serial killers of ancient myth and history killed their victims on highways and left the remains discarded on the roadside or tossed them over nearby cliffs. Roving bands of highway robbers, a common real-life danger in antiquity, sometimes murdered their victims and left them by the roadside or hid them, leaving many accounts of people who simply vanished. Still, it is not accurate to generalize and label these bandits as serial killers, because most worked in groups, robbing and often beating their victims, killing them only to leave no witness, with material gain as their main motivation. Aside from a few extreme examples, such as the murderer in Libanius's story, the behavior of highway bandits from antiquity does not share many characteristics with that of serial killers.

Apart from these cases of highway robber gangs, descriptions of serial murders from ancient times show most of the behavioral characteristics of modern serial killers—the same characteristics that now allow criminologists and law enforcement authorities to know they are in pursuit of a serial killer. And these characteristics are not unique to serial killers in the United States. Criminal profiling in other countries shows that serial killers all over the globe share these common traits. The idea that serial homicide is a problem specific to the United States has been a surprisingly persistent misconception even among those who study such crimes for a living. Only recently have people begun to realize that incidents of serial killing in other countries are not isolated or unusual events, but that such crimes occur regularly around the world. Popular encyclopedias of serial killers now include many entries of international serial murderers. One principal cause for the lag in recognizing the extent of serial killing is that regular documentation of such crimes began only in the nineteenth century. This is also a main reason why many people generally think of Jack the Ripper as the first serial killer: widespread, sensationalistic journalism publicized his crimes to an extent not previously possible. As the internet and other modern media continue to open the world, the true extent of serial murder becomes clear. Nevertheless, although many TV shows (especially police procedurals) focusing on serial murder give the impression that such crimes occur with alarming frequency, serial murder remains a rare phenomenon.

Also, people who study serial murder have only relatively recently and very gradually come to the conclusion that such crimes are both much older and more widespread than previously believed. Forensic psychiatrist Helen Morrison, who has devoted decades of her life to examining the nature of serial killing, wrote in 2004 that "serial murder is not a phenomenon only of Western society. It happens around the world. . . . Serial murder is not a new phenomenon. It probably began with the most primitive of societies thousands of years ago."[9] The international and long-standing nature of this abnormal behavior provides proof that it is not simply the problems critics often associate with modern Western culture—materialism, too much individual freedom, inadequate mental health care, easy access to weapons—that have caused such crimes. The motives expressed by convicted serial killers, along with their methods, show that this sort of behavior is not unique to any particular time or place.

CHAPTER 3

Motives for Serial Murder across the Ages

One of the most critically acclaimed episodes of *The X-Files*, a speculative fiction TV show that originally ran for nine seasons, from 1993 to 2002 (with tenth and eleventh seasons in 2016 and 2018, respectively), was "Clyde Bruckman's Final Repose" (season 3, episode 4). Clyde Bruckman, played by Peter Boyle (who won an Emmy for the role, while the episode itself won an Emmy for Best Writing), is an elderly and cynical insurance salesman with a specific and highly disconcerting clairvoyant power: he can see how people will die. He reluctantly aids FBI agents Fox Mulder and Dana Scully in their investigation into a series of murders of local fortune-tellers. When the killer meets Bruckman, the two have the following exchange:

> **Killer:** There's something I've been wanting to ask you for some time now. You've seen the things I do in the past as well as in the future.
> **Bruckman:** They're terrible things.
> **Killer:** So tell me, please, why have I done them?
> **Bruckman:** Don't you understand yet, son? Don't you get it?
> **Killer:** [Shakes his head]
> **Bruckman:** You do the things you do because you're a homicidal maniac.

In this paradoxically grim and humorous conversation, Bruckman means that people may commit horrific crimes for no discernible reason at all. They cannot necessarily help themselves, and do not always understand their own motivations. They may exhibit certain patterns, such as targeting a specific type of person, following a ritual method of torture and killing, and/or taking trophies from their victims. Besides observing such outward behavioral patterns, psychologists who analyze and profile serial homicides can also often distinguish psychological patterns that many (though not all) serial killers exhibit. Some of these killers suffer from severe mental illnesses that cause hallucinations. For example, they might hear external or internal voices commanding them to kill specific individuals, or they might come to believe it is their mission to exterminate certain types of people, such as prostitutes or homeless men. But most serial murderers commit their crimes because they have various urges to fill. A very large number act for sexual satisfaction or for a feeling of power; some act on the desire for financial gain. Criminologists and psychologists have many different ways to classify serial killers, but new categories of behavior constantly emerge and overlap. In short, "the motives for serial murder are as diverse as those for any other type of crime."[1] Even so, many serial killers from both antiquity and modern times fall into various recognizable types—far too many to enumerate here. But the following discussion of several main examples will prove useful for examining certain cases from antiquity.

Some serial murderers kill primarily because they get a certain kind of gratification from their crimes, such as material gain. They may be the most basic, least complicated type of serial killer. They tend to kill their victims quickly because they get no particular pleasure from torturing them, and their crimes usually lack a sexually aggressive aspect. They also will not mutilate the bodies unless they need to get rid of the evidence quickly.[2] Many serial poisoners fall into this category, and many of them are also female. Starting in her fifties (relatively late for a serial killer), Dorothea Puente of Sacramento murdered more than half a dozen people out of greed. Dorothea ran a boarding house in the 1980s. Her boarders were mostly elderly, alcoholic, and/or mentally disabled, all on Social Security. Though such people often fall through the cracks of society, when one went missing, a social services worker noticed and investigated the disappearance. In 1988 the police were finally called in, and working from reports of odd activity in the basement and garden, they began digging up the yard. They uncovered a body almost right away—but, to their surprise, it was not the body of the missing man, but of an unknown woman. The remains indicated that she had been dead for some time. The police ultimately found seven bodies in the yard, and discovered that Dorothea had killed them and others so that she could cash their Social Security checks—she claimed that they all died of natural causes. Police suspected that she gave them drugs and then suffocated them to death. Sentenced to life in prison, she died there in 2011 at the age of eighty-two.

Many of the characters in antiquity who exhibit characteristics of serial killers fall into the for-profit category. One notable example from ancient Rome is Statius Albius Oppianicus, rumored to have killed at least eight people, mostly various family members, for money. Oppianicus supposedly married for wealth, and one of his earliest victims was his wife, whose death left her substantial dowry to her husband. His political enemies also accused him of killing his own brother and his brother's pregnant wife, the latter to prevent her from bearing a son who would inherit his brother's property. In this way Oppianicus remained the sole heir. But Oppianicus himself was later murdered, and his stepson, Aulus Cluentius Habitus the Younger, was accused of the crime, standing trial in 66 BCE. Cluentius's own mother had brought the charges, claiming that the young man had poisoned his stepfather. Luckily, Cluentius had a first-rate defense lawyer: none other than Marcus Tullius Cicero, who gave such a successful speech that Cluentius was found not guilty. In this speech, the *Pro Cluentio*, Cicero repeatedly describes Oppianicus as a man of unusual wickedness and boldness.[3] The "boldness" hints at an important characteristic common to many serial killers, and Cicero appears to have attempted, intentionally and successfully, to characterize Oppianicus as what we would identify as a serial murderer, whether Oppianicus really was one or not.

Other serial killers who murder for gratification do so not for financial profit or other material gain but because they derive immense psychological and sometimes even physical pleasure from the act of torturing, mutilating, raping, and/or cannibalizing their victims. Some feel pleasure at the act of killing itself: they strongly desire to kill and will not feel complete until they do. After his arrest, Jeffrey Dahmer specifically said that lust played a large role in his actions. He had killed nearly twenty young men, having first experimented on many of them in the hope of turning them into his sex slaves. While they were still alive, he drilled holes in their skulls and injected acid into their brains, thinking that the damage would render them more submissive. Despite the fact that every single victim he tried this procedure on died, Dahmer kept up his ill-conceived experiments. He also cooked and ate several victims, all for his own sexual gratification. As we have seen, the early criminal career of Nero provides a possible ancient example of similar motivation, as before becoming emperor he allegedly raped, beat, mutilated, and stabbed an unknown number of victims simply because he enjoyed doing so. Serial homicides committed for gratification, whether for profit, lust, or the pleasure of torture and murder itself, are often referred to as "hedonistic" killings (from the Greek *hedone*, "pleasure").

Many serial killers commit their crimes not mainly for pleasure and not because they enjoy causing pain, but because they relish the feeling of power they get from torturing and killing their victims. Their process may include

CAN PHYSICAL INJURIES CAUSE SERIAL KILLING?

Aside from delving into the psychological makeup of serial murderers, psychologists and neurologists have examined the question of whether traumatic head injury can cause a previously benevolent person to undergo a complete personality change that could include lack of empathy and willingness to kill. There is certainly no doubt that mass and serial murder results from "a highly complex interaction of biological, psychological and sociological factors," and scientists admit the possibility that some such killers may have had neurodevelopmental disorders that could include head injury. It has been estimated that perhaps 10 percent of serial and mass murderers suffered a head injury in their younger years, a figure higher than that found in the general population. At the same time, however, subjects who had suffered these injuries had also experienced emotional and environmental risk factors, such as turbulent and abusive home lives. Overall, the evidence is too scanty to state with any certainly that head injuries form an underlying cause for serial killing.[4]

In classical antiquity, physicians observed that head trauma often resulted in speechlessness and torpor, but they did not observe a connection with violent acts. Rather, extreme violence was associated with madmen, and even then mainly in literature such as tragedy. In ancient medical texts, by contrast, insane patients were not observed to be especially violent, though there were, of course, exceptions.[5] One treatise describes how a man, who was suffering from a type of insanity called *phrenitis*, threw a friend out a window, causing the young man to be crushed.

sexual abuse and mutilation, but their motivation—the satisfaction they derive from murder—is the feeling of domination, not lust. Though rape often figures in their crimes, it generally occurs as the assertion of control over a victim rather than emanating from sexual desire. Psychologists describe both Ted Bundy and John Wayne Gacy as such "power-/control-oriented" killers. "The I-5 Killer," Randy Woodfield, is also considered a power-control killer. Initially convicted of three murders, he may have committed more than forty along the main highway running through Washington and Oregon. Woodfield sodomized at least two of his victims, and his main motivation seems to have been to demonstrate his superiority. Among other things, he had expressed resentment at having been cut from the Green Bay Packers training camp in 1974, stating that they simply did not appreciate his skills.

This type of killer existed in antiquity, too, as seen in the myth of Theseus. Procrustes was actually the last of six serial killers Theseus encountered on his way to Athens. Before meeting Procrustes, Theseus passed by the territory of the career criminal Sciron, who robbed strangers passing through his section of the main road and forced them to wash his feet, keeping a basin of water nearby for just this purpose. When they crouched down, he kicked them over the cliff into the sea. They died from smashing into the rocks on the way down, from drowning, or from being eaten by a giant sea turtle that made its home at the base of the cliff. In his apparent need to humiliate his victims, Sciron resembles the "power-control" serial killer type: he aimed less to cause pain and suffering than to control and dominate his victims (for more on Theseus and these characters, see chapter 8).

Similarly, another type, the "power-assertive" serial killer, starts out initially planning a rape rather than a murder but ultimately kills the victims in an attempt to control them. This killer is motivated by a strong desire to assert power, again most likely prompted by feelings of inadequacy. He has an exaggerated need to exert his masculinity.[6] Joseph Ture targeted waitresses in Minnesota during the 1970s, raping dozens of them and killing at least six people, including three waitresses, before being caught and convicted for one of the murders. Despite (or perhaps because of) his own blue-collar background—his father was an autoworker and he himself was a drifter without steady work—he believed that he was superior to these women and that they should acknowledge his superiority and yield to him. When they refused, he raped them. He beat one of them to death and used an ax to kill another. At least one rather complicated story from ancient Greece tells of a sailor who, during a shore leave, got drunk and raped a local girl, and then started killing the townspeople until he was caught. His general motivation may have been to compensate for feelings of inadequacy by proving his dominance over the locals (this case is discussed further in chapter 10).

Other serial killers, motivated by feelings of anger and a need for vengeance, may plan murder in advance but do not see themselves as committing crimes so much as exacting well-deserved revenge. They believe their victims deserved to die. Such a general description could apply to Clytemnestra, wife of King Agamemnon, at least as portrayed in Aeschylus's *Agamemnon* (458 BCE). Relishing a certain amount of power while Agamemnon was away for ten years fighting in the Trojan War, Clytemnestra seemed moved to murder by many factors: Agamemnon's sacrificing their daughter Iphigenia to attain fair weather for the trip to Troy, her own desire to retain power, her relationship with a new man (Agamemnon's cousin

Aegisthus), and her resentment toward Agamemnon when he arrives home with a prominent slave-mistress in tow (the Trojan princess/seeress Cassandra). Agamemnon expects his household to return to its prewar hierarchy, but Clytemnestra has other ideas. She hacks him to death in his bath and soon after kills Cassandra, then boasts about the murders, showing no remorse whatsoever:

> While he lay there,
> I struck a third blow . . .
> And so, fallen, he gasped out his life's breath,
> coughing out gobbets of gore in spasms,
> daubing me with dark drops of dewy slaughter.
> (Aeschylus, *Agamemnon*, lines 1385–1390)

This "anger-retaliatory" type of killing usually contains a sexual element, such as rape. One could argue that Clytemnestra's brutal stabbing of Agamemnon, with its repeated penetration, qualifies—especially when contrasted with poisoning, the type of murder most frequently chosen by females, and when we consider that Clytemnestra's troubled background included her own rape at the hands of Agamemnon after he killed her first husband and infant son.

Most anger-retaliatory killers are men, however, and most feel extreme hatred toward women. They plan rape-murders driven by misogynistic rage, often stemming from an immense resentment against a particular woman in the killer's past who made him feel belittled, disrespected, or otherwise inferior in some way. These killers tend to focus their attacks on substitute victims who symbolize their frustration rather than on the actual perceived offender, and the rage manifests in unusually excessive violence that frequently continues after the victim is dead, resulting in mutilation of the corpse. The killer takes on a dominant role that he was unable to achieve with the original offender, although some do ultimately kill the original offender as well.[7]

One prominent example of the anger-retaliatory killer is Ed Gein. Raised in rural Plainsfield, Wisconsin, by an alcoholic father and dominant mother, who, in her religious zeal, firmly believed sex was a sin, he ended up with some severe psychological issues. He loved his mother but increasingly resented her for not allowing him to socialize with women. After his father and brother died, Ed lived with his mother for another year before she died of a stroke in 1945, leaving him alone on the family farm. Her death may have triggered his subsequent aberrant behavior. He sealed off

John Collier, *Clytemnestra* (1882). The artist depicts her just after she has murdered Agamemnon and Cassandra, with blood dripping from her ax.

his mother's room, leaving it the same as when she died. He began reading volumes about the human experiments performed by the Nazis. He seemed confused about his sexuality and at times considered a sex-change opera-tion, although this remained unknown to the townspeople of Plainsfield, to whom he seemed reclusive but also polite and harmless. They did not know that for nearly ten years after his mother's death he regularly dug up freshly buried corpses from the local cemeteries, brought them back to the farm-house, and mutilated them by fashioning them into unusual home furnish-ings. Gein made himself a pair of stockings and a vest out of human skin, a soup bowl from a human skull, masks from dead women's faces, and other macabre decorations.

Eventually, Gein stopped being satisfied by fresh corpses and killed his first victim in late 1954, at the age of forty-eight. He murdered a local woman at her tavern, leaving behind a puddle of blood. Initially unable to solve the crime, police finally caught Gein in 1957 after he abducted and killed a fe-male clerk at the local hardware store; someone remembered seeing him in

EDMUND KEMPER

Another solid example of the anger-retaliatory killer is Edmund Kemper, nicknamed the "Co-ed Killer" because he murdered at least five female college students who were hitchhiking in the Santa Cruz area of California. Kemper had been abused and dominated by both his mother and older sister, more so after his parents divorced and his father moved out. After many years with his alcoholic mother, he ended up living with his paternal grandparents. But this ended badly. In 1964, at the age of fifteen, he grew tired of how his grandmother constantly belittled him, so he shot her and then his grandfather, fearing the latter's disapproval. These were his first murders. Kemper spent several years in a psychiatric facility before being released to live with his mother in 1969, but after violent arguments with her he began to take out his rage on female hitchhikers. In 1973 he finally vented his anger toward his mother herself by beating her to death with a hammer. This seemed to have done the trick; after the death of his mother—whose decapitated head he sodomized and then used as a dartboard, in addition to cutting out her vocal cords and grinding them up in the garbage disposal—Kemper next killed his mother's best friend, and soon after confessed to the authorities. As played by actor Cameron Britton, he featured prominently in season 2 of *Mindhunter* (2019), the television adaptation of Douglas and Olshaker's book.

the shop shortly before the woman disappeared. When police arrived at his farm to investigate this lead, they discovered not just the unique home decor but also a human heart in a pan on the stove, human entrails in the refrigerator, and, most importantly, the headless, gutted corpse of the missing woman, which was hanging from the kitchen rafters. Robert Bloch, author of *Psycho*, lived just forty miles from Gein's farmhouse, and after hearing Gein's well-publicized story, wanted to write a novel "in which a seemingly normal and ordinary rural resident led a dual life as a psychotic murderer."[8] His fictional killer, Norman Bates, embodies the quintessential mama's boy, alternately too attached to and furiously resentful of his domineering and restrictive mother—so much so that Norman develops a psychosis.

For an example of the anger-retaliatory type in antiquity, we can look to Nero, whom one might call "the Norman Bates of ancient Rome."[9] Descriptions of the emperor's life and crimes strongly suggest that simmering rage toward his demanding, overbearing mother ultimately influenced the development of his depraved, murderous personality. According to the

Roman historian Suetonius (ca. 69–122 CE), Nero's father, Domitius, himself a hateful man accused of treason and incest, died of illness when Nero was three. Around the same time, Nero's mother, Agrippina, went into exile. For most of his childhood, Nero was raised in the household of his paternal aunt, where he was attended to almost entirely by two servants who did not appear to have any particular childcare qualifications—a dancer and a barber. Agrippina eventually returned from exile when Nero was thirteen, having been absent for a decade. He seems to have struggled to win any approval, recognition, or tenderness from her; when she demonstrated none of these feelings, he began to resent and hate her. At the same time, Suetonius suggests, Nero developed incestuous feelings toward her, eventually taking on a concubine who physically resembled his mother.[10]

Ancient historians and biographers describe Agrippina as highly critical and controlling (and as not beyond committing the occasional homicide herself; see the box below). Eventually he grew so tired of her that he plotted her death. He first tried to have her poisoned, but, having anticipated this possibility(!), she had built up an immunity and survived no fewer than three attempts at murder by poison. Nero next tried tampering with her bedroom ceiling, loosening the boards so that they would fall on her and crush her while she slept. But evidently word of this plot got out, so he scrapped it and came up with yet another plan. He ordered a collapsible boat built and invited Agrippina to go on her own private pleasure cruise. The boat indeed sank, but she unexpectedly proved to be a capable swimmer. After this last failure, Nero gave up any attempt at subtlety and simply sent some soldiers to run her through with their swords. Supposedly, as one

---

HOW HOMICIDAL WAS AGRIPPINA THE YOUNGER?

Nero's mother, Agrippina the Younger, did not exactly serve as an upstanding role model for her son. She exhibited her own sociopathic tendencies, showing little hesitation or moral regret in plotting and committing a number of political murders. She offered to marry Lepidus, her widowed brother-in-law, if he would assist her in assassinating Caligula, but the emperor discovered the plot, consequently ordering Lepidus to be killed and Agrippina to be exiled for several years. At least two of her husbands died of mysterious illnesses, and she arranged for the deaths of several notable people, including her enemy Messalina (who racked up quite a body count herself; see chapter 11).

Arturo Montero y Calvo (1859–1887), *Nero before the Corpse of His Mother, Agrippina the Younger.* Nero, center, examines the body.

of the centurions drew his sword for the final blow, she pointed to her belly and uttered as her last words, "Strike my womb!," thereby instructing the hired killers to destroy the part of her body that had produced such a monstrous offspring.[11]

Unlike Gein or the fictional Bates, despite his mother issues Nero directed his hostility toward females and males alike, and the ancient accounts emphasize his sexual deviancy. Nero sexually abused boys and castrated at least one, going through a kind of mock-wedding with him that included having the boy wear a bridal veil for the ceremony. Upon seeing this, an anonymous witness remarked that it would have been good for the world if Nero's father, Domitius, had had that kind of wife—one who could not bear children. Nero also seduced married women and raped a Vestal Virgin. He killed both of his wives. He put his first wife, Octavia, to death on a false charge of adultery, having first unsuccessfully tried to strangle her, and later killed his second wife, Poppaea, by kicking her to death when she was pregnant. He did not take rejection well, and had Antonia, daughter of his predecessor Claudius, killed when she (understandably, if not wisely) refused to marry him after Poppaea's death. He poisoned Burrus, a prefect of the Pretorian Guard. He also poisoned several elderly freedmen who had advised him over the years. The list of people Nero murdered is suspiciously excessive, a fact that is almost certainly due in large part to negative political bias on the part of his biographers, who may have intentionally chosen to depict him as a serial killer, especially given that they describe him as having killed a large number of people himself rather than hiring others to do so— although he at least balked at killing his mother with his own hands.

Given that one important aspect of serial killers is their (initial) anonymity, is it even reasonable to consider Nero among them? Serial killers aim for privacy; as we have seen, they effectively keep their murderous persona a secret from family and friends. They usually do not publicize their deeds, though occasionally some, such as Jack the Ripper, the Zodiac Killer, and the BTK Killer, intentionally contact the press to boast about their own cleverness, perhaps also subconsciously hoping to be caught. And serial killers work with partners only rarely, and equally rarely as a family unit, as the Benders did. So, should we think of Nero's actions as those of an abusive autocrat rather than of a serial murderer? Yes and no. Various kings and emperors throughout history have abused their power and condemned many people to death, often with the excuse of protecting their own power and safety. Ancient historians frequently characterize rulers as paranoid and quick to anger, worried about being overthrown, and seeing nonexistent conspiracies everywhere, and consequently they are willing to kill many of their subjects, most of whom were innocent of any wrongdoing. The emperor Tiberius exemplifies this description. But the characterization of Nero far surpasses that of a typical abusive ruler. His background, his psychology, and his methods all closely align him with serial killers. In this case, the source material matters. Many Romans despised Nero, whose conduct grew increasingly erratic after Agrippina's death, and his biographers, writing after his death, saw no need to flatter him (to put it mildly). And as in the case of Oppianicus, it was not unusual for Roman writers to intentionally attribute exaggerated characteristics of vicious killers to anyone they wanted to discredit. The point here is not whether Nero was really a serial killer, but that Suetonius, Tacitus, and other writers were so familiar with the actions and mindset of serial killers that they could attribute such characteristics to an emperor they feared and hated.

CHAPTER 4

Murderous Greek Roof-Tiles and Other Legal Problems

Many Greek and Roman accounts of serial killings, whether appearing in fictional or historical narratives, share certain characteristics that reflect ancient cultural attitudes toward homicide. These stories contain recurring features: prominent citizens are killed, which results in a public outcry, which then causes the state to institute certain laws to deal with the cases. The ancient Athenians even created an origin story for their homicide laws, centering it on Ares, the Greek god of war. Known in the myths for his rudeness, aggressive nature, and black moods—not to mention his penchant for encouraging confused, loud, bloody violence—Ares was extremely unpopular among his fellow deities as well as among men. There was a relatively small temple to Ares in Athens' city center, but the Greeks built no grand sanctuaries to him and instituted no major holidays in his honor; he was worshipped very little, except among the Spartans. If Ares had a decent quality, it was probably the protective attitude he demonstrated toward his children—overly protective, some might say, because when the son of fellow Olympian god Poseidon attempted to rape Ares's daughter, Ares did not appeal to any higher authority, such as Zeus, head of the Greek pantheon and god of justice (among many other things). Instead, Ares took vengeance himself and killed the young man, whose furious and grief-stricken father demanded that the gods put Ares on trial for murder. The jury, composed of other Olympian deities, acquitted him. The myth omits the reason for the acquittal, but it would have been in keeping with historical Athenian law to acquit a defendant who had killed to uphold the honor of a woman in his family and with it his family name and line. Despite this paternal devotion, Ares would hardly qualify for father of the year given that his son Cycnus committed far worse offenses, exhibiting behavior akin to that of a serial killer (see chapter 7). And Ares, though well aware of his son's unorthodox hobby, did not discourage it.

According to Greek myth, Ares's was the earliest homicide case tried in ancient Greece. This etiological story explains that, ever after these court proceedings, the Greeks have called the hill in Athens where the trial occurred the Areopagus ("Hill of Ares"), because the god himself was tried for murder on this spot. The story provides a place name for the rocky outcropping, but, more importantly, explains why the Areopagus was the earliest court in Athens that oversaw cases of homicide. Over time, the Athenians established other courts to try different types of homicide (literally, "the killing of a human being"). Historical documents show that they felt very strongly about prosecuting this type of crime. The same held true for the Romans. But for these ancient cultures the importance of an individual human being was relative: the Greeks and Romans took notice mainly of the killing of fellow citizens, with the Romans chiefly concerned about citizens of high status, such as aristocrats and politicians. They remained largely unconcerned about the killing of a low-status foreigner or a slave, whose lives counted for little or even nothing. In both Athens and Rome, any slaves not tied to the land were considered the physical, moveable property of their masters.

These distinctions in Greek and Roman attitudes toward murder matter because understanding them helps dispel the misconception that, because Greece and Rome were different and long-ago cultures, and because these ancient peoples valued certain human lives differently from the way we do now, their attitudes and actions regarding homicide remain somehow irrelevant. It is true that the Greeks and Romans were more inured to pain and suffering than most of us are; they often experienced agony during illness (especially in the absence of modern anesthetics), and far more commonly saw dead bodies than most of us ever do. And people's status made a significant difference in society's regard toward them and consequently a considerable difference in their legal rights. The Greeks and Romans also believed that homicide of any type, if left unavenged, could jeopardize the state's relationship with the gods; ancient societies believed in the concept of *miasma*, a "stain" or "pollution" that came from spilling (human) blood, and considered punishments for such crimes necessary to avoid or appease divine wrath. As Ares's case demonstrates, even the gods themselves were not excused from having to atone for certain crimes.[1] Given these contexts, the Greeks and Romans considered homicide the worst possible crime. And, as made clear from the mythological and historical evidence, they recognized *serial* homicide when they saw it, even if they did not have a specific term or phrase to distinguish it from other types of homicide.

For these reasons, many books on the subject tend to gloss over serial murder in the ancient world without looking closely at the Greek and Roman attitudes toward killing. For example:

> It is difficult, however, to construct a modern criminal dynamic for the killing perpetrated by ancient despots such as Nero and Caligula. During an era when death circuses were attended by thousands of spectators in arenas, accusing Roman emperors of serial homicide would be like handing out traffic tickets at the Daytona Speedway.

It is certainly true that systematic death was a form of public entertainment in arenas throughout the Roman Empire, and the Roman games have even been called "a form of mass participatory serial murder."[2] But these sorts of observation, humorous and knowingly exaggerated though they might be, have several significant flaws. For one, they ignore important social distinctions. The "circuses" involved slaves—and, less frequently, Roman citizens—fighting against animals and occasionally each other, sometimes to the death. Many of those forced to fight in the arena were convicted criminals, and the spectators would have considered themselves to be rooting for the side of justice.[3] Such observations as the excerpt above also do not explain why any "modern" explanation would be necessary for ancient attitudes toward killing, and ignore the similar modern predilection for violent sports and games, such as American football, boxing, auto racing, and other such pastimes in which participants can be (and often are) seriously injured, maimed, or killed. And such comments distort the definition of serial murder by occasionally merging the concept with that of mass murder (e.g., "mass participatory murder"), so that stories of mass murders—such as mass poisonings—are often incorporated as examples of serial killing from the ancient world. It can be difficult to spot true examples of serial murder in Greek and Roman literature, but a closer look at ancient attitudes toward homicide may help.

Understanding Homicide in Ancient Greece

Unlike, say, the United States, made up of many different states with their own governments and all united constitutionally by a federal authority, ancient Greece for hundreds of years consisted of many different and highly individual city-states known as *poleis* (*polis*, singular). They generally shared a common language (if different dialects), religion, and certain customs,

Thomas Degeorge, *Odysseus and Telemachus Slaughter the Suitors of Penelope* (1812).

and as far as the law was concerned the Greek city-states also shared basic concepts, such as the need for justice when harm was done.[4] But individual Greek city-states formed their own law codes with their own details. One *polis*, for example, might have marriage and property laws that differed greatly from those of its neighbors.

As far as we know, in prehistorical times the ancient Greeks had no official laws. Punishment for various crimes took the form of retaliation by relatives of the victim. In the case of murder, this most likely meant that the victim's family sought out and killed the murderer. The problem with this system is that it could lead to near-endless blood feuds, such as the one at the end of Homer's *Odyssey*. Probably set sometime in the twelfth century BCE and written down in the late eighth century BCE after several centuries of oral transmission, the *Odyssey* describes how the Greek warrior-king Odysseus returns from the Trojan War to his home, the island kingdom of Ithaca, only to find that during his twenty-year absence an obnoxious and unruly group of more than one hundred suitors has been harassing his wife, threatening his son, and making themselves at home in his palace. He and his son slaughter them all.

But word of the massacre spreads quickly, and the families of the slain suitors furiously demand revenge. The bereaved father of one dead suitor addresses the crowd:

> Odysseus has harmed us irreparably. After taking many of our best men away with him in his fleet [to fight at Troy], he lost both the ships and the men. And now that he's back, he has killed these Ithacan noblemen. So come on! Let's get him before he flees to Pylos or to Elis, or we'll be ashamed forever after if we do not avenge the murder of our sons and brothers. (*Odyssey* 24.426–435)

The vengeful families descend upon Odysseus, whom the goddess Athena saves just in time.

Since the ancient Greeks did not, in reality, have a *dea ex machina* such as Athena to help them avoid such blood feuds, in the seventh century BCE the Greeks began establishing specific laws. Regarding homicide, the most complete information we have comes from ancient Athens. As Christine Plastow points out, "Although we cannot know how often homicide occurred in Athens, and therefore whether Athenians experienced it as an occasional horror or a more regular part of life, we can be sure from our sources that it held an inherent conceptual power for them."[5] The earliest homicide legislation dates to approximately 620 BCE, when the politician Draco produced the first known written Athenian law code. This code established varying penalties for different crimes, including homicide. Importantly, these laws recognized the presence or absence of basic intent: a homicide was either intentional or unintentional, though the Greeks did not yet recognize degree of intent, in part because Draco's laws also did not distinguish between concepts such as premeditation (our "malice aforethought") and unplanned but intentional killing, such as might happen when one person intentionally kills another in a sudden fit of rage. These shades of intent currently differentiate first- from second-degree murder in various US penal codes. Rather, a main purpose of Draco's homicide laws was to assert the city-state's jurisdiction over homicide and consequently to suppress retaliatory killings by victims' families, although the *polis* still consulted families regarding the manner of punishment.[6] But the Athenians eventually recognized different circumstances even for intentional and unintentional homicide, as illustrated in the box on the next two pages, delineating the five homicide courts that existed in ancient Athens in the years following the initial institution and later modification of Draco's law code. The Areopagus, as the only court that oversaw cases of clearly unlawful, intentional homicide, hosted any cases of what we would call serial murder.[7]

THE FIVE HOMICIDE COURTS OF ANCIENT ATHENS

Pop-culture depictions of ancient Greece and Rome tend to stress the violent aspects of those cultures, as in movies such as Zack Snyder's *300* (2006) and Ridley Scott's *Gladiator* (2000), leaving the impression that the Greeks and Romans lacked sensitivity concerning the killing of fellow humans. But although killing a foreign enemy (as in battle) was understandable and expected, killing a fellow citizen certainly was not. Ancient Athens had five special courts in which to try cases of homicide, and which court was used depended on the circumstances of the case, the intent of the killer, and the status of the victim.

1. The Areopagus saw the most serious cases, those involving a defendant charged with intentionally killing an Athenian citizen. Conviction on such a charge usually resulted in a mandatory death sentence.
2. The Palladion tried cases of defendants charged with unintentionally killing a citizen. This court also heard cases of defendants charged with killing noncitizens, regardless of intent. Conviction on any of these charges usually resulted in exile from the *polis*.
3. The Delphinion tried cases of defendants who claimed that they killed for lawful reasons. This included, for example, accidentally killing someone during an athletic competition; accidentally killing a fellow soldier in battle (our "friendly fire"); killing a highway robber in self-defense; and killing a man caught in bed with one's wife, mother, sister, or daughter. In these cases, the penalty depended on the intent of the defendant and the status of the victim.
4. In the Phreatto, the Greeks held a very specific kind of homicide trial: that of a defendant accused of homicide while already in exile for a previous crime, specifically anyone who, after being exiled for unintentional homicide, was then charged with committing another homicide intentionally. This might include a second homicide committed either before the defendant was banished for the first homicide, or one committed while in exile, by killing an Athenian outside of Attica (the territory that included Athens). So, if a person was in exile and charged with another homicide, how could this defendant plead his case if he could not come back into Athens? The Phreatto was situated on the coast. The accused stood in a boat offshore while the jury listened to the defense speech from the beach.
5. The Prytaneion may seem especially strange to us. This court held not only homicide trials in cases where the killer remained unknown, but also trials for nonhuman killers, including animals and, most oddly to modern audiences, inanimate objects. Convicted animals were executed, possibly because the Athenians believed them capable of conceiving in-

tent. But convicted inanimate objects were merely exiled, a sentence accomplished by throwing the offending object across the border out of the territory of Attica and into neighboring Boeotia. So, for example, a roof-tile that had fallen from a housetop and killed a person on the street below would be taken to the Prytaneion for trial and punishment!

Some homicide laws might have actually contributed to the proliferation of highway killers. How likely was it that people exiled for crimes would join other communities, as opposed to becoming career criminals? The need for the Phreatto hints at this problem.

Despite legally recognizing several different types of homicide, the Greeks did not have many terms to describe them. They had no equivalents to our "murder in the first degree" or "manslaughter," for example, though as described in the box above they did take into account one's intent or state of mind during the commission of a homicide. They also had no distinction between terms for "murder" and "homicide," as the current US legal system does; although these terms are often used interchangeably by laypersons, technically and legally they describe two different acts. *Homicide* means simply "killing a person" and includes any kind of killing, such as killing in battle, execution by government, and murder; *murder* is a subset of homicide, and refers to intentional and malicious killing. The list below indicates some of the more common ancient Greek terms used to describe murder and murderers. These terms will be useful in examining the main evidence for serial killing in ancient Greece.

1. The most general Greek term for "killing," *phonos*, also meant "murder" in the sense of intentional killing of a human being, and sometimes specified a legal term with that meaning, as in Draco's law.
2. More specifically and frequently, *androphonos*, literally "man-killing," was the technical legal term for "a person who kills a fellow human."
3. The term *kakourgos*, literally "evildoer," frequently described criminals of all types, especially thieves. But by the fourth century BCE the word was mainly used to refer to murderers.
4. Especially useful when considering serial killing in ancient Greece is the term *sphageus*, which meant "murderer," but which more often occurred in the stronger sense of "butcher" or "cutthroat" because of its regular use during religious animal sacrifices in which the priest ritually cut an animal's throat. That is, the Greeks used this term most regularly in the context of ritual animal slaughter for sacrifices to the gods. It appears far less

frequently in relation to the killing of men, and when it does, it relates either to those who carry out mass murders or murders of unusual brutality, including what we would identify as serial murders. The related term *sphage* is a much stronger word than *phonos*, often denoting massacre rather than homicide.[8]

"Against a Murderer"

Although we know a lot about the different courts, surprisingly few historical cases of homicide have survived from ancient Athens. Most information comes from surviving speeches written for plaintiffs or defendants in homicide cases. We also have a number of fictional "practice" speeches from antiquity that reflect real-life homicide cases and how they might have been argued. One of these fictional speeches contains what may be the best example of serial killing from ancient Greek society. This is Libanius's "common topics" exercise about the fictional highwayman who did much more than merely rob his victims. A closer look at this speech provides even more information about serial killing in the ancient world.[9]

In ancient Greece and Rome, teachers of rhetoric assigned common topics exercises to teach students logical and rhetorical skills. Typical exercises asked students to argue for or against a plaintiff or defendant; they might be asked to prosecute an acknowledged (though fictional) criminal, such as an adulterer, thief, traitor, or murderer. The "murderer" was a standard figure in rhetorical handbooks, and a fictional defendant, like one in real life, might even demonstrate two criminal aspects, such as "murderous thief."[10] Libanius wrote dozens of these rhetorical exercises for his pupils to study, and his mock-speech called simply "Against a Murderer" shows that the Greeks recognized many characteristics that we usually associate with modern-day serial killers. Significantly, although the murderer in the speech is fictional, Libanius must have modeled him after real murderers, or the exercise would have been useless. As later chapters of this book explain in more detail, the figure known as the "highway robber" was a legitimate danger to people venturing outside the boundaries of their villages and cities. Libanius's speech also provides information on the ancient Greek attitude toward homicide laws, "which of all our distinguished laws are much more precise than the rest," because of all crimes committed against men, homicide ranks as the most terrible, and endless blood feuds must be prevented.[11] Regarding the accused murderer, here called by the term *androphonos*, Libanius says,

This man alone of all of us has stood in opposition to the laws and, regarding them as being in reality idle chatter and empty words, has made his own right hand more authoritative than our divinely-ordained laws, donning the proper demeanor but exercising wicked intentions and adopting a character contrary to appearances; in our midst, mild, but in deserted places, harsh; in word, humane, but in action, most savage; in the marketplace, self-controlled, but outside the walls, like a wild beast. Taking up his position in a lofty and precipitous spot, he observes travelers from afar, and he hides his victims, taking the night as his accomplice in this audacious act. By Heracles, the sort of dramas with which he has filled the road! One man was hurrying to get to his village and was killed. Another was returning to the city and perished. Someone else went in pursuit of a runaway slave and was murdered. . . . Casting aside all human reasoning, he thrusts his sword without mercy.[12]

In this description of the murderer, which comes early in the speech, Libanius describes several characteristics that happen to be typical of serial killers down the centuries. He hints at what we would call sociopathy, the mental disorder in which a person lacks a sense of moral responsibility or social conscience, and which is characterized by a lack of empathy or remorse and by a lack of behavioral inhibition. Sociopaths excel at mimicking "normal" or "neurotypical" behavior, which explains why serial killers often fit the "friendly neighbor" stereotype. Libanius also demonstrates intent on the part of the defendant, and implies that he seeks a specific type of victim, given that he watches the road from high ground and targets travelers who appear vulnerable. This is not a surprising tactic for highway robbers or criminals in general, but it indicates both premeditation and selectivity of victim. In this case, the defendant has his eye on men traveling alone at night. Significantly, he deliberately hides the victim's bodies. This becomes an issue later, when Libanius suggests that such an action goes far beyond the cruelty of the typical brigand, because hiding the bodies denies the families the chance to bury their dead properly: "The most terrible part of the disaster was that the majority of those who died could not even be taken up for burial," both because most victims' bodies had been hidden and because, after some victims had been found, people were too afraid to go outside the city gates to search for others, for fear of being killed themselves.[13]

In a subsequent section of the speech, Libanius demonstrates the rhetorical device of addressing a recriminating aside to the murderer. Here, he provides details explaining how the man's crimes went beyond the typical robbery-killing: "You were in the habit of striking down suppliants and slaughtering those who beseeched you and cutting to pieces those who grov-eled at your feet."[14] In this sentence Libanius moves from the general to the specific and describes the killings in ritual terms. For example, he says the victims were "beseeching" or "begging" (*hiketeuontas*), the Greek word usu-ally used to describe religious supplication, especially when praying to a de-ity. The word for "groveling" (*proskulindoumenous*)—in the sense of being on one's knees and begging for favor—also more usually occurs in a religious context. And the word "slaughter" (*apesphattes*) is now followed by "cut up" (*katekoptes*). This detailed Greek terminology warrants discussion because such specific wording in the passage accomplishes several things that relate very closely to modern serial killing. First, Libanius equates the killer with a god; modern serial killers are often diagnosed as being megalomaniacs and as having narcissistic personality disorder, considering themselves god-like. Next, Libanius uses religious language that configures the killings as a kind of ritual, which is often very important to modern serial killers even if the ritual has no obvious religious overtones or symbolism. Last, the ex-tended description of the murderer as ignoring his victims' pleas and cut-ting up his victims indicates a level of torture and mutilation considered ex-tremely unusual for a highway robber in antiquity, suggesting instead the behavior often associated with modern serial killers. Many brigands in the ancient world did not find it necessary to kill their victims. Those who did kill them usually did so swiftly. But Libanius indicates that this murderer delayed killing his victims, instead listening to them plead, which perhaps even gave them false hope that he might let them go. Then he not only killed them but also chopped them up, although Libanius's phrasing leaves unclear the specific extent to which the bodies were mutilated.

In a later section, where Libanius explains the murderer's inclinations by providing evidence from the man's previous behavior, he presents the pat-tern familiar in the psychology of modern serial killers:

> He has now been caught having committed the most terrible crime, but he seems to me to have arrived at this point by progressing from lesser crimes. He got away with stealing many items, he broke through not a few walls, he plotted against marriages, he committed violent acts, he plundered with ease what does not belong to him. By not paying the penalty for each of these crimes, he was taught to shrink from nothing, and by remaining un-punished for his other crimes, he has come down to us as a murderer. On what evidence do I say this? Every evildoer [*kakourgos*] naturally begins with actions not very terrible and not done out of wickedness. Then, test-ing himself at the first level, he advances to the second, and from there he

moves on to harsher crimes, and finally he comes to the very crowning act of wrongdoing.[15]

Recalling the typical criminal development serial killers often demonstrate, this murderer started out with petty theft and burglary, progressed to destruction of property, and then to unspecified "violent acts." The Greek term used here, *bebiastai*, often refers to assault and battery and possibly rape, but Libanius probably used the intentionally general word to leave the exact nature of these crimes to the audience's imagination. Notably, Libanius presents the killer's background as already typical for someone committing multiple murders. In short, nearly two thousand years ago Libanius recognized a pattern that has proven to be characteristic of many serial killers: starting early in life with less serious crimes and progressing in adulthood to repeated murders. Libanius's description indicates that this pattern appeared long before modern psychologists and criminologists formally acknowledged it. Suetonius used the same pattern in his vilification of Nero (discussed in chapter 3).

Even the desired punishment for serial murder did not differ substantially in ancient Greece. Libanius's speech, when addressing the jury, notes the inadequacy of the available penalties: "Will you not feel angry at the fact that even if he were to die three times, if that were possible, he could not pay a sufficient penalty?"[16] This rhetorical question highlights a main difference between how the ancient Greeks dealt with multiple homicides and how we deal with them today. All the homicide laws from ancient Greece address the issue of single killings, and the penalty was usually either death or exile. But Libanius's question indicates a concern for the lack of any contrast between the penalty for killing one person and killing several, and laments that the courts could offer no punishment greater than death. Today, a serial killer or mass murderer can be charged with multiple homicides and brought up on separate charges for each. Modern-day serial killers often receive consecutive life sentences or even more than one death sentence. Such penalties are necessarily symbolic rather than literal and serve mainly to acknowledge the suffering of the victims' families, but they remain quite common. Ted Bundy, for example, received three death sentences in two separate trials for homicides he committed in Florida, and was executed there in 1989. Jeffrey Dahmer, found legally sane despite having been diagnosed with borderline personality disorder, was convicted of fifteen of the sixteen murders he had committed in Wisconsin and was sentenced to fifteen life terms in prison. He never got to serve them, because a fellow inmate killed him just two years into his first term. "BTK Killer" Dennis

Rader received ten consecutive life sentences, with an earliest possible release date of February 25, 2180.

The Greeks, in short, took homicide and especially murder very seriously, at least when Greek citizens were concerned. The government enacted homicide laws and cases were tried in public court, a main motivation being to avoid ongoing blood feuds between families. But the Romans adopted a different position. For much of their history, the government did not concern itself with murder—not even the murder of Roman citizens—other than in exceptional cases when the murder posed a potential threat to the government itself.

CHAPTER 5

Murder and the Advantages of Roman Citizenship

After Draco developed his law code in ancient Athens, the Athenians continued to adjust and refine his homicide laws. They added various details over time, such as the types of case handled by the different courts. But in Rome, unlike in Greece, the attitudes and laws concerning murder shifted considerably over the centuries, depending on the prevailing form of government. Rome started out as a monarchy, ruled by kings from 753 to 509 BCE. During this time the Romans started developing laws concerning murder. According to their traditional version of this historical period, the second king of Rome, Numa Pompilius (r. 715–673 BCE), was the first Roman ruler to enact a law prohibiting murder. He did this partially out of self-interest, in that kings preferred to control the power to kill and consequently assigned such power to themselves and limited or prohibited it for others. Numa and the kings who came after him had jurisdiction to try and to punish offenders in cases of intentional homicide, and they often meted out death as the penalty. Numa's law distinguished between intentional and unintentional homicide, and in the case of the latter, a ram or other animal could be sacrificed in place of the killer.[1] The Roman record from this time contains nothing regarding multiple or serial murder, but we know that the usual gangs of brigands roamed the highways, sometimes killing their victims after robbing them.

The Roman monarchy fell in 509 BCE, and the republican form of government that replaced it lasted until 27 BCE. This republican government basically consisted of a legislative assembly with different public officials overseeing various aspects of running the state. The republican constitution continued to evolve over several centuries, but it was nearly always characterized by an ongoing conflict between the upper and lower classes. This tension was reflected in the Roman attitude toward homicide. During the republican period, murder was not a legally defined crime, at least not one actionable by the government.[2] The earliest known Roman law code, the Twelve Tables (ca. 450 BCE), did not include any laws specifically concerning murder, although the Tables did tangentially incorporate laws on certain types of justifiable and unintentional homicide, including the legality of killing a thief caught in the act on one's property (a type of killing also permissible in ancient Athens), and the illegality of poisoning, the penalty for which was death. Over the centuries the state sometimes also concerned itself with kin-killing (*parricidium*). Like the Greeks, the Romans had no specific word for murder, but instead used general words that translated as "murder" depending on context, including *caedere, interficere, occidere,* and *necare,* each of which had its own nuances but could also refer to justifiable or unjustifiable homicide. The English word "homicide" itself comes from the Latin *homicidium,* but that term does not appear until the first century BCE in the works of the Roman statesman Cicero. The crime of *homicidium* is otherwise unknown in the Republic and was never proscribed by law.[3]

The absence of murder laws for many centuries during the Republic did not mean that the Romans lacked concern for the unjustified taking of human life. Although the government usually remained uninvolved, Roman citizens had recourse to other methods of dispute resolution not requiring government action,[4] such as arbitration or, more often, the kind of familial blood feud that the Greeks tried so hard to avoid—death being the preferred penalty for murder as far as the victim's relatives were concerned. In fact, during the Roman Republic the injured families themselves dealt with most occurrences of homicide. Only if the killings somehow threatened the stability of the government did the state get involved. Suspicious deaths of high-ranking officials, for example, attracted the attention of the Roman Senate, which would order a formal investigation and, if suspects were identified, a trial. An investigation was even more likely in the event of more than one such death. Since most of our literary sources for Roman history were written by and focused on the aristocratic classes, several narratives survive that describe what might have been serial murder during the Roman Republic.

The Case of the Sila Forest Murders

One peculiar and disturbing occurrence that caught the attention of the Roman government was the case of multiple murders in the Sila Forest. Located in the Calabrian region of southern Italy, the Sila Forest was rich in pine and fir trees. The Romans exploited these natural resources, especially the valuable pine resin, which they used in various glues, such as caulking for ships. In 138 BCE, a number of contractors working for a pine resin factory were found murdered. Our main account of the incident comes from Cicero, writing nearly one hundred years after the event:

> By order of the Roman Senate, the consuls Publius Scipio and Decimus Brutus tried a heinous and important case [*re atroci magnaque*]. In the Sila Forest a slaughter [*caedes*] had occurred and prominent men [*noti . . . homines*] had been murdered. A number of slaves were accused of the deed, and even some freedmen working for the company, which had contracted for the resin-works from the censors Publius Cornelius and Lucius Mummius. Consequently, the Senate had decreed that the consuls should investigate and present their conclusions about the incident. (Cicero, *Brutus* 85)

The case was so complicated that the consuls, after investigating and listening to the evidence on both sides, decided that they needed to hear more. Ultimately, after the talented orator Servius Galba argued their case, the defendants were acquitted.

It may seem odd to a modern audience, but Cicero's main interest in bringing up this case was not the unusual multiple murders but the reputation and effectiveness of the eloquent orator Galba. So, unfortunately for the history of serial murder, Cicero does not provide any clear details about the nature of the killings. Was this a mass murder, with bodies found at about the same time and same place, or were the bodies discovered scattered throughout the forest over a period of days or weeks? The Latin word *caedes*, used by Cicero to describe the killings, is nonspecific. It contains the suggestion of "cutting," and sometimes means "slaughter" or "massacre," implying a mass murder, but can also refer to murder more generally, including the murder of individuals. Given the context, particularly the suspicion that a large number of people carried out the killings, a premeditated uprising resulting in mass slaughter seems more likely than serial murder. The case remains mysterious, and among other missing details, Cicero does not explain why the slaves and freedmen would stay in the area to be accused of the crime rather than fleeing elsewhere if they had indeed slaughtered Roman citizens.

The incident disturbed the Roman government enough to warrant their involvement, but the Senate technically did not assign the consuls Cicero mentions (Publius Scipio and Decimus Brutus) to investigate homicide. They were sent to conduct an investigation concerning "a heinous and im-

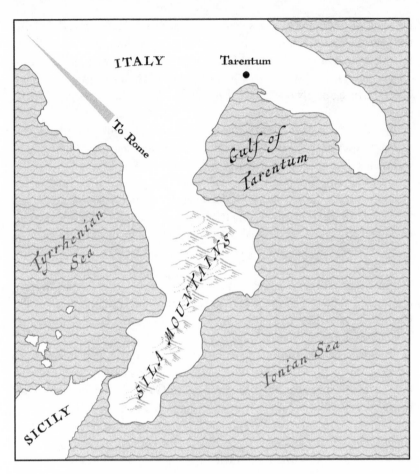

Reference map of ancient Italy, southern part, showing the Sila Mountains region. Map by Michele Angel.

portant case," which was not a specific legal charge.[5] Rather, the magnitude and egregiously atrocious nature of the incident compelled the senators to send consuls to make inquiries. The Senate focused not on the fact that many people died, but that the victims were "prominent men" allegedly killed by people of lower status, that is, slaves and freedmen (see the box on the facing page). Cicero also mentions that the company leased the pine-pitch factory from the censors, the officials in charge of various state finances, so the Roman government already had direct involvement in the company's activities and thus had a vested interest in the success of its endeavors. In short, the disruption of the social order, the high status of the victims, the seriousness of the act, and the governmental ties of the victims all helped to bring about senatorial participation in this trial. Therefore, rather than illustrating murder as a crime in which the government regularly took an interest, this example shows only that an act of murder could come to the attention of the government under certain circumstances, such as those involving prominent citizens and the government's own financial interests.

The type of slaughter carried out in the Sila Forest was very rare in ancient Rome, at least until a number of political uprisings in the late Republic resulted in multiple deaths. Less rare in the republican period were cases

---

CLASSISM AND RACISM IN
(SERIAL) MURDER INVESTIGATIONS

In the Sila Forest case, the fact that aristocrats had been killed was a main factor in gaining attention for and investigation of the crime. The same largely holds true today. When a serial killer goes after members of society considered somehow less important, such as the homeless, or prostitutes, or, say, African American children, authorities pay far less attention and allot far fewer resources to the case than when a killer targets white college co-eds or prominent citizens. As Trudier Harris points out regarding the Atlanta Child Murders of 1979–1981, "Indeed, we could argue, reasonably and easily, that the Atlanta Child Murders are the best-known ignored and unsolved murder cases in American history. Though Wayne Bertram Williams was convicted of killing two of the victims, the remaining cases have not been solved."[6] Similarly, when the serial murder of Black prostitutes was clearly under way in the 1980s in Los Angeles, "the authorities seem to have sung an indifferent tune. . . . This degree of underrepresentation and unwillingness to cooperate is rooted in the ongoing tensions of gender, class, and race. In fact, the authorities did not release pertinent information until twenty-two years later, leaving many unaware of such a crime spree and therefore, unable to take preventive measures. When questioned as to why they did not release any witness-sketches, which they had at their disposal, the police claimed that such tools were unreliable. . . . If this had happened under different circumstances with different people (consider a White blonde girl in the Valley), things would have panned out in a whole other way."[7] Conversely, the murders of four petite, largely middle-class, white brunette co-eds at the University of Florida in Gainesville in 1990 attracted immediate and widespread media attention, and the police wasted no time in identifying and arresting the murderer, Danny Rolling, within just a few months of the crimes.

---

of alleged poisoning of multiple individuals, that is, mass poisonings, and several of these cases share characteristics with serial murder. In the government's view, perpetrators of poisoning, *veneficium*, posed a significant threat to Rome's security. *Veneficium* was one of the few crimes that had a long history as an actionable offense in Rome, even before the creation in the second century BCE of a standing court concerning assassins and poisoners (*quaestio perpetua de sicariis et veneficiis*). The first mass poisoning occurred in the late fourth century BCE. Like the case of the Sila Forest killings, this one illustrates why the government became involved in trials for poisoning: prominent citizens died, and the number of deaths suggested a potential threat from the poisoner(s) to the stability of the Roman state.

The Case of the Roman Matrons

In *The Encyclopedia of Serial Killers*, author Michael Newton cites this case of mass poisoning, which occurred in Rome in 331 BCE, as the earliest recorded case of serial murder. This is a highly debatable claim—both in its characterization of the case as serial murder and in its statement that this is the earliest serial murder recorded—but one very much worth discussing, if only to elaborate on the difficulties of such distinctions given the nature of our evidence, as with the Sila Forest murders. The Roman historian Livy (ca. 59 BCE–17 CE), our main source for the story, writes that the year in question was notorious for a plague but that a high number of deaths among the foremost men of the state (*primores civitatis*) led to rumors that they had been intentionally killed by poison rather than dying from the pestilence.[8] The afflicted all appeared to suffer from the same ailment. A maidservant approached Quintus Fabius Maximus, the official in charge of public order at that time, and said that she would tell him the cause of this ailment as long as he promised that she would be spared from any blame. Fabius secured immunity for her, upon which she revealed the danger to the state from a "female crime" (*muliebri fraude*), that is, a crime being perpetrated by women. She said that Roman matrons—women of married status—were brewing poisons, and that if officials would follow her right away, they might catch these women in the very act. Following their informant, they indeed found a group of women cooking up batches of drugs and other potions already finished and hidden away. Officials seized the prepared potions and arrested approximately twenty matrons at whose homes they found the alleged poisons.

When the accused women appeared before the magistrates, two of the matrons, Cornelia and Sergia, both from aristocratic families, argued that the potions were medicinal. The maidservant, faced with this refutation, suggested that they drink some of their own potion to prove that her accusations against them were false. The authorities allowed the two women a little time to discuss the matter, and after they conferred with the other matrons they all agreed to drink the potions, which evidently really were poisonous, since they all died. This caused much consternation among the officials, who then arrested many other women also implicated in the crime. In total, nearly 170 Roman matrons were found guilty of poisoning.

Up to that time, according to Livy, there had never been a charge of poisoning investigated in Rome. People considered the affair to be a portent from the gods; in the absence of any understandable reason for the matrons' behavior, people believed the women were struck mad rather than being inherently evil. Because the event disrupted civic order and people worried what such an event meant for Rome's well-being, city officials decided to follow an old tradition undertaken during times of strife: they drove a nail into the Temple of Jupiter Optimus Maximus, an action symbolically meant to dispel pestilence from the city.

Livy himself expressed a great deal of skepticism about this story. He believed that disease, rather than poison, was the more likely cause for so many deaths. His thinking is understandable, particularly since his sources apparently gave no motive whatsoever for these women to poison so many people, and Livy was highly conscientious about recording reasons for people's actions when such information was available to him. There are several other interpretive problems. Possibly the women truly were trying to cure people of the disease, not kill them, meaning that the matrons may indeed have been attempting to create medicine. This might explain why, when authorities suggested that they drink the potion they themselves had brewed, they agreed to do so.[9] But Livy's account of the incident raises more questions than it answers. If the potion had already killed a large number of people rather than curing them, why did the women keep administering it? Maybe they really were aiming to poison prominent citizens, because otherwise how could the women fail to notice that their "medicine" did not work? But then what would their motive have been? Or did the potion appear to work on some people and not others, possibly explaining why they continued to use it? Livy mentions that some of the afflicted survived the plague, so it seems possible (if not plausible) that not everyone who ingested the potion necessarily died from it, but then why would the women not point this out? And if, as medicine, the concoction was ineffective, the women had no reason to think the potion would not kill them, too. Perhaps they drank it themselves because they knew they were facing execution and chose suicide. Only a few aspects of this case appear to be solid fact: high-ranking citizens died, the women brewed a potion of some sort, and the Roman government became involved.

This story of the Roman matrons appears not only in Newton but in various other sources about the history of serial murder.[10] The main reason for its inclusion in such sources, and here, is the alleged murder of so many people by the same method over a period of time. But given the number of alleged killers and several other aspects of the case, does this episode really present as serial murder? Possibly. The poisonings were supposedly enacted by a group of women working together, and although most serial killers act alone, some do in fact work with partners or as family units, such as the Benders of Kansas and, in modern times, the Manson family (which also intentionally targeted the upper classes).[11] The claim that 170 women worked in concert to kill dozens of aristocrats seems like the product of a government overreaction, because such an act would not only be highly unusual but would qualify as a political conspiracy, which is precisely why it came to the attention of the Roman government in the first place, as with the Sila Forest murders.[12] In short, the story of the Roman matrons contains the basic elements characteristic of serial murders, but, like the Sila Forest murders, drew attention mainly because of its suspected conspiratorial nature.

Since the Roman government regularly ordered investigations into mass killings of prominent citizens, news of such events reached a broad population. This would not have been the case with any multiple murders that might have occurred in the slums of Rome, such as the lower-class Subura district (notorious for prostitution), where such deaths would have remained largely ignored by officials. State investigations routinely showed up in the works of Roman annalists (recorders of major events). Livy, drawing on such information, wrote about several other trials for poisoning. Like the case of the Roman matrons, most of these also involved large numbers of high-ranking victims, often also during times of plague, and, predictably, attracted the attention of the Roman Senate.[13] Another incident, from the second century BCE, presents a more typical case of serial murder. This one, too, involved a woman.

The Case of Quarta Hostilia

A series of deaths occurred in Rome around 180 BCE.[14] A number of very prominent men, including powerful politicians, died under mysterious circumstances. During a serious outbreak of disease, people began to suspect that at least some of the more notable deaths were the work of criminals who might have been taking advantage of the pestilence to assassinate important officials. The Senate therefore ordered the deaths to be investigated as poisonings. A widespread inquiry ensued, encompassing everything within a ten-mile radius of the city of Rome, and even various market towns and other public meeting places beyond that. Suspicion eventually fell upon a woman named Quarta Hostilia. Her husband, Gaius Calpurnius Piso, came from an illustrious Roman family and held one of the two consulships, the highest elected office. He had been one of the first to die, and under questionable circumstances. His stepson, Quarta Hostilia's son by a previous marriage, became consul in his place. This would not have been quite so suspicious if she had not been overheard bragging, just two months previously, that she would manage to have her son made consul within a few weeks. As a result, rumors quickly spread that she had murdered her husband. Her boast, along with much other (unspecified) evidence, was sufficiently damning that authorities charged Quarta Hostilia with murder in the death of her husband and in the other cases in Rome.[15]

Various Roman officials believed that Quarta Hostilia had not worked alone. As the ongoing investigation into the alleged poisonings extended far beyond the city, one official in charge of the investigation managed to sentence no fewer than 3,000 people. In fact, the investigation took so much time that the official remarked he would have to give up either the case or the administration of his province, because he could not possibly devote himself to both. Ultimately, Quarta Hostilia was executed, along with several thousand others.[16] So again, is this a case of mass murder, serial murder, or something else entirely? Did all of these eminent men succumb to disease, or did criminals use the ongoing pestilence as a cover for murder? Did Quarta Hostilia kill her husband and other important officials to make room for her son? Such an agenda would place her among the earliest known politically motivated individual serial killers. At minimum, this case, like that of the Roman matrons, shows how the Roman government was strikingly unconcerned with homicides of any kind until they affected the upper classes.[17]

The *Sicarii*, or "Dagger-men"

This attitude of the Roman government toward homicide remained consistent throughout the Republic. The government, always concerned about threats to the stability of the state (and to their control over it), tended to

The *sicarii* also gave their name to a genus of spider, *Sicarius* (of the family *Sicariidae*), native to various Southern Hemisphere regions. Like the Roman *sicarii* from which they take their name, these spiders are expert ambush predators. They attack their victims with dagger-like fangs.

obsess especially about poisoners, but also kept watch for another type of political assassin. Along with those accused of poisonings, a class of criminals known as *sicarii* were tried in public courts even before the relatively late creation of the formal homicide court mentioned above.[18] The term *sicarius*, "dagger man" (from the Latin *sica*, "dagger"), originally referred to a hired killer or assassin, but came to mean any person who carried a concealed weapon, as authorities believed such an act threatened the public order (cf. modern Spanish *sicario*, "hitman"). Unlike most murderers, the *sicarius* posed a threat to the government because he was essentially a gangster, and as such either killed or arranged killings for a price, although some *sicarii* merely robbed people at knifepoint. A *sicarius* might kill more than one person over a period of time, might be like a criminal with power issues, and, given his choice of career, might be a sociopath or psychopath, having joined a gang in order to indulge his violent tendencies. But other than these characteristics, we have few details about individual *sicarii*. Can we really call the *sicarius* a serial killer? The question seems worth asking given that, aside from poisoners, the *sicarii* were the only murderers to draw any real attention from the Roman government.

Like many of the other questions raised here, whether to view a *sicarius* as a serial killer is complicated. The *sicarius* often belonged to a gang and was usually politically motivated. But neither of these characteristics completely disqualifies him from being a serial killer. Not all criminologists and psychologists view hitmen as serial killers, but some assassins enjoy their work excessively, deriving both psychological and financial rewards from it, and some commit personally motivated murders on the side, separate from their contract killings. Some criminologists also do not consider gang members to be serial killers, no matter how many murders they commit.[19] Then there are the problems of whether politically motivated gangs of *sicarii* should be considered terrorists and whether terrorists should be regarded as serial killers, but such discussion extends beyond the scope of this book. For example, many people would probably balk at calling Eleazar ben Ya'ir a serial killer, even though he was a leader of the *Sicarii* (with a capital "S"), a specific group of Jewish "dagger-men" working in Judaea during the mid-first century CE. As revolutionary extremists, these *Sicarii* made it their goal to drive the Romans out of occupied Judaea, and they did so by assassinating as many Roman officials as they could. It is not unreasonable to view them as terrorists or guerillas given their activities and context. But were they serial killers? As far as we can tell from the historical accounts, they lacked the personality traits more typical of serial killers, and as a group they believed that they were acting on behalf of an oppressed community, which was demonstrably not the case with the *sicarii* who carried out contract killings in Rome and its environs.

Nevertheless, the ubiquity of poisoners and *sicarii* became a matter of increasing concern for the Roman government by the first century BCE. As Rome became entangled in a series of wars, including a war against the Numidian king Jugurtha (112–106 BCE), three wars against King Mithradates of Pontus in Asia Minor (between 89 and 63 BCE), and civil wars (between 88 and 81 BCE), an influx of "professional poisoners" from various regions including Asia and northern Africa set up shops in Rome.[20] In response, in 81 BCE the politician Cornelius Sulla, a self-proclaimed dictator, passed the *Lex Cornelia de sicariis et veneficiis*, the "Cornelian law concerning assassins and poisoners." The law had disturbingly broad applications. It was originally intended to allow governmental prosecution of murderers who killed by stealthy means (hidden weapons, including daggers and poisons), but officials also employed this law to prosecute people suspected of practicing magic, which often involved drugs that might be poisonous when prepared in certain ways. The *Lex Cornelia* was not principally concerned with homicide in general, but with very specific types of killing that, because of their nature, posed a particular threat to the state and therefore to Sulla's authority. Like other men in positions of power, such as the Roman kings, Sulla himself retained the right to kill, and he started to publish lists of people who could be killed with impunity. These lists, or proscriptions, officially identified and condemned alleged enemies of the state and provided a method to legitimize the political power to kill,[21] but in many cases the proscribed were simply stripped of their property as a means of replenishing the state treasury.

From the Roman monarchy through the Republic and into the early Empire, Rome was known more for its fantastically improbable number of politically motivated killings rather than for what we would call serial killings. Highway banditry, too, posed an immense problem for the Roman authorities, at times serious enough to undermine the authority of the Roman Empire on a large and embarrassing scale.[22] The evidence tells us that even for cases that sound suspiciously like serial murder, the Roman authorities felt insecure enough to see conspiracies against the state rather than individual killers at work, and acted accordingly, usually quite out of proportion to the crime. Sometimes they punished thousands of people as a deterrent to future conspiracies, but an ineffective deterrent at that, since the government—whether the Senate, a powerful politician like Sulla, or an emperor—tended to see conspiracies everywhere.

Neither the Greek nor Roman legal systems noted the "serial" nature of what we call serial murder. Murder was murder, at least if it involved the killing of a citizen. But the record indicates that what we know as serial murders certainly occurred, and that authorities dealt with them in the same way that they would have dealt with a single murder. They investigated reports of homicide, with the intent behind the crime taken into consideration in both societies. But Rome differed from Greece in several important respects in its dealings with homicide. Whereas both societies concerned themselves with the murder of citizens, Rome apparently never had the same concern about potentially endless blood feuds that Greece did. So, in Rome the only cases that received attention were those that were likely to affect the government, such as the case of the Sila Forest and the various multiple poisonings among the upper classes. Also, the Romans policed their territories in ways that the Greeks did not, which may have contributed both to a lack of more individually based crimes and to a lack of reporting crimes perpetrated upon individuals. Even so, the literary and historical evidence shows that serial killers already existed, that they exhibited the kinds of behavior now recognized as sociopathic, and that the Greeks and Romans had a legal framework for recognizing various types of homicide. One significant difference, though, was that the Greeks took homicide seriously enough to create no fewer than five different courts in which to litigate it, whereas the Romans demonstrated a high level of indifference toward homicide except in exceedingly prominent cases.

CHAPTER 6

The Popularity of Serial Poisoning

Both the Greeks and the Romans had good reason to be concerned about poisonings, whether as part of a plot to kill large numbers of people all at once or as a means to carry out serial murder. As early as the *Odyssey*, the young men who have taken over Odysseus's palace in his absence mock his ineffectual son, Telemachus, joking that "he wishes to go to Ephyra . . . to bring back life-destroying drugs and place them into the wine-jugs, and kill us all" (2.328–30). Less of a joke was the use of the toxic plant hellebore to poison the town water supply of Cirrha in Greece during an internal conflict known as the First Sacred War (ca. 590 BCE).[1] Yet although it has occasionally been used in military actions, poisoning has far more frequently been a preferred method of serial (and other) murderers throughout much of human history, if perhaps less so since the twentieth century, when methods to detect the presence of various poisons in the body as well as for finding out who was responsible for the poisoning became increasingly reliable and more widely available. But until the modern era many murderers favored poisoning as a less personal, more efficient, and difficult-to-trace method of killing. Poisoning has also been the most popular method of serial murder employed by women, who are generally less likely than men to prefer hands-on violence and bloodshed, but men, too, have resorted to poisoning, especially when targeting family members. Oppianicus supposedly used poison for at least one of the murders he allegedly committed, according to Cicero's speech *Pro Cluentio* (discussed in chapter 3).

Serial poisoners appear far less frequently in Greek myth and history than in Roman literature of all kinds. When they do appear in Greek literature, they are usually female and often witches or women accused of witchcraft. The mythological sorceress Medea, for example, in addition to murders she committed with swords, killed several people via poisonous drugs (*pharmaka*), including the princess and king of Corinth. She also attempted to poison Theseus. Her motives were partially vengeful and partially political. Greek literature also describes female suppliers and users of unreliable herbal remedies and love-potions who inadvertently became serial poisoners through improper administration of such drugs. Sometimes such women stood trial and were found guilty of poisoning, even if they lacked the intent to cause death and thus clearly lacked a (serial) killer mentality.[2]

In ancient Rome, however, poisoning as a method of murder reached a bizarre peak. Many highly effective poisons, from slow- to quick-acting, were readily available. These included hemlock, henbane, various mushrooms, yew berries, nightshade, and the highly potent aconite. The venoms of certain animals, such as scorpions, various insects, toads, and fish, were also used regularly. Poisoning became especially popular among female members of the imperial court during the Roman Empire, but occurred with alarming frequency among all social classes and for a wide variety of motives, such as to gain an inheritance, to eliminate a husband or other irritating family member, or to get rid of one's personal or political enemies.[3] Poisoning became such a concern for the Romans that even before the Empire, the dictator Lucius Cornelius Sulla passed a law in 82 BCE that not only allowed for prosecution of cases of poisoning, but also contained provisions against anyone who made, sold, bought, possessed, or gave poison for the purpose of poisoning another person. This *Lex Cornelia de sicariis et veneficiis* ("Cornelian law concerning assassins and poisoners," discussed in the previous chapter), in effect for several hundred years, also contained provisions against anyone suspected of armed robbery or murder, most notably the *sicarii*. The punishments allowed by the *Lex Cornelia* varied and changed over time, but the main penalty was banishment, including loss of property and Roman citizenship. The most serious problem with this law was its interpretation: one had to prove that a person carrying a knife or a little bag of poison actually intended to harm another person with it—and proving intent could be tricky. Also, courts interpreted the law so broadly that it was even used to accuse some people of witchcraft, because the Romans, like the Greeks, believed that witchcraft often involved poisonous potions. The first-century BCE poet Horace, for example, accuses the fictional witch Canidia of routinely dispatching her enemies with poison.[4]

Given poison's prevalence as a method of surreptitious assassination in ancient Rome, it is not surprising that many prominent figures died this way, if only occasionally as victims of *serial* poisoning. The historian Tacitus relates that when the emperor Tiberius's nephew Germanicus died under unusual circumstances in Antioch in 19 CE, suspicion fell upon the notorious poisoner Martina, a friend of Piso, the Roman governor of Syria, who was not on good terms with Germanicus. Martina was sent to Rome, where the Senate planned to interrogate her as part of an investigation into Germanicus's death, which they believed had been ordered by Piso. But she died suddenly on the journey, and authorities found poison hidden in a knot in her hair; she had evidently committed suicide.[5] Drusus, the son of Tiberius (r. 14–37 CE), supposedly died from poison administered by his wife, Livilla, though she did not generally make a habit of killing people and had, in this instance, merely aided her lover Sejanus, who wanted Drusus out of the way. But in many cases of poisoning, serial or otherwise, authorities never discovered the perpetrator. On the other hand, in several famous cases the authorities blamed particular people or groups of people for the crimes. Many of the accused were prosecuted; some of those were acquitted, others were found guilty, and several fit the profile of a serial killer.

Calpurnius Bestia: An Early "Bluebeard"?

One curious story about an (alleged) serial poisoner appears in the writings of Pliny the Elder, a first-century CE natural philosopher who compiled an extensive encyclopedic work called *Naturalis Historia*. In his section about various poisons, Pliny devotes some space to aconite, describing it as the fastest of all toxins and adding that if it is applied to the genitalia of female animals they die that same day. The Romans provided a mythological origin for the powerful drug, saying that aconite derived from the saliva of the monstrous dog Cerberus, three-headed guardian of the Underworld. When Heracles, to fulfill his twelfth and last labor, brought Cerberus up from the darkness of Hades to the light of earth, the dog vomited, spewing a poisonous saliva that infected the soil. The plants that grew there became poisonous themselves, and were named *aconitum* in Latin.[6] The witch Medea, for example, supposedly used aconite in her failed attempt to poison Theseus.

In discussing this highly effective poison, Pliny says that, when it is applied to the genitals of female animals, it "brings death on the very same day." As an example, Pliny tells the story of Calpurnius Bestia, a prominent Roman citizen of the first century BCE. According to Pliny, a young man named Marcus Caelius Rufus accused Calpurnius Bestia of using aconite to murder a succession of wives for their money, claiming that Bestia had applied the poison to the vaginal areas of his wives while they slept. Caelius employed an unusual tactic in his speech. He did not accuse Bestia himself of the crime, but rather Bestia's finger, which had smeared the aconite on

Johann Köler, *Heracles Brings Cerberus from the Gates of Hades* (1855).

the unsuspecting women.[7] Aconite, if applied to the mucous membrane of the vulva, enters the bloodstream and, as a highly potent neurotoxin, causes cardiac and respiratory failure. Despite the originality of Caelius's argument, Bestia was not charged with these crimes—but Caelius himself was later accused of trying to poison a woman named Clodia and of killing an ambassador. Cicero successfully defended Caelius in the speech known as the *Pro Caelio*. And although Bestia was never charged in the deaths of his wives, this story characterizes him as an early example of the "Bluebeard" male serial-killer type—one who murders a series of wives or fiancées (see chapter 11).

The Ambiguous Case of Nonius Asprenas

Calpurnius Bestia, truly guilty of serial wife murder or not, has (thanks to Pliny) gone down in history as one of the earliest Bluebeards on record. A few decades later, another unsettling case of poisoning, quite different from that of Bestia, shocked the city of Rome. The emperor Augustus, who ruled the city and the empire he created from 27 BCE until his death in 14 CE, numbered among his good friends a certain Lucius Nonius Asprenas. Not much is known about Asprenas aside from the ghastly incident that ruined his reputation. In 9 BCE or thereabouts, he threw a lavish banquet at which 130 of the dinner guests died. Titus Cassius Severus, a skilled orator and lawyer known for his aggressive manner, brought charges against Asprenas, alleging that he had intentionally poisoned his guests. Asprenas was brought to trial.

Both the incident itself and the subsequent charges, however, struck many people as highly suspicious. If the deaths were caused by accidental food poisoning, why had Asprenas himself not also been poisoned? For that matter, why would Asprenas poison so many people in a situation where he would obviously be the prime suspect? Unfortunately, the details of the prosecution's speech have not survived. Our ancient sources focus mainly on the effect this incident had on the emperor himself, because Augustus was at a loss as to how to respond to the situation. He feared that if he supported his friend, he might appear to be shielding a guilty man. Then again, if he did not support him, he would not only seem a poor excuse for a friend, but also might prejudice the court case against Asprenas by remaining at a cool distance. Ultimately, the Roman Senate advised Augustus to attend the trial but not to speak—not even as a character witness. Asprenas's defense lawyer, Gaius Asinius Pollio, was as good an orator as Severus, if not better; that, along with Augustus's presence at the trial, resulted in Asprenas's acquittal. Still, the accusation and trial put an end to Asprenas's career in politics.[8]

Is it reasonable to consider Asprenas a serial killer, as Newton has suggested?[9] Even if Augustus's close friend really had poisoned 130 dinner guests, would that not constitute mass murder rather than serial murder? Probably so. The story does not provide enough details to sort out the spe-

MITHRADATES'S POISON BANQUET

Unlike Nonias Asprenas, King Mithradates VI of Pontus (r. ca. 120–63 BCE) definitely planned to poison his dinner guests. Concerned about a potential threat from the neighboring region of Galatia, Mithradates invited sixty Galatian princes to stay at his royal palace, not in the hope of friendship but merely so that he could keep an eye on them. These "guests" did indeed plot to kill the king, but he discovered the plot and insisted that they all attend a feast. Adrienne Mayor writes, "Enough arsenic was on the Poison King's menu to murder all the guests," but three of them managed to escape.[10] Mithradates knew his arsenic from his hemlock. Ever since he was a child, when his father was assassinated by poison, "he dreamed of making himself immune to poisons."[11] He experimented with many, studying their good and bad effects. This included ingesting very small, nonlethal doses in an attempt to make himself immune to as many as possible, fearing that he would be assassinated just as his father had been. But Mithradates was also a serial killer of sorts. Aside from massacring tens of thousands of people in his wars with Rome, he picked off various family members one by one when suspecting them of treachery, and poison was his favorite (but not only) method for dispatching them. Mithradates's victims included his own mother, his brother, and four of his sons, among many others.

cifics. Most likely the compilers of some popular "serial killer" encyclopedias stretch the definition in an attempt to show that serial murder has a truly extensive history. The case of Nonius Asprenas does not correspond well to what we know of serial killings, but antiquity provides many other suitable candidates, some of whom, such as Locusta of Gaul, are also catalogued in encyclopedic compilations of serial killers.

Locusta of Gaul

In contrast to the dubious case of Asprenas, Roman literature contains more than enough evidence to allow consideration of Locusta of Gaul as a serial killer. Katherine Ramsland, a professor of forensic psychology, describes Locusta as "noted by many criminologists as the first documented serial killer."[12] Probably the single most famous poisoner from ancient Rome, Locusta lived during the first century CE, hailing from the Roman province of Gaul (much of which is now modern France). We know little else about her background but a great deal about her career. She made her living as a poisoner-for-hire and, as Ramsland observes, has been widely considered the first well-documented serial killer, probably because of her detailed and lurid (if probably largely fabricated) history. Technically, she was more professional assassin than serial killer (depending on where one stands in the debate about whether assassins are a type of serial killer). In fact, although she frequently supplied poisons to others, particularly for the right price, we have scant evidence that she administered her poisons personally. Still, Locusta became infamous as a poisoner even in her own time, and has her own entry in so many popular histories and encyclopedias of serial killing that we cannot overlook her. Suetonius called her "foremost among poisoners."[13]

According to Tacitus, Agrippina the Younger hired Locusta to poison the emperor Claudius.[14] Agrippina was Claudius's niece and also his fourth wife. She had a son by a previous marriage, and Claudius formally adopted this son, Nero (yes, that Nero), who became heir to the throne because he was older than Claudius's own son, Britannicus. Yet Agrippina, evidently impatient for Nero to become emperor, formulated a plan to poison Claudius. With Nero most likely lending a hand, she considered the various options. If she used a fast poison that killed him quickly, his death would be highly suspicious. But if she used a slow poison and Claudius lingered for days, he might guess that she had betrayed him, and might then have time to reinstate Britannicus as his heir. Agrippina decided to use a poison that would work slowly but confuse his mind, so that he would be unaware of exactly what was happening.

Agrippina next had to find a person skilled in poisons. She chose the highly qualified Locusta. As Tacitus (with his wry sense of humor) puts it, Locusta had recently been convicted and sentenced for poisoning, which made her especially well-suited to serve the imperial family.[15] She used her skills to mix a potion, while Agrippina arranged matters with the emperor's food taster. Rumor had it that the taster sprinkled the poison over a bowl of mushrooms, one of Claudius's favorite dishes. But because Claudius was already sluggish, or drunk, or both, the poison had no effect on him. A bowel movement apparently cleared his system. Agrippina, terrified that Claudius had survived this attempt on his life—she had been so sure the poison would work!—did not feel she could turn back. She now solicited the help of the emperor's doctor. Under the pretense of helping Claudius to vomit, the doctor stuck a feather smeared with a quick-working poison

Sixteenth-century woodcut illustrating scenes with Agrippina, Nero, and Claudius, including Agrippina feeding Claudius poisoned mushrooms (scene on the left).

down the emperor's throat. That did the trick. Claudius died in excruciating pain in the early hours of the morning. The year was 54 CE. Agrippina's plan had succeeded. Nero was declared emperor.

Even in his new position of power, Nero worried about his stepbrother Britannicus, who was now nearly fourteen years old, the age at which he could officially be considered an adult in Roman society. As Tacitus tells it, the boy was very popular, so naturally Nero wanted to be rid of him and any potential political influence he might have.[16] But Nero could not find any crime with which to charge the boy and order his execution. Following in his mother's footsteps, Nero decided to go the stealthy route and poison Britannicus, enlisting the services of Locusta. She was quite notorious at this point, having been convicted yet again in another case of poisoning shortly after helping Agrippina. When Nero sought her aid, he had to make arrangements by going through an officer of the Praetorian Guard, into whose charge Locusta had been placed. Locusta provided a poison, and Nero had Britannicus's tutors administer it, first ensuring their disloyalty to the boy. As had initially happened with Claudius, though, the poison, perhaps too diluted, did not work properly, and having succeeded only in upsetting the boy's stomach, exited his system via a bowel movement.

Nero was furious. He threatened the officer and ordered Locusta to be tortured. Suetonius tells us that, in her defense, Locusta said that she had tried a relatively small dose so that the crime would be less obvious. Nero compelled her to mix a stronger potion as quickly as she could, in his presence. She did so, and they tried it out on a young goat, but the kid took nearly five hours to die. Locusta promised that she would produce a more effective poison, one that would bring death as quickly as a sword. This time, she mixed a lethal dose. Nero tested it on a pig, which died instantly, so Nero immediately ordered this poison to be given to Britannicus with his meal.

The effects were indeed alarming. At the time, the imperial young men customarily dined with their peers at a slightly less fancy table than that reserved for the adults (the Roman equivalent of the "kids' table"), but in the same room. Here Britannicus sat. Usually a special servant tasted his food and drink to ensure its safety, but the murderers had thought of a trick to circumvent this obstacle. A harmless but very hot drink was brought in; the servant tasted it with no ill effects, and passed it to Britannicus. But the boy found it too warm, and pushed the cup away. Then cold water containing the poison was added to cool the drink. As soon as Britannicus tasted it, the poison pervaded his entire body so quickly that he dropped dead before he could even utter a word.

A great fear seized the dinner guests. Some fled immediately, not understanding what had happened. The less ignorant guests sat fixed in their seats, staring at Nero, who, not bothered in the least, still reclined at his table. He calmly remarked that this sort of fit was normal for epileptics, and that Britannicus had been afflicted with the disease since infancy. The guests should not worry, he said; in a little while the boy's vision and other senses would return. This did not happen, of course, and even Agrippina, who had clearly not been in on this particular plot, was terrified and dismayed at Britannicus's sudden death. Nero arranged for an uncharacteristically quick cremation and burial of the boy's body, apologizing for the haste by claiming that it had been an ancestral practice to avoid displaying the bodies of those who had died bitterly grievous deaths, and that they should therefore avoid a public display of sorrow. Most likely he simply wished to conceal any evidence of his crime and avoid the chance for Britannicus's supporters to rally.

Nero rewarded Locusta by pardoning her for past crimes and granting her immunity from execution during his lifetime. He also presented her with large country estates, and even sent students to her to learn the art of poisoning. When the people finally turned against Nero, he visited Locusta

Joseph-Noël Sylvestre, *Locusta Testing in Nero's Presence the Poison Prepared for Britannicus* (1876). Here the poison is evidently being tested on a slave rather than on a goat or pig.

one last time before fleeing Rome, acquiring some poison from her that he kept in a little box, apparently preparing for suicide.[17] But he never did use it. Instead, he commanded one of his servants to stab him in the throat.

Locusta, for her part, did not fare as well under Nero's successor, the emperor Galba. According to the historian Dio, writing in the late second to early third centuries CE, Galba ordered the poisoner Locusta, along with certain other unsavory elements who had surfaced and been tolerated during the time of Nero, to be led around the city in chains and then executed by an unspecified method.[18] This dates her death to 68–69 CE, as Galba ruled for only seven months after Nero before being assassinated.

There exists one very lurid but entirely inaccurate account about the circumstances surrounding Locusta's death. This false story claims that before her execution she was first raped by a specially trained giraffe at a public ceremony after being smeared with secretions from a female giraffe in order to attract the male. This tale does not appear in any ancient source.[19] Quite possibly the confusion about Locusta's fate arose from a conflation of her story with other stories of executions during the Empire. Various literary sources describe how being raped by specially domesticated animals before being torn to pieces by wild beasts was indeed a method of execution for convicted murderesses. The *Metamorphoses* of the second-century CE author Apuleius provides one graphic example. In this novel, the main character, a young man named Lucius preoccupied with learning magic, accidentally turns himself into a donkey and becomes involved in all sorts of misadventures, including the case of a vile woman responsible for several murders. Although the story is fictional, many of the events Apuleius describes have their basis in real life, including aspects of the murders and executions.

The woman in question began her career of slaughter by savagely torturing and killing her husband's sister out of misplaced envy, first beating her with a whip and then shoving a burning torch up her vagina, causing the poor girl an astoundingly agonizing death. But the woman's preferred method of murder was poison. When her husband became inconsolable at his sister's death, his wife decided to get rid of him, too. She purchased a quick-acting poison from an equally villainous doctor. But when the doctor came to administer the potion, the woman forced him to drink the poison as well, not wanting to leave a potential witness to her husband's murder. Both the husband and doctor expired in a matter of minutes. Realizing the doctor's wife knew about the situation, the wicked woman then plotted to kill her, and next decided to kill her own daughter so that the dead husband's inheritance would not pass to the girl. Proving herself to be as depraved a parent as she was a wife, she used the same poison on her daughter and the doctor's wife.

The little girl died quickly, but the doctor's wife lived long enough to inform the governor of the province about the woman's crimes. The governor took immediate action, sentencing the woman to be thrown to the beasts and raped by none other than Lucius, still in donkey form. Disgusted and ashamed at the thought of being forced to have sex with this wicked woman, Lucius escaped through the nearest gate as quickly as possible. What ultimately became of the condemned woman with her penchant for serial poisoning, Apuleius does not say. But it seems highly unlikely that the governor would have commuted her sentence.

By the second century CE, murder by poison was so rampant in Roman society that the satirist Juvenal expressed disgust at what he perceived to be an incredibly lax attitude toward the perpetrators, lamenting that (as we might say) "crime pays," and that killers receive welcome publicity, much like the attention showered on notorious criminals by today's media:

Take the case of a high-ranking wife who, before offering
mellow Calenian wine to her husband, mixes in dried toad's venom,
doing Locusta one better by teaching her inexperienced neighbors
how to bury their poison-blotched husbands, earning her fifteen minutes
   of fame.

NO GIRAFFE, BUT LASTING INFAMY

Compounding the false rumor about Locusta being raped by a giraffe is an equally inaccurate rumor about the *bestiarius* ("wild animal wrangler") known as Carpophorus. As a *bestiarius*, Carpophorus may have trained and most definitely fought multiple fierce animals in the Flavian amphitheater; according to the poet Martial, Carpophorus fought boars, bears, wild oxen, panthers, and lions, and during one of his appearances in the area killed no fewer than twenty such animals. The rumor about this *bestiarius*, the origins of which remain unclear, claims that he trained giraffes to rape women, supposedly by waiting for female animals to be in heat so he could collect samples from them to arouse the males. Carpophorus would then rub these samples against women brought into the arena, causing the male giraffes to force themselves upon the women, several of whom were supposedly killed by this experiment before he got the animals properly trained.[20] At some point, this false story about Carpophorus was combined with the equally unsupported story about Locusta being raped by a giraffe. Aside from these entirely incorrect accounts, Locusta's reputation as a professional poisoner was so unusual that it has lived on for two thousand years. She was infamous enough that Alexandre Dumas, in his 1844 novel *The Count of Monte Cristo*, had his characters compare the poisoner Mme de Villefort to Locusta (chapter 80, "The Accusation"), even naming a later chapter for her (chapter 101, "Locusta," in which Mme. de Villefort tries to poison the young girl Valentine).

If you want to be someone, dare to do something worthy of prison. . . .
Crime gets you the fancy gardens, mansions, feasts and antique silver.
(Juvenal, *Satire* 1.69–76)

Here and elsewhere Juvenal describes a reputation as a poisoner as almost a status symbol.[21] Of course, it was virtually impossible to diagnose poisoning after the fact, so most cases were merely suspected rather than definitively proven. But deliberate poisoning occurred so frequently in imperial Rome that people who considered themselves to be potential victims tended to prepare in advance by taking "remedies," such as smaller, nonlethal doses of poison, to build up their resistance. Nero's three attempts to poison his mother, Agrippina, failed miserably because she had foreseen this possibility and already "fortified herself with antidotes," as noted in chapter 3.[22] Mithradates VI intentionally ingested nonlethal doses of various toxins over the course of several years in order to develop an immunity, certain that his foes would try to kill him by poison.[23]

What emerges from all these cases of poisoning is the importance of social and political context. Incidents of mass poisoning in early Rome, such as the cases of the Roman matrons and Quarta Hostilia, often coincided with crises such as wars and epidemics. During those times popular superstition, including the belief that scapegoats would solve the problems, contributed to wild accusations. The late Republic, on the other hand, a more well-documented era, produced written accounts that mention serial poisoners, including the (dubious) cases of Oppianicus and Calpurnius Bestia. By the first century CE, in the early days of the Empire, reports of serial poisoning reached their peak. During this unstable time, ambition and political intrigue must have played an important role in the incredibly large number of suspicious deaths. But the second century CE, encompassing the reigns of the so-called Five Good Emperors and generally regarded as the most peaceful and prosperous period in Roman history,[24] saw a significant decline in poisonings. Any serial poisoners working during this time must have gone far underground, as virtually no reports of suspicious activity survive.[25]

Although poisoning remained a popular, often untraceable, method of murder, a far more widespread concern during the Roman Republic and Empire was the danger posed by highway bandits, who were recognized as a significant menace not just during Roman times but also in ancient Greece, as evidenced in some of the earliest Greek literature. Working in groups or alone, some highwaymen seemed more inclined toward murder than robbery. The next two chapters examine this phenomenon in more detail.

CHAPTER 7

Heracles and the Headhunters

Many cultures, including those of ancient Greece and Rome, regarded criminals as representatives of disorder, of the chaos that existed before men formed societies and began enacting law codes. In both myth and history, rulers and heroes who freed their lands from such criminals as highway bandits garnered praise for bringing peace, and the suppression of robbery marked a transition from barbarism.[1] Most ancient accounts of robber bandits describe them as operating in dangerous gangs that roamed the countryside and attacked travelers. Loosely organized, robber gangs fought in a way civilized people did not (to the extent that any type of fighting can be considered civilized); they waged a type of guerilla warfare. Being too dishonorable to engage in formal battle, their sudden assaults on innocent passersby marked their barbaric nature. The *latro* (Latin for "robber bandit") was the enemy of social and political order.

Occasionally, in certain genres of ancient literature—such as Greek and Roman novels—some bandits act nobly by sparing a virtuous victim here and there. But for the most part, these robbers exhibited lawless, reprehensible behavior. They were rarely romanticized as dashing heroes, such as the likes of Robin Hood (late medieval period) or Dick Turpin (eighteenth century), outlaws infamous in England for their daring exploits and popular enough to be fictionalized so that audiences could continue to read about their exciting adventures. In this regard, Romulus and Remus, mythological ancestors of the Romans, were anomalies in antiquity, because the two young men attacked other brigands, stole their plunder, and distributed the spoils among the poor.[2] These exceptions aside, classical authors depict highway robbers as people who pose a serious threat to law-abiding society. Being such unsavory characters that they attacked innocent travelers for profit, highway bandits were considered crueler than common thieves and more depraved than most other criminals. One of the most despicable things about these robbers was that, in giving in to their greed—in their inability to control their basest passions—they gave up any vestiges of the quality of reason that would allow them to belong to the society of men.

The main problem contributing to the existence of such criminals was that for many hundreds of years the rudimentary roads across the ancient Mediterranean lands were not secure. Travelers within Greece, Italy, and elsewhere had to pass through long stretches of sparsely settled countryside where gangs of highway robbers could easily ambush them. The rich could afford bodyguards; robbers sometimes spared the poor, who had nothing worth taking. But stories indicate that even servants were glad to have armed companions on their journeys. In his *Satyrica* (61–62 CE), the Roman author Petronius tells the story of a slave who, traveling from the city to the country to visit a friend, sought the company of a soldier as a traveling companion. But even the slave himself was armed with a sword, so unsafe did he consider the roads outside the cities to be. (The slave was even less happy when his companion turned out to be a werewolf, but that's another story; see chapter 9.) A woman traveling outside the city would likely be told not to wear her jewelry, but instead to carry it concealed.[3] Despite such precautions, both women and men remained vulnerable to attack by robbers intent not just on stealing wealth but on kidnapping, with plans to sell their victims elsewhere as slaves or into prostitution for a keen profit.

Unlike the typical highway robbers of the ancient world, however, the criminals described in many Greek myths, such as those about Heracles and his younger cousin Theseus, seemed completely uninterested in merely stealing riches from unwary travelers. Instead, they took delight in torturing and killing their victims. Notably, they worked alone, not with others as part of organized bandit gangs. The accused murderer in Libanius's rhetorical exercise provides a good example of this distinction (see chapter 4). If the typical robber of antiquity, who participated in lawless gang activity, was already considered the lowest form of humanity, a robber who acted alone and gained a reputation not for looting but for killing was something else entirely: a travesty of a human being, a monster. Both Heracles and Theseus famously encountered highway "robbers" who specialized in various forms of torture and murder. Heracles also faced a number of cruel, xenophobic kings and landowners who acted much the same as highwaymen, ambushing and killing travelers trying to pass through their lands. Although these traditional myths are fiction, the types of crime described in them resemble modern real-life serial killings in many ways.

Heracles, like many Greek mythological heroes, had a mortal mother and a divine father—the latter being Zeus, leader of all the Olympian deities. This lineage contributed to Heracles's outstanding trait: his immense strength, which far surpassed that of other humans. Even in the cradle, his extraordinary ability manifested itself when he strangled two serpents sent by Zeus's envious wife, Hera, in an attempt to kill the illegitimate child whose very existence humiliated her. Hera's enmity followed Heracles into his adult life. After he married and had children, Hera sent a fit of madness upon him, causing him to murder his entire family. To atone for killing his wife and children, Heracles agreed to perform the Twelve Labors, which became the main source of his heroic fame as he fought and vanquished terrifying beasts and monstrous hybrid creatures. Before, during, and after these labors, as he traveled all across the ancient Mediterranean world, Heracles had a number of side adventures, or *parerga* (literally "additional deeds"), sometimes also referred to as the "Minor Labors." Lists of what these *parerga* included vary considerably, but most mention adventures such as freeing the Titan Prometheus from his torture in the Caucasus Mountains, saving the princess Hesione from a sea monster, and retrieving Queen Alcestis from the hands of Thanatos ("Death").

The majority of *parerga*, though, involved Heracles fighting against savage human or humanlike characters who exhibited such monstrous behavior that these human antagonists were at least as disturbing as the mythological monsters Heracles faced during his Twelve Labors—possibly more disturbing, since their actions fell within the realm of the possible, inasmuch as the typical mortal Greek traveler was just as likely as the semidivine Heracles to encounter a murderous highway bandit.[4] But Heracles's victories over an unusually high number of such opponents, like his victories over the monstrous beasts, may have represented to the Greeks the abstract triumph of a "civilized" society over the perceived savagery of earlier cultures. His adventures may then reflect a number of cultural shifts in the early Mediterranean world, such as the development of roads, the crossing and opening of geographical boundaries, and a movement away from specific ritual practices seen as barbaric by the seventh century BCE and toward what anthropologists consider more humane customs, as Hellenic culture spread and the Greeks started developing formal law codes to maintain an orderly society.

Lethal Encounters during the Twelve Labors

One of Heracles's first encounters with a lone highwayman occurred during his fourth labor, the quest for the Erymanthian Boar, which took him to the regions of Elis and Arcadia in southern Greece. Passing through Elis he met Saurus, who assaulted not only travelers passing through but even people living in the surrounding area. The Greek word *saurus* means "lizard" (as in *tyrannosaurus*, "tyrant lizard"), and although no ancient author explains the reason for this nickname, he may have acquired it from his ability to creep up quietly and ambush unsuspecting victims. Alternatively, the Greeks and Romans generally considered lizards untrustworthy and ill-omened creatures,[5] making "lizard" a fitting alias for a criminal. Saurus attacked Heracles but was no match for him; the hero easily killed his assailant in self-defense. Despite (or possibly because of) Saurus's infamy, the locals commemorated Heracles's deed by naming a ridge along the local river Erymanthus after the bandit and placing his tomb there, while nearby they raised a shrine in honor of Heracles for having made their territory secure again. According to the Greek author Pausanias (second century CE), the ruins of both the tomb and the shrine were still visible during his time,[6] but no later record mentions them. It is worth noting that, although the stories do not explicitly state that Saurus killed his victims, they very strongly imply that he did so. And even if Saurus was a robber who only assaulted rather than killed his targets, his case provides an example of how, early in his adventures, Heracles made the roads safe for travelers.

More blatantly homicidal was Cacus ("Wicked One"), a monstrous criminal who robbed passersby, killed them, and, as the literary evidence clearly suggests, ate them. The stories describe Cacus as a half-human, three-headed, fire-breathing giant. Supposedly a son of Vulcan, the Roman god of fire and the forge, Cacus lived in a vast, labyrinthine cavern on the Aventine Hill in the area that later became Rome. He decorated the entryway to his cave with the rotting faces and limbs of his victims, and the floor of his dwelling was covered in blood and littered with blanched human bones, stripped of their flesh. Hence the implied cannibalism:

> the ground was always warm with fresh blood,
> and the heads of men were insolently nailed around the entryway,
> pale with grim putrescence.
> (Vergil, *Aeneid* 8.195–197)

> Heads and arms dangled over the entryway,
> and the gruesome ground was white with human bones.
> (Ovid, *Fasti* 1.557–558)

Heracles encountered Cacus while passing through Italy on his way back from his tenth labor, capturing the cattle of Geryon far across the western

Mediterranean. Cacus had stolen some of those cattle, and when Heracles traced the missing beasts to Cacus's cave, he beat the giant to death. Later versions (after the first century CE) rationalize the mythological aspects of the story by downgrading Cacus to an ordinary robber with no divine or cannibalistic associations. After Heracles's victory, the local people instituted a ritual honoring the hero for saving them from this danger.

A similarly murderous character was Antaeus, whose name, appropriately enough, means "Opposed" or "Hostile." Described as a giant nearly as broad as he was tall, Antaeus ruled over Libya and was reputedly the son of the sea god Poseidon and Gaia ("Earth"). Like Heracles, Antaeus had immense, nearly invincible strength; unlike Heracles, Antaeus did not use this asset for the good of society. Instead, reflecting the xenophobia evident in many early stories of encounters with foreigners, he challenged every traveler passing through his kingdom to a wrestling match. Inevitably, because of his superior strength, Antaeus won. Not content with merely winning each bout, he killed his exhausted, unwilling opponents, cut off their heads, and used their decapitated skulls to roof a temple to his father.[7] As we saw in chapter 2, it was not unusual for certain tribes in the ancient world, such as the Scythians, to cut off the heads of their conquered enemies. The taking of human body parts from one's enemies is documented throughout most of human history and occurs even in modern times, as discussed below. But Antaeus, like the other lone killers Heracles met in his travels, hardly falls into the category of "warrior engaging with an enemy." He confronted unsuspecting travelers who had no wish to fight him. Unfortunately, they had no choice.

Heracles encountered Antaeus when passing through Libya on his way to the far west of North Africa for his eleventh labor, obtaining golden apples from the tree in the Garden of the Hesperides. In those mythological times the ancient kingdom of Libya stretched across most of North Africa, and the two characters came into conflict on the Atlantic coast near the river Lixus (the modern river Draa, Morocco's longest), not far from Antaeus's palace. As he did with all strangers passing through his territory, Antaeus forced Heracles to wrestle with him. At first, the match did not go well for the Greek hero: Heracles was immensely strong, but Antaeus seemed to be even stronger, and Heracles noticed that every time he wrestled his opponent to the ground, Antaeus appeared to gain new energy. Finally, the goddess Athena, who often watched over Heracles, advised him to lift Antaeus up from the earth during the contest. When he heard this, Heracles realized Antaeus's trick: contact with the earth, his mother, restored his strength. So Heracles, clasping the giant by his waist, held Antaeus tightly and lifted him up into the air, depriving him of contact with the earth. He did not allow Antaeus to fall or even to accidentally touch the ground. In this way Heracles defeated a weakened Antaeus, crushing his torso and squeezing the life out of him, driving his rib bones into his liver and his breath from his lungs.[8] Notably, the move of lifting one's opponent into the air was the exact opposite of the objective of an ancient Greek wrestling match, which, even as early as the Archaic period, was to throw your opponent to the ground three times without first suffering three falls yourself. Heracles's adventures constantly required him to think outside the norm. With Antaeus vanquished, "the Greek civilization of Libya began."[9]

As in the story of Saurus, the myths mention that the local inhabitants gave Antaeus a proper burial. Not to do so might offend the gods. The alleged tomb of Antaeus, which formed an elongated hill in the shape of a huge man stretched out at full length, was exhibited as a local attraction for centuries near the town of Tingis in ancient Mauretania, formerly a part of ancient Libya and now part of Morocco and Algeria. Local folk belief held that whenever anyone removed part of the earth covering the tomb, rain fell until the hole was filled up again. The Roman general Quintus Sertorius, while waging a campaign in Mauretania in the early first century BCE, reportedly opened the grave, but upon finding in it a skeleton more than eighty feet long was so horrified that he ordered the tomb covered over again immediately.[10]

Although local legend mentioned Antaeus's tomb, no sources tell us what happened to that temple to Poseidon roofed with the skulls belonging to Antaeus's unfortunate victims. But this aspect of the story recalls the need of many serial killers, during or after committing a murder, to perform a ritual that involves taking a souvenir or trophy of the crime. As Vronsky explains, "The taking and keeping of souvenirs is essential for the serial killer to somehow create, and maintain the bridge between his dreamed desires and the reality of acting out his fantasy. Without the souvenir, some serial killers may not even be sure that they had acted upon their fantasy. Others use the souvenir to perpetuate the pleasure and excitement they sparked during the murder."[11] Modern examples of killers who took souvenirs include Jeffrey Dahmer, who had an altar in his bedroom decorated with human skulls, and Ed Gein, who saved human body parts and displayed them in his home, reminiscent of the heads and limbs Cacus kept as boasts or warnings affixed to the entry to his cave.

After Heracles killed Antaeus in Libya he passed through Egypt. When he came to the Nile River at Memphis, he fell into the clutches of King Bousiris. Known in many versions of the myth for his cruelty, Bousiris—yet another son of Poseidon—hated foreigners and killed any who entered

Heracles killing Bousiris on the altar. Greek red-figure vase by the Troilos Painter, ca. 480 BCE, found in the Etruscan town of Vulci in Italy.

his kingdom. An alternate but equally well-known version of his story says that a seer from Cyprus advised Bousiris to sacrifice a stranger to Zeus once a year to restore prosperity to the kingdom, which had suffered from nine years of bad harvests. In this latter version, when Heracles arrived in Memphis he had the bad luck to be chosen as the annual sacrifice. In both versions, the Egyptians took him captive, but he broke his bonds and killed Bousiris, the king's son, and several servants near the altar upon which the king ritually slaughtered foreigners.[12] By the fifth century BCE, Greece and Egypt shared friendlier relations, and the historian Herodotus goes so far as to refer to the Bousiris story as "silly" and the Greeks as "utterly ignorant of Egyptian character and customs," arguing that the Egyptians could never have practiced human sacrifice since their religious beliefs forbade them from sacrificing nearly every kind of animal.[13]

The story of Heracles and Bousiris may well have arisen from Egyptian xenophobia toward Greeks and others.[14] In that case, the Greek characterization of Bousiris, itself xenophobic in depicting the king as a merciless killer disguising his actions as ritual, carries with it shades of serial killing, often a highly ritualistic act. At minimum, Bousiris seriously abuses his royal power, with the Greek author Plutarch (second century CE) accusing him of "deceitful hospitality."[15] But the second version presented above provides the motivation of a yearly sacrifice for the sake of the community at large, a theme that relates to Heracles's later encounters with Lityerses and Syleus (discussed below).

While on his way out of Egypt, Heracles also crossed paths with a thug named Termerus, known mainly as a pirate who regularly plundered the coastal cities in the regions of Lycia and Caria on the southern coast of Asia Minor. But Termerus also had his own unique method of murder, one that walks the line between a pirate who randomly cuts down people while robbing them and a serial killer with a specific (and oddly unnecessary) modus operandi: he killed people by head-butting them, apparently running at them before violently bashing into them. The stories do not explain how Termerus's own skull remained consistently intact after these encounters. They do relate that Heracles killed him in the same manner, dashing his head against Termerus's skull.[16] The origins of Termerus's peculiar habit remain unclear; possibly the story was influenced by observation of mountain sheep or goats native to the Carian region, creatures that exert dominance by ramming each other. Such a characteristic would serve to align Termerus more closely with beasts than with humans, in keeping with the ancient attitude toward such criminals as sea pirates and highway bandits.

Increasingly Deadly Encounters after the Twelve Labors

After his labors, Heracles participated in a number of military expeditions. While in Thessaly in northern Greece for one such campaign, he encountered another deadly foe, Cycnus, a son of the god Ares (see chapter 4). Cycnus robbed passersby and then decapitated them, using their severed heads as trophies to build a temple to his father, just as Antaeus had done for his father, Poseidon.[17] Cycnus lurked in the sacred grove of Apollo by the Thessalian coast, intercepting travelers coming from the north who were heading far to the south with rich offerings for Apollo at his sanctuary in Delphi. Cycnus had taken over this grove and targeted Apollo's worshippers because of an unspecified grudge. Possibly he was supporting his father's hatred of Apollo, because according to the myths Apollo was the first-born son of Zeus and second-born Ares resented his father's favorite. Ares's son would naturally share his father's resentment. This Cycnus also happened to be the son-in-law of King Ceyx of Trachis, one of Heracles's allies, but Ceyx disowned the villainous Cycnus despite the family connection. The main version of Heracles's encounter with Cycnus appears in the early Greek epic poem known as the *Shield of Heracles* (late eighth or early seventh century BCE), which describes the battle that ensued when Cycnus challenged Heracles to combat.

The *Shield of Heracles* recounts how, while on his way to King Ceyx to report a successful campaign, Heracles, accompanied by his nephew Iolaus, came across both Cycnus and Ares himself in the grove sacred to Apollo. Cycnus rejoiced, hoping to kill both men and strip them of their splendid armor. Armor was a typical sought-after prize of battle, but Heracles's was extraordinary: Hephaestus, god of the forge, had made the shining bronze greaves for the hero's legs, and Athena had presented Heracles with an exquisite golden breastplate. The shield, though, was the pièce de résistance, made by Hephaestus and carved with intricate details of daily life and of war (in a poetic callback to Achilles's shield in the *Iliad*). Heracles and Cycnus dismounted from their chariots and engaged in hand-to-hand combat in what became one of the last great battles of Heracles's career. With his bronze spear, Cycnus struck the hero's shield, barely denting it. Heracles's spear, on the other hand, pierced Cycnus's neck and killed him. In his grief, Ares attacked Heracles, who wounded the god in the thigh, whereupon Ares's sons Phobos and Deimos ("Fear" and "Terror") swept their father away from the combat and up to Olympus to be healed. Heracles and Iolaus stripped Cycnus's armor and continued on their way.

Not long after Heracles returned to Trachis, Ceyx, despite having disowned his son-in-law, arranged for Cycnus's burial. But the river Anauros, swelled by a rainstorm, obliterated the grave and memorial of Cycnus at the command of an angry Apollo, who wanted vengeance for Cycnus's actions against him. As in the case of Antaeus, no myths mention what happened to the shrine of skulls. And no archaeological evidence so far has turned up any skull caches corresponding to the geographical sites of any of these myths, meaning that no material finds provide evidence of events upon which the myths might even remotely have been based, in contrast to those associated with the alleged tomb of Antaeus.

At some point during his various military expeditions—the sources do not agree on exactly when—Heracles again found himself atoning for murder, because he killed his good friend Iphitus. Some versions of the myth say the Heracles believed Iphitus had lied to him; others say that Heracles suffered from a fit of madness, possibly again caused by Hera. In either case, Heracles ended up horrified at what he had done and wanted to atone for the bloodshed and purify himself. This time, instead of being sent out to kill monsters, as with the Twelve Labors, Heracles was instructed by the Delphic Oracle to sell himself into slavery for a period of time to Omphale, queen of Lydia in Asia Minor. While in her service, Heracles "punished those throughout the land who made a habit of pillaging."[18] Out on patrol, he happened to pass the territory of Lityerses, who was well known as a master harvester, albeit one with an odd sense of hospitality reminis-

PUT YOUR ENEMY TO SLEEP, THEN KILL HIM

Heracles was hardly the only character from ancient myth and history to put an enemy to sleep before killing him. The god Mercury used a similar strategy on Argus, the hundred-eyed watchman sent by the goddess Juno to guard Io, one of Jupiter's mortal paramours. The god had tried to disguise her from Juno by turning the unfortunate girl into a cow. This did not fool the goddess, who instructed Argus to keep an eye (or several) on the animal so that Jupiter would not be able to rescue her. But Jupiter enlisted the aid of Mercury, who played on his reed pipe, sang songs, and told stories until all of Argus's eyes closed in sleep—at which point Mercury cut off his head (Ovid, *Metamorphoses* 1.681–718).

Whereas Heracles and Mercury used music to sing their foes to sleep, others used wine to get their enemies drunk. Odysseus famously introduced the Cyclops Polyphemus to wine, encouraging him to drink his fill. Once the man-eating, one-eyed giant was sound asleep, Odysseus and his men blinded him and escaped from the Cyclops's cave with his flock (*Odyssey* 9.307–479). According to Herodotus, when Cyrus the Great of Persia set out to attack a people known as the Massagetae, he left the weaker part of his army behind at camp. Cyrus had gone in the wrong direction, and the Massagetae attacked the camp, slaughtering everyone left behind. But then they took their fill of food and wine, and fell sound asleep. When the Persians returned, they caught the Massagetae off guard, killed most of them, and took the rest prisoner (1.211). The pious young widow Judith, wishing to save the Jewish town of Bethulia from the invading Assyrian army led by Holofernes, left the town and entered the enemy camp under the pretense of having important information for the general. Holofernes was so enchanted with her beauty that he drank more wine than usual; when he fell into a drunken stupor, Judith cut off his head and stealthily made her way back to Bethulia (book of Judith, ca. second century BCE).

---

cent of Bousiris's xenophobia. Lityerses invited travelers passing by his territory to go harvesting with him, but if they refused, he either killed them or forced them to work for him. Sometimes he compelled passersby to participate in a competition to see who could harvest sheaves more quickly. He always won. Whether they had cooperated or not, Lityerses decapitated every one of these unfortunate travelers and displayed their heads on a heap of grain. When accosted by Lityerses just as other passersby had been, Heracles accepted the bloodthirsty man's challenge, but, humming as he worked, made Lityerses drowsy and cut off his head as he slept. Also during his service to Omphale, Heracles was sent to work in the vineyard of Syleus, who apparently shared Lityerses's strange sense of hospitality. Syleus, another of Poseidon's many sons, and described as an "outlaw farmer,"[19] was a wine-grower who forced passersby to toil in his vineyard before putting them to death. Instead of tilling the vines, Heracles tore them up and then killed Syleus with his own hoe.

Interpreting the Encounters

All of these stories allow for various possible interpretations relating to early Mediterranean society. Although we can never know with absolute certainly what such stories meant to the Greeks and Romans, we can speculate about different aspects of the myths. For example, many of the highway criminals Heracles encounters are also mythologically the sons of gods, especially Poseidon and Ares. Theseus also meets a number of savage criminals who are sons of deities. This pattern suggests a reluctance on the part of storytellers and their audiences to attribute such gruesome torture-murders to mere mortals. For a man to commit such a heinous crime there had to be something inhuman about him, though these villains were technically still mortal; having only one divine parent rather than two does not make you immortal, only highly formidable. The excessively violent temperaments attributed to these two particular gods, Poseidon and Ares, partially explain the behavior of their offspring. As the god of war, Ares himself was especially impetuous and bloodthirsty. And since nearly all the major heroes, including Heracles and Theseus, were also sons of gods, their opponents needed to be more than human. Although Poseidon also had noble sons, including Theseus himself, Ares had no "good" sons. Even if Phobos and Deimos usually appear in myth as abstractions who accompany Ares without having adventures of their own, their names, "Fear" and "Terror," are not encouraging. These two characters were violent and murderous, just like their father.

Notably, many of these myths relate to human sacrifice. Heracles's encounters with Bousiris, Syleus, and Cacus all suggest a basis in sacrificial ritual, but the stories of Antaeus, Termerus, Cycnus, and Lityerses are even more specific and may connect to real-life practices in the prehistoric Mediterranean. The archaeological evidence for ritual human sacrifice in ancient Greek society remains ambiguous and highly debated, but material finds confirm that head-taking and the use of skulls in various rites occurred throughout the wider ancient Mediterranean basin from the Euro-

Remnants of the portico at Roquepertuse, now housed in the Mediterranean Archaeology Museum in Marseille. The pillars have hollowed-out niches that housed skulls. Celtic-Ligurian culture, third to second centuries BCE.

pean Mesolithic period through the early Iron Age (very broadly, periods covering anywhere from ca. 15,000 to 300 BCE from beginning to end, respectively). Depending on the culture, head-taking had various meanings. For some, collecting the skulls of slain enemies might indicate social and political power, with display of these heads serving to terrify and impress. For example, two skull clusters found in Mesolithic-era pits in Ofnet, Germany, showed fatal head injuries and other evidence of warlike activity. In other cultures, head-taking might serve as a symbol of spiritual efficacy as part of a religious ceremony. The reconstructed portico from Roquepertuse in southern France, dating to the third and second centuries BCE, was formed from a series of stone pillars originally joined by lintels, each pillar bearing niches carved to hold human skulls. This portico is thought to have served as a liminal (threshold or gateway) structure, as passage through this transitional space seems to have symbolized the transformations associated with death and a journey to the afterlife.[20]

The skull shrines created by Antaeus and Cycnus recall the ritual collection of enemy skulls, if not of actual human sacrifice to Poseidon and Ares; we have only very tenuous, anecdotal evidence for such sacrifice. Termerus's targeting of his victims' heads may also reflect the real-life practice of collecting enemy skulls. Classical literature has a long-standing interest in headhunting; the practice was a recurrent motif in classical writings about Celtic peoples, including the Gauls. Greek and Roman writers from the mid-second century BCE on regarded the collection of human heads as battle trophies as a characteristic Celtic custom that proved the tribe's barbarity. Yet headhunting was practiced not just among the Celts but all over the ancient world; Germans, Iberians, and even the Romans themselves collected enemy heads at various points in their histories. Trajan's Column in Rome, a monumental work of bas-relief sculpture commemorating the emperor's victory over the Dacians in the early second century CE, depicts a Roman soldier holding the decapitated head of a Dacian warrior in his teeth, while coins issued during this time show Trajan himself standing with his foot on the severed head of the Dacian leader. In 1988, several dozen skulls unearthed in a pit dating to Roman London provided evidence that the Romans collected the heads of foreign enemies, slain gladiators, and executed criminals, possibly for public display.[21]

Some headhunting occurred in the context of war and politics, but a widespread ancient belief in links between human heads and the fertility of crops, animals, and people probably lies behind the story of Lityer-

---

OTHER SKULL COLLECTORS IN GREEK AND ROMAN MYTH

According to the Roman poet Ovid, Hercules's eighth labor included a villain who collected skulls. For this labor, Hercules had to travel to the northern wilds of Thrace and bring back the mares of King Diomedes, who had raised his horses on a diet of human flesh. Ovid describes "heads nailed up in Thracian households" (*Threiciis adfixa penatibus ora*) (*Heroides* 9.87). This might refer to the Thracians generally as a people who, as the Greeks believed, practiced human sacrifice.[22] Alternatively, the phrase might refer only to Diomedes's palace. Whichever the case, after he defeated Diomedes, Hercules fed the king to his own horses. And aside from the skull trophies taken by the hero's savage foes, skulls from human sacrificial victims appear in Euripides's *Iphigenia among the Taurians* (ca. 413 BCE). According to the ancient Greeks, the Taurians, who lived on the Crimean Peninsula, carried out ritual human sacrifice. On a mission in the land of the Taurians to retrieve a statue of the goddess Artemis, the character Orestes asks his friend Pylades, "Do you see the spoils [*skula*] hanging from the cornices?" Pylades replies, "Yes, the prime prizes [*akrothinia*] from slain strangers" (lines 74–75). The word *akrothinia* literally means "topmost/highest part," sometimes indicating simply the "best," but here most likely referring to the "topmost" part of the strangers—their skulls.[23]

ses. A range of surviving literature makes symbolic links between heads of humans and heads of grain or flowers, and some evidence, though highly controversial, suggests that in various cultures, human sacrifice, including head-taking, might have had a strong association with the fertility of crops. Because Poseidon was himself linked with fertility, we may be seeing a remnant of this metaphorical connection in his sons' proclivities toward human sacrifice and skull collecting. The story of Syleus also touches upon the relationship between human sacrifice and crop fertility.[24] This metaphorical connection is not limited to stories from antiquity; consider Shirley Jackson's 1948 short story "The Lottery," in which the townspeople annually stone to death one of their own to ensure a good harvest, or Robin Hardy's 1973 film *The Wicker Man*, in which Celtic pagans, led by Christopher Lee as Lord Summerisle, conduct a human sacrifice in the hope of saving their island's crops from a devastating drought. The earliest mention of such a Celtic wicker man ritual appears in the first century BCE in Julius Caesar's *De bello gallico* (*On the Gallic War*): "As a people, the Gauls are seriously inclined toward religious rituals. Because of this, those who are afflicted with serious diseases, and those who face danger in battle, either offer humans as sacrificial victims or solemnly swear that they will do so. . . . Others use immense effigies, whose limbs are woven from twigs. They fill these structures with living men and then set them on fire; the men are killed when the flames surround them from below" (6.16).

But such sacrifices, to whatever extent they really occurred in ancient Greece, gradually fell out of favor, and Heracles's conquest of his "barbaric" foes, depicted as marauding on the outskirts of the Mediterranean—the farther from Greece, the more uncivilized—suggests Greek propaganda regarding the civilizing effect of Hellenic culture. Although Heracles himself was a transitional figure, combining primitive brutality with a civilizing force, literary sources tended to focus on the latter. As we have seen, the myths of Antaeus and Cycnus do not say what became of the skull shrines so triumphantly assembled by their builders, and this lack of narrative interest in the macabre collections may seem odd to us but most likely reflects the myths' focus on Heracles's achievements and dismissal of barbarism, expressing an overall shift in Greek thought toward a more "orderly" society.

Significantly, collecting enemy skulls and using human heads for fertility rituals generally occur as tribal actions, not as the actions of an individual. As the myths depict them, Antaeus, Cycnus, Termerus, and Lityerses did not act as members of communities when they killed their victims. They acted alone, in the absence of community. They preyed on individual, innocuous travelers, not enemy tribes. Their murderous actions were

WHAT ABOUT THE MONSTERS?

Heracles and other heroes frequently faced terrible monsters, which fell into several categories. Some were excessively large and strong forms of real animals, such as the Nemean Lion and the Erymanthian Boar. Others were exaggerated, mutant forms related to known animals, such as the Lernaean Hydra, a snakelike creature but with multiple, regenerating heads. Still others were frightening, impossible hybrid creatures, such as the Chimaera (faced by the hero Bellerophon), which combined features of a lion, goat, and snake. What might such monsters have represented? Very generally, such monsters represented the chaos of the natural world, constantly in conflict with man's impulse to tame and manipulate nature and spread civilization. Certain female monsters, such as Scylla and Charybdis, hint at or outright express a fear of female sexuality. Some creatures might also originally have represented real-life local dangers. The Hydra, for example, might have represented the poisonous gases known to be present in the marshes around the town of Lerna. This theory circulated even in antiquity among authors such as Palaephatus, who tried to rationalize myths. For an accessible, general introduction to Heracles's Twelve Labors and the monsters therein, see Emma Stafford, *Herakles* (2012).

opportunistic and spaced at intervals. They had no personal relationships with their victims. They each engaged in ritualistic killing and mutilation, and their methods were consistent. Three of the four took specific trophies (the skulls). Their actions lacked political or social motivation, and instead arose from a need to feel powerful and assert their authority over other, weaker individuals. According to the stories, Antaeus and Cycnus wanted to impress their dominant fathers, and Antaeus had a dependent relationship with his mother (the Earth). In short, the behavior of these characters resembles that of serial killers,[25] including that of the "anger-retaliatory" serial killer type (the ones with parent issues). The stories of these four, along with other killers Heracles met on the road, such as Syleus and Cacus, may have not only reflected earlier ritual cult practices but also shown an awareness of real-life serial mutilation-murders, characterizing both types of primitive behavior as monstrous.

The location of these murders is also important: early roads. The appearance of so many highwaymen as serial killers in the Heracles myths suggests several things. The ancient Greeks and Romans did not tell these stories only to make Heracles look good; rather, to a large extent the stories reflected the reality that the rudimentary and unpatrolled roads were very dangerous, and that travelers regularly fell prey to bandits, some of whom were violent enough to kill and mutilate their victims. But even in the mythological time of Heracles, such criminals were considered extremely unusual. Heracles came across them occasionally, in very remote locations, and as super-strong but still mortal characters they played a secondary role to the monstrously large, excessively strong and dangerous creatures he had to face during his Twelve Labors, such as the Lernaean Hydra and Cerberus.

The concerns of the time period during which the myths of Heracles circulated (early Iron Age Greece) were still more agricultural than urban, which helps explain the tension between the old ritual of skull shrines, possible crop fertility, and Heracles's conquest of characters representing these older beliefs. Heracles likely served as a transitional figure for the Greeks, bridging the span of time between the Iron and Archaic Ages (ca. 1100 through 480 BCE), as various towns in Greece began to develop law codes and other means of ordering society. Using both primitive force (his club) and more advanced technology (his sword), as well as the chronologically ubiquitous bow and arrow, Heracles was both brutal and civilized, ultimately considered not a savage who unthinkingly slaughtered hoards but rather a culture hero who purged the earth of monsters and tamed the uncivilized world, making it safe for the spread of Greek culture.[26]

The adventures of Theseus relate even more clearly to the growing urban expansion in late Archaic Greece, and they depict highway serial killers in a surprisingly more modern and immediate form. Main roads between cities were just starting to play a major role in ancient Greek society; in the sixth century BCE contact between the city-states grew rapidly, and as a result trade and exploration became increasingly important. Before the sixth century, given that the isolationist tendencies of Greek settlements along with the mountainous geography of Greece (which itself largely caused the isolated settlements) did not lend themselves to the development of major road networks, "most roads were single tracks following stream beds or some other path of least resistance,"[27] and tended to be muddy and narrow. With few exceptions, these early roads were not paved because a widespread road system at that time would have been "expensive to build and hard to maintain." But in the sixth century, travel between Greek city-states became more frequent, and encounters with highway bandits more of a serious concern. The stories of Theseus and his travels reflect this growing technology and the societal concerns surrounding it.

CHAPTER 8

Theseus and the Highway Killers

Many myths involving Heracles, such as his battle with Cycnus, circulated most frequently before the fifth century BCE but maintained their popularity throughout the Roman period. By the fifth century BCE, Heracles had morphed into a pan-Hellenic hero whose adventures took him all over Greece and beyond. Theseus remained a localized hero specifically connected to the city of Athens, partially because, as Athens' importance as a city increased during the late sixth and early fifth centuries BCE, the city wanted and needed its own legendary hero. The myths surrounding Theseus most likely originated in political propaganda intended to increase Athens' reputation, and as part of accomplishing this goal the Athenians modeled him after his famous cousin from the Peloponnese. The Greek writer Plutarch tells of Theseus's adventures in the *Life of Theseus*, a "historical" account of the mythological hero. He begins by providing background for Theseus's adventures:

> That age—the time of Theseus—produced men who were outstandingly strong and tireless but who used this advantage for nothing helpful or productive to society. Instead, they rejoiced in being exceedingly insolent and used their strength for cruel deeds, destroying everything they came across. Heracles cut down some of these men on his journey, but others hid from him as he passed by and escaped his notice. And so in some areas of Greece these men again plied their evil trades, there being no one to stand in their way.[1]

Heracles was among the greatest of Greek heroes, but he could not do everything; there were still plenty of outlaws around for another hero to confront. Like Heracles, who was reputedly the son of Zeus, Theseus too had a divine parent. His mortal mother, Aethra, married a fellow mortal, Aegeus, king of Athens. According to the stories, however, she was impregnated not by Aegeus but by Poseidon. Theseus never achieved the same level of fame as Heracles, but he became immensely popular in Athens after 510 BCE and appeared frequently in sculpture and painting. Eventually the stories that arose around Theseus, especially the one about his encounter with the Minotaur in the Cretan labyrinth, spread almost as widely throughout Greece and beyond as did the legends of Heracles.

But before becoming widely known for slaying the Minotaur and thus saving Athenian youths and maidens from a terrible fate, the young Theseus began to build his heroic reputation by fighting less fantastical, more realistic foes. According to Plutarch, Theseus's adventures started shortly after his mother told him that he was heir to the throne of Athens. At the time he lived with his mother, in southern Greece, but based on what she told him he decided to travel from his birthplace, Troezen, to Athens to meet his father, King Aegeus (see map, facing page). Theseus's maternal grandfather, Pittheus, knew the perils of the land route from Troezen to Athens and described to Theseus six murderous criminals who preyed on travelers passing that way. Pittheus urged Theseus to use the easier route, by boat across the Saronic Gulf, saying that it was difficult to walk the road to Athens because no part of it was clear of the danger from "robbers and evildoers" (*léistês* and *kakourgoi*).[2] Theseus, however, decided to ignore his grandfather's advice and take the land route precisely because of the dangers it presented. He had grown up listening eagerly to stories about his cousin Heracles's glorious deeds and longed to make a similar reputation for himself. But Theseus's motive was not all vanity. He also wanted to help society by making the roads safer. The stories emphasize Theseus's wish to punish the wicked and bring upon them the justice they deserved.

The six outlaws Pittheus described to Theseus, usually referred to in modern translations and retellings as "robbers," were really much more than that. They resemble modern serial killers in many ways. Periphetes, Sinis, Phaea, Sciron, Cercyon, and Procrustes killed primarily for the pleasure they derived from it, and only secondarily for profit. They exhibited sadism and a consistent pattern in their methods of killing. Their brutality far surpassed that of the typical highway marauder; they not only robbed and killed but tortured and mutilated their victims. And although modern versions of these myths refer to these criminals as robbers or bandits, most ancient Greek literary sources do not. Instead, they refer to the criminals by their names or use the generic term that Libanius applies to highway murderer-thieves, *kakourgoi*, the same term applied above by Plutarch. The stories make clear

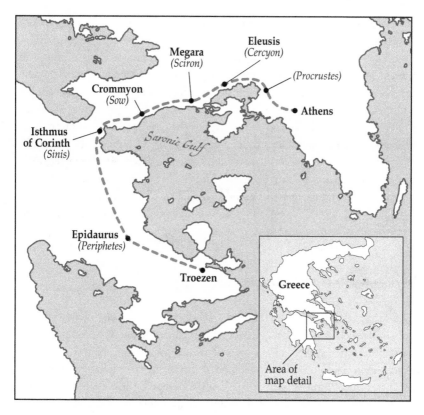

Theseus's journey from Troezen to Athens. Map by Michele Angel.

that plunder was not the main goal of these outlaws. Only one literary source even mentions the actual act of robbery, and the myths say nothing about what these men did with their spoils. Instead, the myths focus on how inhumanely these men disposed of their victims. Ancient Greek artistic representations, too, focus not on these characters as robbers but on Theseus ridding the world of these criminals, killing them by the same methods they had used on their victims.

Did six outlaws really lurk on the road from Troezen to Athens? And if they did, and people knew this and told each other as Pittheus told Theseus, why would anyone other than a foolhardy hero ever have traveled on that road? Such concerns elicit reminders not to take Greek myths too literally; these are the wrong questions. Many myths, like Theseus's six adventures, represented societal concerns. In this case, the stories come from a period of time—the late sixth century BCE—when the Greek city-states were only just beginning to communicate with each other via the ancient equivalent of highways as Greece entered a period of urban and mercantile expansion. Roads generally, as in the adventures of Heracles, remained unpatrolled and fraught with danger. Robbers routinely preyed on vulnerable travelers, who often out of sheer necessity passed along certain thoroughfares and simply had to take their chances. The map on the previous page shows Theseus's route; he was a mythological character, but the cities and the road were real. Possibly some of the villains Theseus met were based on real-life criminals, in some cases for political propaganda, but more likely they reflected real-life concerns, such as sparsely populated roadways and the brigands who lurked nearby watching for vulnerable travelers. Unless people could afford a boat voyage across the Saronic Gulf (and they often could not), they had to traverse the same land route as Theseus.

Periphetes, the "Club-Bearer"

Upon first setting out from Troezen, Theseus traveled some distance without incident. But when he approached Epidaurus, Theseus encountered the outlaw Periphetes, who had a club of wood—or bronze, or iron, depending on the version of the story—so he also went by the nickname "Corynetes," meaning "Club-Bearer." Periphetes was reputed to be the son of Hephaestus, the only Greek god with a physical deformity. God of the forge, Hephaestus was lame in one leg and walked with a limp. Periphetes himself was also a cripple and initially carried the club as a walking stick. When he became a brigand, he used the club to cave in the skulls of anyone entering his territory—possibly a callback to Heracles's multiple encounters with headhunters and skull-bashers. Periphetes tried to do the same to Theseus, but the young man wrested the club away and killed him with it. In one version of the myth, Theseus tricks Periphetes into giving him the club by claiming that he wished to see whether it truly was made of bronze. After giving Periphetes his comeuppance, Theseus kept the club and continued to use it, just as Heracles wore the skin of the Nemean Lion, the first monstrous creature he killed. In this respect, both heroes took "trophies," much like some of the serial killers they met. The club is a primitive weapon, and although Theseus had a sword, he thought it just to kill Periphetes by the criminal's own method, emulating his cousin Heracles, who also chose to vanquish his opponents by their own means.

Less information has come down to us about Periphetes than about the other five criminals Theseus met, possibly because Periphetes was a late addition to the group. He does not appear in the Theseus story much before

GENUS *PERIPHETES*

A vast number of living things, from plants to animals, take their names from classical literature. Several insect names come from the Theseus myth cycle. Cercyon and Procrustes have lent their names to various beetle genera and species. *Periphetes* is a genus in the insect family Phasmatidae, the stick insects. The name "Phasmatidae" itself comes from the ancient Greek word *phasma*, meaning "apparition, phantom, ghost," because so many species in this family resemble (and thus "appear" to be) natural objects, such as sticks or leaves, providing them with excellent camouflage. Some even mimic scorpions or other creatures more dangerous than themselves. The genus *Periphetes* takes its name from Theseus's club-bearing foe, as the stick-like insects resemble Periphetes's favorite weapon. Below, an image of two *Periphetes forcipatus*.

Periphetes forcipatus, a stick insect whose genus name comes from Greek myth. (The species name means "shaped like pincers.")

450 BCE, and never attained the popularity of the other five, who appear in much more detail in the ancient literary and artistic sources. Even so, the stories provide interesting details to consider. Psychologically, Periphetes's use of his club to murder people might have been a way to compensate for his deformity, a motive evident in many modern serial killers. Japanese serial killer Tsutomu Miyazaki, active in the late 1980s and known as a cannibal and necrophiliac, was born with a severe hand abnormality. The joints in his hands were fused to his wrists, meaning that he had to rotate his entire forearm to turn his hand. Because of this disability, other children at school teased him horribly. He became a loner and eventually developed interests in horror films and pornography. Before being caught, he killed four young girls, strangling them with his deformed hands. He also mutilated the hands of at least one of his victims. Edgar Eric Cooke, an Australian serial killer known as "The Night Caller," had a noticeable facial deformity, a scar from surgery to correct a cleft palate and harelip. The operation also left him with a speech impediment. His disfigurement and mumbling speech resulted in Cooke being regularly beaten and verbally bullied at school, and, like Miyazaki, he grew up harboring great resentment toward the world. He killed at least eight people (both men and women) between 1959 and 1963, using a wide variety of methods—stabbing, strangling, and hacking with an ax, among others.

Despite the relative rarity of disfigured criminals, there remains a mistaken popular belief that most serial killers have a physical deformity partially responsible for fueling their resentment and rage. This belief probably resulted from the once popular but thoroughly discredited theory of Cesare Lombroso, a nineteenth-century Italian physician (1835–1909), who pioneered the now-debunked field of "criminal anthropology," which claimed links between the nature of a crime and the criminal's physical appearance. Highly skeptical of the long-standing theory that criminal behavior was a characteristic trait of human nature, Lombroso theorized that people who committed crimes were somehow throwbacks to our prehistoric past, and that consequently they could be identified by certain physical characteristics. He suggested that born criminals had specific physical defects that made them resemble apes, such as thick skulls, large jaws, heavy brows, and wide necks. Social scientists did not take Lombroso's theory seriously for very long, and it was disproven in the early twentieth century. Nevertheless, Lombroso's work left behind the strong impression that criminals must be motivated by their own physical deformities.[3]

The criminal anthropology school of thought still survives in recent depictions of villains and serial murderers in fiction, particularly in graphic

DEFORMITIES AND DISGUISES

Many serial killers in movies wear masks, either to disguise their identity or to cover up a deformity. In Tobe Hooper's 1974 *Texas Chain Saw Massacre*, the principal antagonist, chainsaw-wielding Jed Sawyer, acquired the nickname "Leatherface" because he always wore one of three different leather masks, all made from human skin. He was not deformed, but rather wore the masks to express different personalities ("Killing Mask," "Old Lady Mask," "Pretty Woman Mask"). But the 2003 remake gave Jed a backstory, explaining that as a child Leatherface had suffered a disfiguring skin disease that ate away most of his facial features, and that other children cruelly teased him because of this. Filmmakers Tobe Hooper and Kim Henkel based Leatherface on real-life serial killer Ed Gein, who wore masks made from the skin of female corpses. But Gein was one of only a very few real-life serial killers to wear masks, and he did not do so during the commission of his crimes, but at home, where he donned entire outfits made from women's body parts. Jason Voorhees, the fictional antagonist in many (but not all) of the *Friday the 13th* movies (1980–2009), suffered cranial deformities at birth and eventually adopted a hockey mask to disguise his features and his identity. Michael Myers, the enigmatic killer from the *Halloween* series (1978–2018, so far), wore a mask, but like Leatherface was not deformed. His featureless white mask emphasized the blank nature of his malevolent, seemingly supernatural character.[4] Wes Craven's 1996 film *Scream* and its sequels used "Ghostface" masks to hide the killers' identities. There is no evidence suggesting that robbers and killers in the ancient world wore masks or disguises of any kind. But Periphetes may provide an early case relating a killer's physical deformity to his psychological disturbance.

---

novels and film (see the box above), despite the entirely unexceptional appearance of most real-life serial killers. This persistent mistaken belief in a connection between criminality and physical deformity may have its basis in the wish to believe that a clear reason exists for why killers behave the way they do, and that evil inside a person must be reflected by exterior ugliness. As Glinda, the "Good Witch of the North," exclaims in Victor Fleming's 1939 film *The Wizard of Oz*, regarding the green-skinned, hook-nosed "Wicked Witch of the West"—and to the detriment of girls' self-esteem everywhere—"Only bad witches are ugly!"[5] Cinematic deformed serial killers include the mutant cannibal clan in Wes Craven's 1977 film *The Hills*

Have Eyes and vengeful Freddy Krueger from the *Nightmare on Elm Street* series, disfigured by the horrific burns suffered in the fire that killed him. But most cinematic serial killers tend toward the good-looking and charming type. Take, for example, Anthony Perkins as *Psycho*'s Norman Bates (in contrast to his unattractive literary predecessor in Robert Bloch's novel), Christian Bale as *American Psycho*'s Patrick Bateman, Matt Damon as *The Talented Mr. Ripley*, and Michael C. Hall as television's *Dexter*. Periphetes, though, is unusual in being one of the few serial killers from antiquity for whom we have any specific physical description at all. Most criminals from the ancient world are not described in the sources as deformed or blandly handsome or anything in between. Greek and Roman authors focus instead on these characters' moral turpitude.

Deformity aside, and despite his skull-smashing inclinations, Periphetes proved no match for Theseus. The ancient Greeks probably imagined Periphetes along the lines of the several highway killers in Heracles's adventures, such as Cacus, Antaeus, Termerus, Cycnus, and Lityerses, who focused on their victims' heads, so they may have added Periphetes intentionally to Theseus's adventures to provide another connection to Heracles. But the rest of the criminals Theseus confronted showed more creativity in their murderous methodologies, perhaps in an Athenian attempt to portray Theseus as surpassing Heracles when facing human opponents.

Sinis, the "Pine-Bender"

Having dispatched Periphetes, Theseus safely passed through Epidaurus and continued to the Isthmus of Corinth, where he encountered Sinis, also known as Pityokamptes, meaning "Pine-Bender." According to some variants of the myth, Sinis (whose name comes from the Greek verb *sinomai*, "to harm") was a son of Poseidon and thus a half-brother of Theseus himself. Like Periphetes, Sinis preyed upon anyone who passed by his territory. The Greek author Pausanias calls him a *lēistēs*[6]—the word regularly translated inadequately into English as "robber"—but Pausanias and other authors' versions of the myth concentrate on Sinis's method of killing, saying nothing of the spoils he seized from travelers.

Sinis was amazingly strong. After attacking and overcoming a victim, he bent two pine trees to the ground and tied one arm of the unfortunate traveler to each tree, so that the victim was ripped in two when Sinis released the branches. In some versions Sinis uses only one tree, which flings his victims high into the air, whereupon they smash back (fatally) onto the ground.

Theseus (right) about to kill Sinis by the villain's own method. Interior of a Greek red-figure drinking cup by the Elpinikos Painter, 490–480 BCE.

Theseus killed Sinis by a similar method. Lest this (rather than any other) aspect of the story sound implausible given Theseus's lack of experience with pine-bending, Plutarch specifically explains that Theseus succeeded because "nobility of character is superior to all expertise and practice."[7]

Sinis's unique method of killing may have been inspired by the surrounding landscape. Pine trees grew in abundance around the southern isthmus and appear in other stories about the area. At least one grove of pine trees in the region was sacred to Poseidon, reputedly Sinis's father. Possibly, like Heracles's opponents Antaeus and Cycnus, Sinis intended his victims as sacrifices to his father, but there exists no definite evidence of human sacrifices ever being made to Poseidon (see the box on page 125). The act of splitting people in two may represent man's dual nature, a common theme in Greek myth—our baser inclinations always clashing with more civilizing instincts. This is not to say that Sinis's modus operandi reflected a profound and potentially redemptive conflict within himself, but rather that the myth might have incorporated a metaphorical statement about what we sometimes call the Jekyll-and-Hyde nature within all of us. Perhaps reflecting this concern, one version of the story describes how Theseus seeks spiritual atonement from the blood pollution after slaying Sinis: he undergoes a purification ceremony at a local altar of Zeus. Alternatively, Theseus atoned for the bloodshed and honored the memory of his slain half-brother Sinis by instituting the Isthmian Games.[8]

Phaea, (and/or?) the Crommyonian Sow

After Theseus took care of Sinis he continued across the isthmus around the Saronic Gulf, heading toward the village of Crommyon about 25 km northeast of Corinth. He planned to hunt down and kill the Crommyonian Sow, sometimes called Phaea; this was a monstrous porcine creature devastating the region. Most versions of this adventure explain that the name Phaea originally referred not to the Sow but to an old woman who had reared the creature and trained it to kill humans. The Sow thus took its name from its elderly caretaker, and typical Athenian fifth-century artistic representations of this myth show an old woman urging the Sow to attack the hero. This alarmingly huge and ferocious pig (the offspring of two even worse, more primordial monsters, Echidna and Typhon), killed people indiscriminately, earning itself the endearing epithet "man-slaughtering." A large and aggressive pig can, in reality, easily knock over a grown man and stomp him to death and then eat him, if so inclined. And sows, like male pigs, can have tusks and can gore a man to death (see the box on the facing page). But aside from a monster sow's ability to kill a man, Plutarch notes the rumor that Phaea was actually a murderous female bandit simply nicknamed "Sow" because of her filthy personal habits. Such rationalizations of Greek myth were not uncommon (see chapter 1). It is also possible that a giant pig made its way into the adventures of Theseus in imitation of Heracles's fourth labor, capturing the giant Erymanthian boar. In any case, Theseus's confrontation with the Crommyonian Sow earns its place in an account of serial killing not only because of the disagreement as to whether Phaea was a giant pig or a female serial murderer, but also because, even in most of the Sow versions, an elderly woman with murderous inclinations controls the Sow's actions. Whichever Phaea was—giant pig or human bandit—Theseus killed her and then received widespread praise for making the area around

A SUSTAINABLE METHOD OF CORPSE DISPOSAL

In Steve Minor's 1999 film *Lake Placid*, Betty White plays a seemingly harmless old woman who just happens to raise gigantic, man-eating crocodiles, while the popularity of swine as a method of corpse disposal appears occasionally in fiction, as in Thomas Harris's *Hannibal* (both the book and film versions). It is not unusual for killers to dispose of their victims by feeding the human remains to animals. The presence of the Crommyonian Sow and the man-eating turtle in the myths of Theseus may reflect this long-standing real-life practice. In late nineteenth-century California, farmer Joseph Briggen fed his prize hogs the body parts of butchered farmhands. Carl Panzram, traveling in Portuguese West Africa in the 1920s, killed six locals he had hired to help him hunt crocodiles and fed their bodies to the reptiles. In 1930s Texas, John Ball murdered a number of women and fed their corpses to the alligators he kept in a pond in his yard. In the 1939 film version of *The Wizard of Oz*, Dorothy's fall into the pig pen causes a panic not simply because she might have injured herself, but because *pigs will eat virtually anything*, so Dorothy was in serious danger. In 2002 a jury convicted Canadian pig farmer Robert Pickton of killing half a dozen women; in 2004 came the revelation that he had ground up human flesh and mixed it with pork from the farm, and that he may have fed human remains to the pigs. This infamous case influenced a 2009 two-part episode of the fictional television series *Criminal Minds* (season 4, episodes 25 and 26, "To Hell . . . and Back"). In short, the case of Phaea sounds less odd when we consider that pigs, as omnivores, do not balk at eating human flesh (or even each other). On a farm near Riverton, Oregon, in 2012, authorities found the remains of Terry Vance Garner in his own hog enclosure, where the swine had eaten most of his body. Because one of the nearly 700-pound hogs had previously bitten Garner, officials investigated the possibility that the animals had deliberately knocked him over and eaten him.

Crommyon safe again for its inhabitants. The myths do not tell us whether Theseus also killed the elderly woman who raised and controlled the Sow.

The myth of Phaea lacks details. It says nothing about the old woman's background, how she acquired and raised such a monstrous pig, or why she trained it to kill humans. Possibly she wanted to rob the travelers and was too infirm to kill them herself. Likewise, even if Phaea were "in reality" a murderous female bandit, we have no information about how she killed her victims. But this case still provides some unusual information. For one thing, the Greeks clearly believed that not only men but also women—and not merely mythological women like Medea or Clytemnestra—were capable of using not just secretive methods of killing such as poisoning but also of committing violent mutilation murder. Today, an average of one out of every six serial killers is a woman, a ratio coincidentally represented in Theseus's encounters. Some female serial killers work alone, such as Aileen Wuornos (active in Florida in the 1990s), who targeted lone males traveling along highways. Others work with a partner, although said partner is not usually a monstrous farm animal but rather a male who initiates the murders.

Sciron: Local Hero or Power-Control Killer?

After ridding Crommyon of its menace (whether pig or woman), Theseus continued across the isthmus and in the vicinity of Megara encountered the criminal Sciron, the only one of the six outlaws actively described as "robbing passersby" rather than receiving the generic label "robber."[9] But according to tradition, Sciron, who was yet another of Poseidon's sons, did not simply rob travelers passing his way. He had his own distinctive method of killing them and getting rid of their bodies. After relieving them of their valuables, he shoved them to the ground and forced them to wash his feet, using water from a little basin he kept nearby expressly for this purpose. Then, while his victims were crouching on the ground, he kicked them over the cliff into the sea, where they were dashed to pieces on the rocks, their bodies devoured by a giant sea turtle waiting below. If the fall did not kill them, the turtle did. Theseus eliminated Sciron in the same way, throwing him over the cliff into the jaws of the monstrous turtle.

The story of Theseus's crossing the isthmus and his adventures during this journey reflected the nature of the landscape itself. Before a modern roadway was cut along the cliffs and in a narrow strip along what is now the Corinth Canal, an even narrower old road threaded its way through the rocks, a terrain with clear advantages as a bandit stronghold. For much of the way, the ancient road clung precariously to sheer cliffs.[10] The monstrous sea turtle, analogous to the Crommyonian Sow in its consumption of human flesh, recalls Poseidon's many sea monsters, such as those sent to devour Hesione and Andromeda (see the box on page 125). But Theseus did not slay the turtle, probably because (in addition to living in the sea at the base of the cliff) it did not attack him and posed no threat to travelers in the absence of Sciron.[11]

Plutarch notes that local Megarian authors disagree with the Athenian

Theseus hurling Sciron over the cliff into the sea. Greek paintings of this scene show the turtle as quite small, either for perspective or for an unexpected realism. Interior of Greek red-figure drinking cup, ca. 480 BCE, found in the Etruscan town of Vulci in Italy.

version of Theseus's story. They describe Sciron as neither a violent man nor even a robber, but as a local hero, a just and reasonable man who punished outlaws. In the Megarian version, after Theseus arrived in Athens and established himself as its ruler, he invaded Megarian territory and slew Sciron. Historically, Athens and Megara were embroiled in territorial disputes in the late sixth century at the time when the Theseus myths coalesced, so the appearance of Sciron in them as a villain strongly suggests a political motivation for his characterization. But even if the Athenians intentionally depicted Sciron as a villain, the peculiar details of this characterization warrant a closer look. Why did Sciron make his victims wash his feet? Why kick them over the cliff? Psychologically, Sciron's need to humiliate his victims aligns him with the power-control serial killer type, whose main motive is not to cause pain and suffering but to control and dominate his victims, often sexually, even while using torture as a method of control. The murder itself ultimately expresses the serial killer's control over his victim, and a level of control often continues into death with various postmortem sexual acts and mutilation.[12] Sciron's story implies much of this. Forcing his victims to bend over and wash his feet is sexually suggestive. Kicking them over the cliff involves mutilation, inasmuch as their bodies would have been mangled by hitting the rocks on the way down, and the presence of the man-eating turtle hints at the cannibalistic element sometimes found in serial killings, just as in the story of Phaea (and/or) the Sow.

The Case of Cercyon and His Wrestling Mania

With Sciron dead, Theseus continued toward Athens. About 21 km out, in the vicinity of Eleusis, Theseus met Cercyon, who monitored the road and forced any strangers passing by to wrestle with him. If they lost (they inevitably did), he killed them. He tortured and murdered anyone who refused to wrestle with him. Unlike most of the criminals Theseus encountered, Cercyon already had a notorious background; he had killed his own daughter for having an affair. Compelled to wrestle with Cercyon like every other passerby, Theseus won the match by lifting Cercyon high up into the air and then dashing him to the ground forcefully enough to kill him, in a partial echo of Heracles's bout with Antaeus. But in this case, as with Sciron, the portrayal of Cercyon as the local villain probably resulted from political rivalries. Cercyon was a hero—some say king—in Eleusis, part of the Megarid territory involved in disputes with Athens in the late sixth century BCE. Cercyon also resembles Sciron in fitting the power-control killer type, his primary goal being to dominate his victims rather than to torture them.

Procrustes, Revisited

Arriving on the border of Attica but before entering Athens itself, Theseus confronted the last of the six outlaws: Procrustes ("Smiter," also known as Prokoptes, "Cutter"). Procrustes had a house near the road along a river and invited exhausted travelers to spend the night there. Then he made sure they fit his guest bed exactly. If his visitors were too tall, he cut off the excessive extremities with an ax or a saw; if they were too short, he stretched their limbs with weights and pounded them out with a hammer until they fit the bed. Some versions of the myth say that Procrustes had two beds and intentionally mismatched travelers to them. From this myth comes the English adjective "procrustean," used to describe something that has been unnaturally forced to conform to a narrow standard.

Of all the criminals in Theseus's story, Procrustes most closely displays the behavior of a modern serial killer. His implements include a hammer,

Theseus attacking Procrustes with the killer's own ax. Note the bed. Greek red-figure vase by the Alkimachos Painter, 470–460 BCE.

saw, and ax, and his method of killing is the most detailed, torturous, ritualistic, and personal of all the ones described here. Procrustes fits the "anger-excitation" type of serial killer, whose primary motive is to inflict pain and terror and whose crime involves prolonged torture and mutilation of the victim; the murder itself is a lower priority than the process leading up to it. This type of killer is initially friendly to his victims until he has them where he wants them, and his need to express power and control results in a highly ritualized crime that includes a "murder kit," such as particular instruments of torture.[13] The case of Procrustes, along with those of several other outlaws Theseus faced, hints at the sexual domination aspect so often a feature of serial killing. Certain objects and actions in these myths allow for sexual interpretations: Periphetes's club serves as a phallic symbol, the pine branches in the Sinis story suggest a certain invasiveness,[14] and Sciron's forcing his victims to bend over and wash his feet is at best creepy and at worst sexual. Cercyon's wrestling contest was hardly a fair competition, and his actions may imply rape. Procrustes killed his victims in a bed. All of this is not intended to strain the point, but only to suggest that these crimes do, in fact, appear to contain sexual elements.

NICKNAMING THE KILLERS

Descriptive names rather than individualized monikers are highly characteristic of folktales and legends. The heroines of the Brothers Grimm tales, for example, bear such generic names as "Little Red Riding Hood," "Sleeping Beauty," "Snow White," and "The Brave Little Tailor." These general names allow the audience to relate to the characters and also contribute to the characters' legendary quality. Typical serial killers' nicknames work the same way. "Jack the Ripper," had he been known as "Steve," would probably not have captured the public imagination in the same way, but of course the unsolved nature of his crimes, along with their appalling gruesomeness, contributed greatly to his infamy. Elizabeth Báthory, who was active from the late sixteenth to the early seventeenth centuries and who became the most notorious female serial killer in history, gained the epithet "The Blood Countess" because she reportedly bathed in the blood of virgins to sustain her youthful appearance. The modern media continue to assign such nicknames to serial killers, especially before the killers are caught and identified. Kenneth Bianchi and Angelo Buono, for example, were "The Hillside Stranglers" (1977–1978), and Gary Ridgway was "The Green River Killer" (1982–1998 or later), both phrases referring to the locations where they discarded their victims' bodies. Through such nicknames serial killers become legendary rather than mundane. The nature of their crimes is also far from mundane, but the descriptive names ensure that their crimes will not easily be forgotten. This practice of nicknaming goes all the way back to classical antiquity. Heracles's antagonist Saurus ("Lizard") may have been so called because of his ability to creep up on his victims (see chapter 7), and several highway killers in the Theseus stories had descriptive names that, like those of modern serial killers, reflected how they killed their victims—"Club-Bearer" and "Pine-Bender" being two prime examples.

Theseus: Vigilante, Serial Killer, or Savior?

After clearing the roads of all six outlaws (or of five outlaws and one giant pig), Theseus arrived at Athens. But he could not enter the city right away. Having shed so much blood, Theseus himself might have been perceived as just the sort of criminal he so loathed—a serial murderer. As we saw, Theseus even took a trophy from one of his victims: Periphetes's club. On the one hand, the Greeks commonly took trophies from enemies slain in battle, such as armor. On the other hand, this was not ordinary warfare. What, then, makes Theseus different from any of the villains he killed? Unlike Heracles, who unintentionally encountered various criminals such as Antaeus and Cercyon, Theseus intentionally sought out these six criminals hoping to get the better of them, viewing his actions as a rite of passage from youth to adulthood or from anonymous man to hero. There existed no organized police force or garrisons of any kind monitoring the roads in ancient Greece (in myth or reality). People who knew about dangerous territory where brigands attacked simply tried to avoid passing through those areas. But having mythological heroes do the job provided wish fulfillment in addition to political propaganda: Theseus confronted the killers when no one else dared. His motives differed vastly from those of the pathological killers he faced. But how and why is a hero allowed to murder? How does Theseus differ from or appear morally better than, say, the fictional Dexter, who also stalked and killed only those who "deserved" it? The Megarians, for one, certainly viewed Theseus as a nefarious killer. But in the majority of (admittedly Athenian-biased) stories describing Theseus's road trip, Theseus did not demonstrate a true longing to kill. Unlike Dexter, he was not trying to find a constructive outlet through which to channel an inner desire to murder. Rather, Theseus wanted to make the world safer and, in doing so, to gain a noble reputation. This problem, that "what it takes to catch a serial killer is tantamount to being one,"[15] shows up frequently in modern fiction, where the criminal profilers and other lawmen in pursuit of serial killers find themselves trying to think like the killers in order to catch them. Films such as Michael Mann's 1986 *Manhunter* (based on Thomas Harris's 1981 novel *Red Dragon*, the novel that introduced Hannibal Lecter) create "uncomfortable affinities between protagonist and antagonist" that partially undermine the barriers between monster and human.[16] To a modern audience, Theseus might appear similar to the killers he pursues, given his trophy-taking and his imitation of the killers' methods.

But the ancient Greek audience, especially the Athenians, would not have viewed Theseus as a criminal. Quite the opposite. Even if Theseus had been a real person and was put on trial, Athenian homicide law probably would have exonerated him. The law addressed the issue of killing in self-defense when ambushed on the highway, though one could perhaps argue that Theseus's intent (if he admitted it in a court of law) might have precluded a plea of self-defense. But these are not the important points. The significant difference between Theseus and the criminals he killed is that whereas the outlaws insolently sneered at the concepts of reverence, justice, fairness, and human kindness,[17] Theseus and other pious heroes upheld these ideals and regretted having to shed blood. This is why they sought ritual purification. And according to the stories, Theseus underwent purification and ritual atonement, either shortly after killing Sinis or after he had killed all six criminals. Most versions say that when Theseus reached the river Cephisus just outside of Athens, members of the Phytalidae clan (an ancient race living in the area) greeted him, and he asked them to purify him from all the blood he had shed. They agreed, and after cleansing him with the customary rituals, they helped him make the necessary propitiatory burnt offerings to the gods. This sort of ritual purification was not merely fictional but a real-life practice reflected in many myths. In contrast, unrepentant criminals did not seek purification.

Theseus went on to other adventures, including saving Athenian youths and maidens from the Minotaur in the labyrinth on the island of Crete. He eventually became king of Athens (after having been inadvertently responsible for the death of his father, Aegeus). His later life was not exactly scandal-free and he eventually met a dismal death, as did many heroes after they tried unsuccessfully to settle down into mundane everyday life. But Theseus was certainly the subject of a good story and a focus for Athenian patriotism. Even more, as Ward explains, Theseus "was a powerful influence in practical terms on the daily life of the Classical Athenians. He was the object of a hero cult with far-reaching moral implications, and his name was closely associated with the democratic institutions of which Athens was so proud. The legend's propaganda value was extended even beyond the borders of Attica by making Theseus . . . the personification of the Athenian ideal of democracy, progressiveness and philanthropy."[18]

Theseus, by ridding the highway of those six horrific murderers, exemplified the morality that the Athenians expected in their leaders. The Romans, too, remembered Theseus principally for making the roads safe. The poet Ovid may have said it best:

> It was because of your public service, your effort
> that the Crommyonian farmer now plows untroubled by the Sow
>
> . . . .
>
> And since Sciron met his match in you, the road to Megara lies open.
> (Ovid, *Metamorphoses* 7.435–436, 443–444)

The Dangers of Highway Travel Then and Now

The importance in antiquity of being able to travel the roads safely cannot be overstated. If highwaymen constituted a concern for the Greeks, they were practically an epidemic for the Romans, whose vast empire and strained military resources were often sorely tested by the number of criminals roaming the vast road network through Italy and across the Roman provinces. Murderous highway robbers remained a stark reality in ancient Greece and Rome. Anyone traveling beyond a city's limits probably came across tomb inscriptions indicating as much, since in those days cemeteries were placed outside city walls. Many such inscriptions survive, especially from Roman times, for which we have an immense compilation known as the *Corpus Inscriptionum Latinum (CIL)*. This collection from all over the Roman Empire contains nearly 200,000 Latin inscriptions from various sources, including tombstones, law codes, boundary stones, wine jars, and even jewelry. *Interfectus a latronibus* ("He was killed by robbers") and similar phrases appear on many dozens of tombstones, indicating that death at the hands of bandit gangs occurred with some regularity.

Highway bandits, those robbers who prey specifically on travelers, have been a problem all over the world throughout history. The Thugees of India, for example, plagued the roads of that country from at least as early as the fourteenth century and continued to do so until the British ruling officials eradicated their gangs in the nineteenth century—but the word "thug" survives (and with increasingly mutated meanings). Britain itself has a well-documented history of cutthroat highwaymen from the seventeenth and eighteenth centuries. In ancient Greece, in the sixth century BCE, when previously isolated Greek city-states began to interact more via highways, the myth of Theseus expressed the dangers of such travel. Highway robbery and murder have been common crimes for such a long time because of the vulnerability of travelers. Travelers are often isolated; they are strangers to an area, stopping to rest in unfamiliar places; they rarely know the local lore, and often do not know which areas to avoid. All of this makes them easy to rob and to kill. Even more advantageous for a killer is that days or even weeks may elapse before such disappearances are noticed. Today's major thoroughfares provide a similar backdrop. Highway violence in the United States increased dramatically following the period of rapid interstate construction in the 1950s under Eisenhower's highway program. As in ancient Greece, one purpose of all these new thoroughfares was to aid and increase the growth of trade, agriculture, and industry. In ancient Rome, advancements in road construction and maintenance were also motivated by the need for official communications and troop movements across the Empire. Similarly, in the United States, highways were also part of the Cold War effort to increase the nation's civil defenses, designed to allow troop and tank movement and evacuation of cities. But the new highway system and the growing car culture that accompanied it also increased the mobility and anonymity of both travelers and criminals. Stranded motorists, hitchhikers, drifters, and prostitutes, along with people living in the suburbs, became increasingly vulnerable to roving predators who now had easy access to serpentine road systems.[19]

The murder spree of Charlie Starkweather and his girlfriend Caril Ann Fugate in 1958 was probably the first explicitly linked with America's burgeoning car culture and new mobility, and after that, serial murder along highways slowly increased. Notorious cases also include Edmund Kemper, who killed six young female hitchhikers between 1972 and 1973. In the mid-1980s, more than four dozen women disappeared from the Seattle and Tacoma areas in Washington State, their strangled bodies later found in wooded areas along the Green River. The "Green River Killer" eluded capture for many years. Finally, in 2001, DNA evidence led police to Gary Leon Ridgway, who admitted to picking up the women along Pacific Highway South. But because of the anonymous nature of highways, many serial highway murders remain unsolved. The "New Bedford Highway Killer," responsible for murdering at least nine women in New Bedford, Massachusetts, in 1988 and 1989, has never been caught. A stretch of Highway 16 in British Columbia between the cities of Prince Rupert and Prince George acquired the nickname "Highway of Tears" because of the dozens of murders and disappearances of women recorded there since 1969. Authorities have considered a number of suspects over the decades for these cases, many of which are unrelated; Canadian citizen Cody Legebokoff (b. 1990) was convicted on four counts of first-degree murder for killings that occurred in 2009–2010, but most of the perpetrators remain unknown. Yet one significant difference distinguishes modern highway killers and those in the Theseus myths: in antiquity it was the travelers who moved around, whereas the killers remained stationary. They had their lairs and killed strangers passing by. In modern highway killings, often both the killers and victims travel. Perhaps two dozen or more truckers are currently serving time in US prisons for serial murder; most picked up prostitutes at truck stops, killed them, and dumped the bodies miles away along the highway.

In short, a disturbingly large number of modern serial killings have occurred and continue to occur along highways. Helen Morrison, a psychiatrist specializing in the psychology of serial killers, has said, "I sometimes joke that if it weren't for the interstate system of highways, serial killers would probably stay in one place and be a lot easier to apprehend."[20] FBI analysts have discovered patterns of highway killings all over the United States—so many, in fact, that in 2001 the FBI began its (regrettably named) "Highway Serial Killings Initiative" to raise awareness of the phenomenon among law enforcement and the general public. FBI analysts have called highway killings an "emerging trend," but clearly the FBI is not familiar with the nearly 3,000-year-old stories of Heracles and Theseus. There may also be a familiar environmental lesson buried in these stories, both ancient and modern: roads mar the landscape and intrude upon the wild. Civilization, encroaching upon nature, meets danger in doing so.

CHAPTER 9

From Murderous Contests to Olympic Sports

The quadrennial Olympic games, which, according to ancient Greek tradition, were founded in 776 BCE, marked the formal development of Greek athletic competition. Some Greek literature, including the *Iliad* and *Odyssey*, describes foot races, chariot races, and other sports that adhered to various rules. But the Olympics, originally held in Olympia in southern Greece in honor of Zeus, organized multiple athletic contests to an extent previously unknown in the ancient Mediterranean. Athletes from any Greek city-state could participate, and people all over the Greek world considered the Olympics so extraordinarily important and prestigious that a sacred truce, known as the *ekecheiria* ("holding of hands"), constituting an armistice among any hostile city-states, covered a period of several weeks before the games so that both athletes and spectators could travel in safety to the games from near and far.[1] At first, the Olympics included only footraces of varying lengths. The Games then added boxing sometime in the late eighth or early seventh century BCE, along with several other competitions, such as wrestling and, eventually, chariot racing.

But there was a long period of time before sports in the ancient Greek world were regulated and recognized as legitimate competitions that they formed a productive outlet for otherwise hostile impulses. Heracles and Theseus, who (mythologically) lived in the generation before the Homeric epics, each encountered many savage antagonists who, under the guise of friendly competition, attacked and killed people they wanted to eliminate. This included Antaeus, the king who forced strangers to wrestle with him; Cycnus, who gave travelers no choice but to engage in armed combat; and Cercyon, who, like Antaeus, challenged passersby to a wrestling match. These killers all exhibited an exaggerated and deadly passion for unsanctioned athletic contests forced upon unwilling participants. A large number of other myths and legends from ancient Greece describe similarly blood-thirsty, belligerent killers. What becomes apparent in many of the stories about murderous athletic confrontations, however, is a gradual shift in con-text, whereby these sports change from savage, primitive fighting meth-ods to skilled Olympic competitions. The myths' subtext suggests that the Greeks turned these barbaric sports into civilized, legitimate, accepted ath-letic contests in which the goal was to demonstrate admirable expertise while adhering to a set of rules rather than to randomly slay as many re-luctant and terrified opponents as possible. We have already seen several stories about wrestling, and will see examples of brutal pre-Olympic foot racing and chariot racing. This chapter, meanwhile, presents two stories centering on antagonists who exhibit characteristics of serial killers as ex-pressed through deadly boxing competitions.

The Sadistic Hobby of King Amycus

Amycus was king of Bebrycia, a land in Asia Minor on the southern shore of the Black Sea. A physically gigantic, temperamentally vicious monarch, the xenophobic Amycus did not take kindly to strangers passing through his territory. His subjects lived in fear, and so obeyed his order to capture all intruders. If the travelers seemed weak and puny, and therefore not worth fighting (they would provide no challenge), Amycus simply took them up to a cliff-top and hurled them into the sea as sacrifices to his father, Poseidon. But if the strangers were stout and strong, Amycus forced them to engage in a boxing match. Inevitably winning the bout, Amycus enjoyed pulverizing, mutilating, and killing his ultimately inferior opponents.

The Greek hero Jason and his crew, the Argonauts, stopped to rest in Bebrycia on their way to obtain the Golden Fleece from Colchis on the east-ern end of the Black Sea. Jason sent his scout Echion ahead to reconnoiter the unknown territory. Going just a little way inland, Echion came across a young man lamenting the murder of a friend. Upon seeing the stranger, the young man urgently warned him to flee. Echion was astonished at this un-expected and alarming greeting, but when the young man persisted, Echion led him back to the *Argo* where the youth told his story to the other sailors, describing how the region was ruled by Amycus, a cruel king with a raging temper who physically towered over other men and forced strangers to box with him until he beat them to a bloody pulp. This had happened to his de-ceased friend, the young man said. Jason cautiously inquired as to how the young man himself had survived: Hadn't Amycus forced him, too, to fight?

HUMAN SACRIFICES TO POSEIDON?

Several classical myths mention humans offered up to Poseidon, often as retribution for dishonoring the sea god. In one story, King Laomedon of Troy broke a promise to Poseidon, who then sent a sea monster to plague the Trojans. The oracles told Laomedon that the trouble would cease if he offered up his daughter Hesione as a meal for the creature. The king did so, but the girl was rescued by Heracles. When Queen Cassiopeia of Aethiopia insulted the sea nymphs by claiming that her daughter Andromeda was more beautiful than any of them, a furious Poseidon flooded the city until an oracle instructed King Cepheus to appease the god by presenting Andromeda as food for a (different) sea monster. So Cepheus reluctantly tied her to a rock by the sea, where she awaited her horrible fate. But the hero Perseus, on his journey home from slaying the Gorgon Medusa, saved her by killing the sea monster with his sword. In neither of these cases are there any repercussions from Poseidon after the heroes rescue the maidens, which suggests that the "sacrifices" were intended mainly to build up the heroes' reputations as saviors, or, at the very least, that Poseidon simply wanted to test the kings' willingness to offer up their daughters to appease him.[2] Similarly, the Hebrew God tested Abraham with Isaac (Genesis 22). But the Greek tales differ from the biblical one in many respects, given that the kings are not themselves required to physically kill their children, and that Poseidon, unlike the biblical god, does not interfere in the sacrificial process (although he also does not object to such interference). It is also worth noting, as Dennis Hughes points out in his study on human sacrifice in ancient Greece, that language relating to sacrifice is entirely absent from these two Greek stories.[3] In contrast, the Latin *Argonautica* of Roman author Valerius Flaccus (first century CE) describes King Amycus as throwing trespassers off a "sacrificial ridge" (*sacrifici iugi*) into the sea to honor his father, Neptune (the Roman version of Poseidon), joining the ranks of other sons of the sea god (such as Antaeus, Lityerses, and Sciron) whose human victims were, at least in part, dedicated to the deity.

The young man mournfully and truthfully explained that, after the death of his comrade, Amycus had not deemed him worth fighting and instead left him to weep for his friend.

Greatly disturbed by this story and wanting to see the evidence for themselves, Jason and his crew insisted that the young man show them the spot where Amycus took his victims. The youth led the way to a cave not far from the shore, overshadowed by a rocky cliff. At the base of this cliff, by the cave entrance, were strewn various horrors: mangled arms torn from lifeless torsos, but with boxing gloves still attached; bones, moldering where they lay, unburied; a chilling row of severed heads. The men noted how Amycus's blows had obliterated the victims' faces, leaving the bodies unidentifiable.[4]

As the Argonauts viewed this dismal scene, Amycus himself arrived. When the men saw his giant stature and heard his dreadful boasts, they grew fearful and momentarily wished that Heracles, who had accompanied them for part of their voyage, had not left them. But then one of the crew, Polydeuces, renowned for his own boxing prowess, stepped forward to meet Amycus's challenge. Although Amycus dealt several serious blows that left him staggering, Polydeuces managed to gather his strength and deliver a fatal strike to Amycus. Then the Bebryces, who, as it turned out, had no love for their sadistic king, allowed the Argonauts to depart in peace.

This story clearly bears strong similarities to various adventures of Heracles and Theseus. Amycus's display of body parts resembles the skull-shrines set up by Antaeus and Cycnus as well as Cacus's macabre cave decorations (the rotting faces and limbs of his victims). Unlike those stories, this one is related in much more detail, particularly by first-century CE Roman author Valerius Flaccus in his *Argonautica* ("The Voyage of the *Argo*"), an epic poem about the quest of Jason, his crew, and their ship. Working with traditional lore about Amycus dating back at least to the fifth century BCE, the poet elaborates on Amycus's behavior, describing how he exults in killing and mutilating his victims. Although the king's highly public demonstrations contrast with the usually private predatory nature of modern serial killers, in most other respects his actions and attitude strongly align him with the "power-control" killers: highly organized and extremely sadistic, although causing pain and suffering is only their secondary motive. Their primary goal is domination of the victim, with murder the ultimate expression of control. And they do not lose interest once the victim dies. Instead, the control often continues into death as the killer keeps the corpses in a safe place where they can be revisited and, often, mutilated.[5]

The similarities between Amycus's story and those of Antaeus, Cercyon, and others are unlikely to be coincidental, and not simply because early Greek hero myths naturally influenced later hero tales. Rather, stories about savage monarchs probably reflected a growing Greek dissatisfaction with hereditary kingship and other forms of authoritarian rule. During the sixth century BCE, a number of Greek city-states, including Athens, began developing aspects of a democratic government (such as a general assembly), and by a century later basic democracy had taken such a firm hold in various parts of Greece that antimonarchy sentiment became the norm. In both their fiction and nonfiction, the Greeks repeatedly characterized kings as unreasonable, paranoid, and unusually cruel and sadistic, and sometimes even as outright insane. And from the Greek point of view, any non-Greek was by nature a less civilized "barbarian," because the Greeks viewed their society as enlightened and rational compared to other cultures they knew of in the Near East and Mediterranean regions.[6] The characterizations of Antaeus, Cercyon, Amycus, and other foreign kings as sadistic serial killers follows the trend of viewing outsiders and especially foreign monarchs as unenlightened, savage barbarians.[7] Amycus's use of a cave—part of the natural landscape rather than a human construction—only reinforces this impression.

The Serial Killer of Temesa

As an example of Greece's opinion of its own civilizing influence in the Mediterranean and how this influence extended even to the sport of boxing, consider the following local legend from Pausanias, a Greek travel writer of the second century CE. The story describes a series of ritual killings in the town of Temesa in Magna Graecia, a region of Greek settlements in southern Italy. Pausanias records the legend as part of his biographical description of the boxer Euthymus of Locri, a famous real-life athlete of the early fifth century BCE. Like the fictional heroes Heracles and Theseus, Euthymus had notable, supposedly supernatural, origins. According to Pausanias, Euthymus's father was a human named Astycles. But the people in the boxer's hometown of Locri in southern Italy claimed that he was the son of Caicinos, god of the river bordering the Locrian territory. Material and textual evidence tells us that Euthymus was unquestionably a historical figure; he won Olympic victories in boxing in the years 484, 476, and 472 BCE (losing only in 480 BCE), and the Greeks raised a statue in Olympia in his honor. The marble base of this statue, discovered there in 1878, survives today, and bears an inscription honoring Euthymus that indicates his status and calls the athlete "Euthymus, a Locrian, son of Astycles." So why would the Locrians assign him a divine origin? How did Euthymus gain such a reputation? And what does a prizewinning athlete have to do with a series of ritual killings?

In Pausanias's time, more than six hundred years after Euthymus won at Olympia, the people of Temesa still told the story of how Euthymus vanquished a frightening creature that killed the inhabitants at random unless they offered a maiden to him once a year. After Euthymus won his first victory in the 74th Olympic Games of 484 BCE, he returned to Italy where, in the town of Temesa, he fought against the local "Hero" (*heros*). The legend refers to the Hero as a *daimon*, a Greek word meaning "spirit" or "ghost," or, in general, a type of being construed by the Greeks as more than mortal but less than god and that, in this last sense, can have a physical presence. The Hero of Temesa incorporates several of these meanings, as both angry spirit and physical presence, a type of superhuman force that can intervene in human life.[8] Before explaining Euthymus's role in the story, Pausanias opens with the Hero's background and then tells of Euthymus's arrival and conquest of the *daimon*:

> They say that Odysseus, during his wanderings after the destruction of Troy, was forced ashore by storm winds to various cities in both Italy and Sicily, including Temesa, where he arrived together with his ships. While there one of his sailors, after a drinking binge, raped a local maiden and was stoned to death by the townspeople for this crime. Apparently quite unconcerned about the loss of his crewman, Odysseus departed, sailing away. But the *daimon* of the stoned man kept killing people in Temesa indiscriminately, attacking those of every age equally until, when the people were preparing to flee from Italy altogether, the Pythia did not allow them to leave Temesa but ordered them instead to appease the Hero. After assigning him a sacred precinct they were to build him a temple and give him every year as a wife the most beautiful maiden in Temesa. And indeed, after they did what the god had ordered there was no more to fear from the *daimon*.
>
> But Euthymus—for he arrived in Temesa at just the same time as the ritual for the *daimon*—learned what was going on there, and greatly desired to enter the temple and, more, to see the maiden. When he saw her he first felt pity, but then passion, and the girl swore an oath to live with him as his wife if he saved her. So Euthymus equipped himself and awaited the attack of the *daimon*. He was the victor in the fight, driving the Hero out of the land; it disappeared, sinking into the sea. Euthymus's wedding was spectacular, and the people of Temesa lived forever free from the *daimon*. (Pausanias 6.6.7–9)

This legend resembles many stories from all over the world in which a heroic man slays a monstrous being and restores order to the region, often winning a (formerly sacrificial) maiden in the process.[9] But unlike most such stories, this one features a real person and offers specific details that, like those in Libanius's model speech, permit a number of wildly varying interpretations. For example, Euthymus's victory over the *daimon* might reflect the Greeks' colonializing conquest of an indigenous Italian people.[10] Alternatively, the nature of the Hero's worship, given that it was ordered by the Pythia herself, might suggest that the Temesians viewed the Hero as a figure connected to the city's founding.[11] These explanations for Pausanias's Euthymus story share a common element—they are local legends grounded in reality. Yet another interpretation sees the Hero of Temesa as a river deity, one given a sacred space and a shrine, who came from the sea and was driven back to it. But all these interpretations focus on the hero cult of the *daimon* and on the cult of Euthymus that superseded it. They only tangentially provide a reason for the excessive violence in the story. Another possibility is that the story also reflects a Greek awareness of serial killing and a tendency toward lionization similar to that seen with killers both fictional (such as Hannibal Lecter and Norman Bates) and historical (such as Jack the Ripper and John Wayne Gacy).

A modern audience might wonder why a killer ghost (who, before his death, was a drunken rapist) would end up being worshipped as a hero. But the ancient Greeks' concept of "hero" differed considerably from our contemporary understanding. For one thing, the term "hero" could refer to any man who was the offspring of a deity and a mortal, and who consequently had abilities beyond those of a man from purely mortal ancestry—abilities such as extraordinary strength and endurance, or unusual courage and determination, as demonstrated by Heracles and Theseus. Also, especially in the Homeric sense, "hero" indicated any warrior, even a man of solely human ancestry, ready to fight for his country's cause, hoping to gain a glorious reputation that would live in the memories of his descendants and bring distinction to his family line. The ancient Greek hero, whether entirely mortal or semidivine, was not expected to be a paragon of virtue, and not only had the flaws of his fellow men but also might exhibit such flaws on a grander scale—the excessive and deadly anger of Achilles in the *Iliad* being a famous example. A man who met all these qualifications still would not usually be considered a hero until after he died and had a cult founded in his honor. The Greeks worshipped heroes, as they did gods, and honored them with shrines, although heroes were more likely to be objects of worship locally, in and near their hometowns, rather than across all of Greece. It also helped if the hero was associated with a miraculous event, such as healing.[12] And heroes could become immortal if the gods chose to make them so, as Zeus did for Heracles.

Given this background, a modern audience may more easily understand why Pausanias referred to the *daimon* as a "hero." But this *daimon* also demonstrates characteristics of a vengeful ghost. When the sailor was stoned to death, even as a justified punishment for a crime, in the context of religious thought the resulting *daimon* would have been considered what the Greeks called a *biaiothanatos*, someone who had "died by violence" and who, in this case, had also not received proper burial. Odysseus had sailed away "apparently quite unconcerned about the loss of his crewman."[13] The dead man's spirit was therefore restless, vengeful, and likely to harm the living until appeased. This explains the indiscriminate killings in the story. As a result of these killings, the Oracle of Apollo at Delphi, known as the Pythia, advised the townspeople to build a temple to the Hero and offer a maiden to him every year. In general, the dedication of annual victims in this and other stories may, among other things, represent a community's attempt to respond to and control a phenomenon that defies rational explanation. Hero worship and ghost appeasement aside, however, what about the likelihood that many details from this story originated from knowledge of real-life events, such as various unsolved rapes and murders that became expressed as legend over the course of several hundred years? The actions of the *daimon* as described in the story, when sifted out from the more clearly legendary aspects (such as a "ghost" who can kill people), present a progression of increasingly violent behavior, the "learning curve" typical of many serial killer types.

This killer starts with a substance abuse problem: too much alcohol. Although wine constituted a respectable and important part of Greek culture, Greek literature frequently warns against the dangers of overindulging in drink, and Pausanias's audience would have understood the problem with the sailor's "drinking binge" immediately. In modern terms, psychologists would label the binge as a "facilitator" for the crime, since alcohol not only decreases inhibitions but also suppresses moral conscience and any sense of propriety. From the rape onward, the sailor exhibits behavioral characteristics common to the "power-assertive" serial killer, who is motivated by the assertion of masculine power over his victims (who are usually, though not always, women) via sexual defilement. In this respect, these killers differ from power-control killers, whose crimes are not overtly sexually related. Power-assertive killers' first crimes are almost invariably rapes, but they end up committing murder as they become increasingly aggressive and violent while trying to control their victims. Yet they normally do not mutilate their victims, nor is there a prominent element of sadism; the first murder may even be accidental. In Pausanias's story, the sailor, already identified as an outsider to Temesa and thus isolated from the community, rapes a girl and his (alleged) *daimon* goes on a killing spree. A serial killer in the early stages may initially kill at random but later establish a pattern, following a learning curve in which he becomes more specific in his methods and in his type of victim. In the story, the *daimon* initially kills indiscriminately, but his later victims are only young women.[14]

The power-assertive killer, like other types of serial killer, may murder a number of people with a cooling-off period between each event. The murders may go on for months or years until someone stops the killer or he stops on his own for unexplained reasons, as happened with the Zodiac Killer, a power-assertive type who murdered at least five people between 1968 and 1972 and whose last taunting letter to the police was dated January 1974, but whose activities ceased after that.[15] During the cooling-off period, the killer slips back into his daily routine and identity. Pausanias mentions a year between each offering of a maiden, a length of time typical in folktale and in many real-life rituals, such as birthday celebrations. But some serial killers, such as "BTK Killer" Dennis Rader, do indeed wait years between murders.

Several other details about the murders also suggest a power-assertive killer. Such killers obsess about projecting a masculine image, often in a relatively primitive physical manner, such as bodybuilding or participation in martial arts. They frequently have military records, but are generally not perceived as "team players" because they exhibit unnecessarily aggressive, arrogant, and condescending attitudes, and tend to be loners.[16] This fits the description of a Homeric warrior alarmingly well. Homeric warriors aimed primarily to win individual glory and an everlasting reputation, and only secondarily thought of themselves as part of a group such as "Greeks" or "Trojans"—but at least they had the excuse of fighting in the context of war. Whether the killings at Temesa occurred during the Bronze Age, in which Odysseus's adventures are situated, or hundreds of years later during the time of Euthymus, and whether Temesa had been making ritual maiden sacrifices for upwards of 700 years,[17] or whether these killings and sacrifices ever occurred at all—whether we have here a conflation of mythological and real events or not—a man responsible for such killings probably had military training, as did most adult men in the ancient Greek world. The military background of a power-assertive killer, though, is usually far less prestigious than that of his associates. Given the anonymity of the sailor in the story, he was apparently not a renowned Greek warrior with a notable reputation. In short, the story provides enough detail to allow speculation regarding how its various aspects relate to serial mutilation murder.[18]

Not to strain the point, but given the highly unlikely probability that a ghost or walking corpse really went around killing people, we can try to picture a more realistic scenario: A sailor got drunk, raped a local girl, and was attacked by an outraged group of townspeople. He escaped the mob but did not get back to his ship, instead hiding in the surrounding woods and hills.[19] His crewmates gave up their search and sailed without him. His criminal tendencies increased after they abandoned him, and he reached his potential as a power-assertive killer. This is absolutely not intended to sug-

WEREWOLVES OR SERIAL KILLERS?

As an epilogue to his Euthymus story, Pausanias reports that he saw a copy of a painting depicting the Hero of Temesa wearing a wolfskin: "His color was dreadfully dark and his whole appearance was extremely frightening, and he was wearing around himself a wolf-skin for clothing. Also, the letters on the picture gave his name as Lykas ('wolf')." The description aligns the Hero with a more brutal, less civilized period of Greek history, but also hints at a characteristic occasionally associated with serial murder: werewolfism. There have been serial killers throughout history who were either believed by their fellows to be werewolves or who actually believed *themselves* to be werewolves, as such beliefs helped explain their unnatural desires. France saw two separate cases of such murders in the year 1521 alone. Pierre Bourgot and Michel Verdung, thinking themselves to be werewolves, killed, mutilated, and ate several children. In Germany in 1589, a man named Peter Stumpf, whom authorities charged with the rape, murder, and cannibalization of fifteen women and children, had supposedly made a pact with the devil to turn into a werewolf, in which form he would attack his victims. And again in France, in 1603, fourteen-year-old Jean Grenier confessed that he would take the form of a werewolf while mutilating and eating pretty girls. Grenier genuinely believed that he took on this form, but the physicians who examined him concluded (somewhat ironically) that he only imagined he turned into a werewolf and that he was in reality possessed by a demon. This "werewolf delusion" has been identified in many other cases of serial killers, and the belief that serial murderers must be possessed by evil spirits has also persisted over the centuries.[20]

Even the Greeks and Romans had stories about people who could shape-shift into wolf form, usually attributing the ability to sorcery (as opposed to a curse). As early as the fifth century BCE, the Greek historian Herodotus wrote about a tribe called the Neuri, living in the region that is now Ukraine, who reputedly turned into wolves for a few days each year.[21] The first-century CE Roman encyclopedist Pliny the Elder, in his *Natural History*, records a tradition from the Arcadian region of Greece that a man chosen by lot every year had to go to a certain marsh, hang his clothes on an oak tree, swim across the marsh, and go into the wilderness, where he was transformed into a wolf for nine years. If he refrained from eating human flesh during that time, he regained human form.[22] The most famous werewolf story from antiquity appears in Petronius's *Satyrica* (first century CE).[23] Here a man, wishing to visit his girlfriend who lived out in the country, persuades a soldier to accompany him, since robbers roamed the roads. Arriving at the cemetery outside the city boundary, they pause for a rest; the man is shocked to observe his companion strip, put his clothes in a pile by the roadside, pee in a circle around them, and then suddenly become a wolf! The wolf runs off into the woods, and the traveler, terrified, continues on to his girlfriend's villa. There he discovers that a wolf had recently attacked the flocks. He soon comes to the realization that his soldier companion is a werewolf, and is too frightened to associate with him anymore. Significantly, the Greek and Roman stories stress that these shape-shifters do not or should not eat human flesh if they wish to retain their humanity.

---

gest that the story of the Hero of Temesa was based on a real person or any specific real-life event. Rather, it suggests only that reports of such events, based on real-life mutilation murders, could easily turn into local legend, with a mortal criminal replaced by a *daimon* whose motives for murdering townspeople indiscriminately would be more understandable. As FBI special agent John Douglas remarked (see chapter 1), the stories and legends that have filtered down about witches and werewolves and vampires may have been a way of explaining outrages so hideous that no one in the small and close-knit towns of Europe and early America could comprehend the horrific violence often now taken for granted. Monsters had to be supernatural creatures; before modern psychology, criminology, and forensics, it would have been difficult to fathom why a real person would commit such horrific crimes.

Whether Pausanias's story about the Hero of Temesa involves conflation of mythological and historical events or not, the story's ending illustrates the shift in how the Greeks perceived the sport of boxing: "So Euthymus equipped himself and awaited the attack of the *daimon*. He was the victor in the fight, and the Hero was driven out of the land and disappeared, sinking into the sea."[24] The "equipment" was probably boxing gloves, as illustrated below. In a departure from most traditional hero stories, Pausanias does not say that Euthymus killed the Hero, only that he vanquished him and drove him into the sea. The story of Jason and the Argonauts, set in mythological times, presented boxing as still a "primitive" means of fighting, but one moving toward respectability as the Greek Polydeuces used his skill and courage as a boxer to defeat the brutal King Amycus. By the time of Euthymus, boxing had been an Olympic sport for many decades. These two stories demonstrate how savage impulses, as embodied by a (foreign) character with the motives and methods of a serial killer, became civilized when con-

Boxing match. Note the gloves wrapped around the boxers' hands. Greek black-figure vase by the Antimenes Painter, ca. 520 BCE.

trolled by heroic Greek characters, such as Polydeuces and Euthymus, and through officially sanctioned sporting events, such as Olympic boxing.

Epilogue: The Sila Forest Region—A Haven for Murderers?

The Caicinos River, mentioned prominently in Pausanias's story of Euthymus, flowed from the Sila Mountains into the Mediterranean between the towns of Rhegium and Locri. This same region was the site of the Sila Forest murders around 300 years after the time of Euthymus, as reported by Cicero (see pages 60–64). This is probably not a coincidence: the Sila Forest has been notorious as a lair for criminals for more than two thousand years. Nineteenth-century Scottish writer Craufurd Tait Ramage, during his travels through Italy, commented:

> In this vicinity [Sila] I hear of nothing but robberies and murders. . . .
> It seems that there is a *comitiva*, or band, of twenty individuals, who are spread in all directions, carrying terror and dismay into the bosom of the inhabitants. They have lately waylaid several, and one of them has had to pay five thousand *piastres*—upwards of eight hundred pounds sterling.

About a month ago they killed a boy fifteen years of age, because his family was unable to pay the ransom they demanded. They have committed upwards of twenty murders in this neighborhood, and yet the government has only lately sent a small force under my friend, the lieutenant of gendarmes, to make an attempt to suppress such a disastrous state of matters. Murder seems to have been the chronic state of the Silve Sila [Sila Forest] . . . from the earliest times.

Ramage continues with Cicero's story about the Sila Forest murders, and concludes: "Here, then, we find still the same insecurity for life and property to exist, and I do not hear that it has ever been otherwise."[25] Similarly, the nearby Aspromonte Mountains overlooking the Strait of Messina have provided hideouts for criminal gangs, including the Mafia: "Originally peasant families who rebelled against rich landowners by stealing their animals and blackmailing the elite, the *'ndrangheta* used the dense, mostly inaccessible mountains as a hiding place for kidnap victims—usually the offspring of wealthy businessmen—and contraband."[26]

CHAPTER 10

Serial Murders in Local Legends

Although the Greeks associated the individual killers encountered by Heracles and Theseus with specific geographical regions, these criminals were and still are even more closely identified with the heroes who killed them. If and when people recognize the name "Sinis," they think of Theseus (and possibly pine trees), but probably not a location as specific as the Saronic Gulf or the town of Megara. Similarly, Pausanias's story about the Hero of Temesa focuses on Euthymus and his boxing prowess, not on the oddity of a "ghost" capable of killing people and fighting an Olympic champion. But Greek myth also contains stories in which monsters remain steadfastly associated with their locations as much as or even more than with the heroes who vanquish them. Rarely if ever venturing outside a narrow perimeter, the creatures in these stories exhibit behavior now associated with serial killers, demonstrating again that these characteristics have been around for thousands of years.

The Theban Sphinx: A Reflection of Serial Mutilation Murder?

As we mentioned in chapter 1, the story of the Theban Sphinx provides a surprisingly apt analogue for modern stories of localized serial killings. Closely tied to the adventures of Oedipus and to his identity as a riddle-solver, the Sphinx is at least as closely associated with Thebes as with the Greek hero; hence her epithet "Theban." In fact, unlike heroes such as Heracles and Theseus, Oedipus is not principally known as a monster-slayer. His fame in relation to the Sphinx came from solving her infamous riddle and thereby saving Thebes, not from killing her.[1] Most versions of the myth say that the Sphinx, rather than being killed by Oedipus, committed suicide in a fit of humiliation, frustration, and rage at having her riddle solved. Thereafter she remained an integral part of Theban local lore.

Oedipus was famously fated to kill his father and marry his mother. He traveled to Thebes in central Greece to try to avoid this prophecy, despite an understanding present throughout Greek literature that trying to avoid one's fate, however well intentioned, constitutes an act of hubris. Along the journey, in an incident perhaps best described as the earliest recorded example of road rage, Oedipus did indeed kill his father, King Laius of Thebes— but without knowing that Laius was his father. When Oedipus arrived at Thebes, he found the city in turmoil because a monster called the Sphinx, a hybrid creature with the head of a woman, body of a lion, and wings of a bird, had taken up residence on nearby Mount Phicium, ambushing people from the cliffs and consequently making travel to and from Thebes highly undesirable. The goddess Hera had sent the Sphinx, whose name means "Strangler," to punish Laius for raping a young man named Chrysippus. The creature would not depart until the Thebans answered a riddle she posed, one she thought no one could solve: "What goes on four legs in the morning, two legs at noon, and three legs in the evening?" When the brave young men of Thebes, hoping to save their city, tried to solve the riddle and inevitably responded incorrectly, she devoured them, leaving the ground strewn with their bones. The Thebans, having already heard (apparently via an unusually speedy messenger) of Laius's death, offered the kingdom and the queen's hand in marriage to anyone who correctly answered the Sphinx's riddle. Oedipus (apparently traveling to Thebes at a much more leisurely pace than the aforementioned messenger, given that the Thebans had time to organize their "kingdom, queen included" reward) encountered the Sphinx upon his arrival at the city boundary. Presented with her riddle, he replied "Man," who as an infant crawls on all fours, as an adult walks upright on two legs, and in old age walks with a cane. The Sphinx, having believed her riddle unsolvable, threw herself headlong down the rocky cliffs to her death (despite having wings). Oedipus received the kingdom and married the queen, who (unfortunately) happened to be his mother, although neither of them realized this for many years. Aside from and despite the parricide and incest (and eventual self-blinding and exile from Thebes upon discovery of these crimes), Oedipus remained famous ever after as the one who solved the riddle of the Sphinx.

Although best known today for her famous riddle, the Theban Sphinx as a riddler does not appear in classical literature until the fifth century BCE, quite late compared to most monsters of Greek myth. Cerberus, the Cyclopes, the Gorgons, and many others showed up in the earliest Greek literature, the works of Homer and Hesiod, whereas the Sphinx did not even originally appear in Oedipus's story. In the eighth century BCE, long before the Sphinx started to systematically kill the young men of Thebes, Oedipus was already infamous for parricide and incest (Homer, *Odyssey* 11.271–274). Various theories try to explain the Sphinx's eventual introduction into the Oedipus story. One popular explanation posits the need for the hero to overcome a monster in order to bring him in line with other Greek heroes, such as Heracles and Theseus. But tradition does not have Oedipus himself slay the Sphinx, even if by causing her death he saves Thebes as other heroes saved other places by ridding them of monstrous existential threats. Another explanation suggests that the Greeks wished to connect Oedipus, in his role as hero, with the common folkloric motif of riddle-solving and besting a monster to win a bride. The myth hints at such a possibility, given the sort of person who would usually attempt to answer the Sphinx's riddle. Although the myths do not elaborate on this point, the context suggests that young men were the most likely. Since the Thebans were offering the kingdom along with marriage to the queen as a prize, a adult man already settled into life with a wife and children had less reason (other than sheer suicidal patriotism) to risk his life than a young, unmarried man. But using folkloric tradition to suggest that Oedipus needed to solve a riddle to win his bride comes across as odd when there was a much bigger riddle he needed to solve, namely, who his parents were. After Oedipus becomes king of Thebes, he also has to solve the mystery of who killed Laius, the previous king; for years, Oedipus had no clue that Laius was the man whom he had killed on the road to Thebes, nor that Laius was his real father. Sophocles's *Oedipus the King* emphasizes this weakness: Oedipus was able to solve the Sphinx's riddle but not a crucial murder case, and thus did not live up to his clever reputation. The riddle may help in this characterization of Oedipus as being blind to the truth. But the Sphinx's late appearance in the Oedipus story seems less puzzling overall if we remember that the ancient Greeks initially associated her not primarily with her riddle but with the deaths of young men, and if we consider the possibility that this local legend may be another good example of how the Greeks recognized the phenomenon of real-life serial mutilation murder and incorporated it into various characterizations of villains and monsters in their stories.

The Sphinx's association with the Oedipus story probably occurred in a roundabout way. Along with other hybrid creatures, such as griffins, sphinxes abounded in art of the ancient Near Eastern and Mediterranean regions. The Egyptians depicted their sphinxes as primarily male, but the Greeks envisioned sphinxes as predominantly female, occasionally even with a woman's breasts on the lion's torso. The earliest sphinxes in Greece, which were probably imports from Egypt, appeared in the late Bronze Age (ca. 1700 BCE). Highly stylized sphinxes, griffins, and other fabulous animals and vegetation became popular motifs in Greek vase paintings over the next few centuries, especially during the Orientalizing period of the eighth and seventh centuries BCE when designs from the East (including Anatolia, Syria, and Phoenicia) and Egypt influenced Greek art and culture. In the Archaic period of the sixth century BCE, sphinxes as design elements appeared commonly in Greek tomb art, where they were often depicted perching on grave monuments.

By this point, a crucial difference had developed between Egyptian (and Near Eastern) sphinxes and those of Greece. The former perhaps represented a pharaoh's strength (lion part) and intelligence (man's head) but served mainly as benevolent guardians at the thresholds of palaces and necropolises, whereas the latter evoked dread as harbingers of death and chaos, a change also reflected in the shift from male to female. And at this time a new, more popular motif developed in Greece: sphinxes chasing, catching, and killing young men, with artistic representations containing a distinctly erotic component touching on the association between sex and death. And this was long before the myth of Hera sending the Sphinx to Thebes in retaliation for Chrysippus's rape. By the late sixth century (530 BCE), the sphinx figure as a killer of young men was almost completely associated with Thebes in central Greece, and by the mid-fifth century the sphinx appeared frequently in art in connection with Theban hero Oedipus. How did the formerly ubiquitous sphinx end up with such a specific association?

The legend of the Theban Sphinx, which contains the elements of sex and cannibalism often present in serial killings, may reflect the ancient Greeks' recognition of serial mutilation murder, such as an occurrence of localized ritualized killings of young men. In the fourth century BCE, about two hundred years after the Sphinx became closely tied to Thebes, the Greek mythographer Palaephatus tried to provide a rational explanation, suggesting that the Sphinx was simply a robber woman who attacked travelers to and from Thebes. According to Palaephatus, Oedipus (a real person, in this telling) pretended to join her band and killed her after earning her trust. Though his main intent was to record myths for future generations, Palaephatus was denounced by his fellow Greeks for his rationalized interpretations of traditional stories. But a similar account appears in Pausanias's *Description of Greece* (second century CE). Pausanias's method of recording and verifying information included gathering oral histories, and he concluded from his interviews with local people that they based the legend of the Sphinx on the

A sphinx "abducting" a young man; she seems to be living up to her name's meaning ("strangler"), as she appears to be pressing on the young man's chest. Greek red-figure vase by the painter Poilion, ca. 420 BCE.

true story of a female bandit who had terrorized Thebes for an extended period of time, occasionally emerging from her hideout in the surrounding mountains. She raided Thebes frequently and continued to plunder the region until Oedipus arrived from Corinth with an army and killed her. Pausanias also records a different local legend explaining that the "Sphinx" was actually a daughter of Laius who believed that she was the legitimate heir to his throne and who therefore killed any man who stood in her way.[2]

In the versions of both Palaephatus and Pausanias, the concept of a robber woman was never in question. The Greeks had no difficulty accepting the idea that a killer bandit could be female, just as they could accept the story of Clytemnestra slaughtering her husband, Agamemnon, and his concubine Cassandra. Women could be as vengeful and cold-blooded as men,

CRIMINAL RIDDLERS

More so than other types of criminals, serial killers enjoy taunting their victims and especially the authorities with riddles and other puzzles. Letters sent to several London news agencies in 1888, supposedly from Jack the Ripper, alluded to his crimes and teased new murders, sending clues such as half a kidney (allegedly from a victim), leaving police on the alert but unable to find the notorious murderer. In 1969, the Zodiac Killer, active in California from 1966 through the early 1970s, sent letters to three Bay Area newspapers, each containing part of a boastful cryptogram, eventually deciphered by a local high school teacher and his wife: "I like killing people because it is so much fun," the message began, expanding on the killer's motives. A separate Zodiac cipher from 1969 was only just deciphered in December 2020, also by private citizens. "BTK Killer" Dennis Rader sent police eleven separate letters and packages in 2004–2005 with cryptic evidence of his crimes until they finally caught up with him. Other serial killers, such as South Carolina's Todd Kohlhepp, who in 2017 pled guilty to seven murders, taunt the police with claims of more, as-yet-unknown victims. Many killers may do this in the hope of gaining both leniency in sentencing and greater notoriety by continuing to stymie the police. By provoking the police with letters, sometimes using these letters to provide their own nicknames, as the "Zodiac" and "Son of Sam" (David Berkowitz) did, the killers reinforce their perception of themselves as intel-

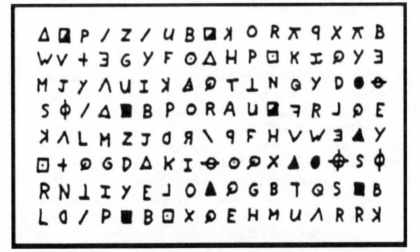

Zodiac Killer cipher, deciphered by Donald and Bettye Harden, August 1969.

HARDEN worksheet

```
Δ/▣ P / Z / U  B ▣ X O R  T  ⌐ X ⟋ ⌐
I   L  I K E / K  I  L  L  I N G / P E O P L

W/V +  ⊒ G Y F O/Λ H P ◻ / K  I /◍ X  L
e / B E C A U S E / I T  I S / S O  M U (C) (H)

M⌐Y  Λ/U I ⋰N  A ◍ T L  N/Q Y D ◍ €
F U N / I T / I S  M O R e / F U N / T H

S Φ/Λ  ▣ B P O R/A U ▣ ⊒/R J ◍ E
A N K I L L I N G / W I L D / O A H E I

X Λ L M  Z / J ◌ ◌  ⟍ Q F  H/V W ⊒ Λ Y
I N T H E / F O R R E S T / B E C A U

◻ + / ◍ G  D /Λ K / ⟐ ⊖  O / ◍ X Δ ◌ ◌ S Y
S E M A N / I S / T H E / M O S T  D A N

R N  + I Y ⊑ / J O  ⋀ ◍ G C B / ⊓ C/S  ⊑ ⊒
G E R O U E / A N A M A L / O F / A L L

L ◌ / ⟋ P ◌ B/◻ X ◍ E H M U Λ R R  X
T O / K I L L / S O M E T H I N G !
```

A was found to mean A and S. Serious

Zodiac Killer cipher (*continued*)

lectually superior to the authorities in addition to achieving a desired level of publicity backing up this perception. The fictional "Riddler" (also known as E. Nigma) from DC Comics, one of Batman's perennial foes, delights in leaving puzzles and clues to his future crimes for authorities to ponder. In issue 26 of DC's *The Question* (a solo series based on a character of the same name), the Riddler teams up with a criminal named Sphinx Scromulski. The two of them take hostages on a bus, and the Riddler asks each passenger a riddle. If the passengers answer incorrectly, Sphinx shoots them, completing the metaphorical shift from mythological creature of Greek myth to serial murderer.

although in so doing they were considered to be taking on and exhibiting masculine qualities. Later Byzantine tradition of the fourth and fifth centuries CE, almost certainly influenced by these earlier rationalizing writers, describes the Theban Sphinx as a beastly, possibly physically deformed female robber and murderer killed by Oedipus, who cleverly presented himself as a fellow bandit but then ambushed her. And again, this story takes no issue with the presence of a female killer, and like the other versions emphasizes not so much the robberies but the murders. Female serial killers have been historically rarer than males, but no less infamous.

The rationalized versions presented by Palaephatus and Pausanias remain far too reductionist, and unlike those authors I do not wish to claim that the story of the Theban Sphinx absolutely must have been based on a real-life incident. Rather, I would like to draw attention to the many ways in which her story resembles that of modern-day serial killers and might, therefore, reflect an ancient Greek understanding of serial murder. For example, the Sphinx's story contains a sexual subtext. First of all, mythologically, Hera sent the creature as punishment for Laius's rape of Chrysippus. The myth also provides a consistent victimology, with the targets apparently all young men, and a consistent modus operandi—asking a riddle, then killing and eating the victim (hints of cannibalism, or at least anthropophagy). And the Greeks historically associated sphinxes with the deaths of young men, using semierotic depictions in art that presented the creatures in sexually dominant positions over the males in a context suggestive of torture and rape.

A final thought on Oedipus himself. He furiously killed King Laius and all but one of the king's entourage on the road after Laius's charioteer struck him on the head to get him to make way for the king. In his overreaction, Oedipus became little better than other murderous highwaymen. He may not have robbed anyone, but the travelers still ended up dead. In Sophocles's *Oedipus the King*, Oedipus, still obtusely unaware of his crime, works to solve Laius's murder and asks the Chorus what they had heard all those years previously, when news of Laius's death first arrived at Thebes. The Chorus reports the rumor that Laius died at the hands of some "wayfarers" (*hodoiporôn*),[3] which is accurate, apart from the plural; later in the play, characters refer to only one killer. The context implies that *hodoiporoi* meant not simply innocuous travelers but highway bandits.[4] Eventually realizing the truth, Oedipus does penance, much as Theseus did after killing the six criminals he met on the road. Having committed a host of other transgressions, however, Oedipus suffered severe punishment rather than being allowed to simply undergo a purification ritual.

Monstrous Snake or Local Serial Killer?

In his Latin novel *Metamorphoses*, the second-century CE writer Apuleius tells the adventures of a man named Lucius, who, through a botched magical spell, turns himself into a donkey. At one point in the narrative Lucius, still in ass form, travels with a group of runaway slaves along a road somewhere just north of central Greece. After a while they stop to rest in a grove of trees, the only shaded place in an otherwise open and deserted area. They spot a lone shepherd nearby, but when asked, he refuses to pause to give them anything to eat or drink: "How can you think of food or drink or any other refreshment at all right now? Don't any of you understand where you are?"[5] The shepherd's tone of voice and his haste to pass through the area frighten the travelers, who try to learn more about the place but cannot find anyone else around to ask.

Then an old man approaches them, bent over his walking stick, trudging along slowly. Weeping, he begs the group to help him, explaining that his grandson, who was accompanying him on his journey, has fallen into a deep pit that lies unseen near some bushes by the roadside. Still alive but seriously injured, the boy keeps calling to his grandfather, but the old man simply does not have the physical ability to help the poor lad. So he beseeches the travelers to come to the boy's aid. One strapping young man in the group quickly volunteers and follows the old man to the thicket, not far off. After some time has passed and the young man has still not returned, his companions call out to him; they keep shouting his name, but he does not answer. Growing increasingly uneasy over his absence, the unexpected delay, and the need to proceed with their journey, the group sends out another man to search for the first. But this second man returns quickly, agitated and aghast, bringing astounding news about his fellow slave: "I saw him stretched out on the ground, most of him already devoured—a huge serpent was slithering all over him, chewing on his flesh! And that wretched old man was nowhere to be seen!"[6] The men realize belatedly that this is what the shepherd had been warning them about. They immediately flee the area, not stopping until they reach the safety of the next village for the night.

The story leaves no doubt that the old man and the serpent are one and the same. This little tale may be related to ancient lore involving dragons serving as boundary guardians, but no folkloric analogues survive for this particular type of tale, one in which a guardian serpent tricks people in order to kill them.[7] Guardian serpents in Greek and Roman literature simply do not exhibit that kind of behavior. The sentry serpents in a previous section of Apuleius's narrative, for example, are just that: savage, but intent only on guarding the waters of the fountain that feeds the river Styx.[8] They will harm only those who attempt to violate the sacred spring. The lack of any comparable folktale from antiquity suggests that this story originated in a local incident that mutated over the decades and centuries into folkloric form. Although the story is fiction, it reflects a keen awareness of real-life serial mutilation murders. For example, the shepherd's behavior implies that the local residents know to stay away from this particular area. In asking the men whether they realize where they are, the shepherd seems to assume that the men must already have heard about the local danger, an assumption indicating that inhabitants throughout the region know that people disappear from this part of the road. He may even be implying that the local inhabitants occasionally find mutilated corpses in the area, as it is rather unlikely that unexplained disappearances on their own are enough to cause the level of infectious terror he exhibits, whereas partially devoured corpses resulting from the serpent's activity would understandably provoke such a reaction. And the flesh-eating aspect of the story could easily reflect the cannibalism present in so many serial killings throughout history.

Such an interpretation would be consistent with the other main appearance of a monstrous serpent in Apuleius's *Metamorphoses*. Earlier in the narrative, in the inset story popularly known as "The Tale of Cupid and Psyche," Psyche's envious sisters make her doubt her unseen husband's true nature. The readers know that he is the god Cupid, but her sisters maliciously prey on her susceptible mind by telling this lie:

> We cannot hide from you the fact that your husband is really a gigantic serpent with many twisting coils, whose bloody jaws drip with lethal poison, whose maw is a bottomless pit of darkness. . . . Many locals who hunt in the area, and neighbors who live nearby, have seen him returning in the evening from his feeding. (Apuleius, *Metamorphoses* 5.17)

They add that he plans to keep Psyche around only long enough to fatten her up and devour her. Psyche readily believes this story for many reasons, not the least of which is the ubiquity of tales of local, man-eating monsters.[9]

Also, the way the old man in Lucius's adventure lures his victims by feigning helplessness should not be entirely unfamiliar to audiences versed in true crime. Take, for example, this scene from Thomas Harris's novel *The Silence of the Lambs* (a scene that also appears in Jonathan Demme's 1991 movie adaptation), in which serial killer Jame "Buffalo Bill" Gumb acquires his next victim: "A man climbed out of the back of the truck. She could see by the lamplight that he had a cast on his hand and his arm was in a sling. . . . [She] saw the man trying to put the chair into the back of the truck. He gripped it with his good hand and tried to boost it with his knee. The chair fell over." Feeling sorry for the injured man, the girl offered to help. But as she pushed the chair forward into the back of the truck he "brought the plaster cast down on the back of her head," knocking her unconscious.[10] Harris probably based this technique on that of Ted Bundy, whose modus operandi often included using a phony cast on his arm. "He'd wait outside libraries. When the right victim came by, he'd drop the books. The girl would come over to help pick them up." Then he would knock her unconscious and take her away.[11] Bundy frequently used a fake cast or sling but also reportedly appeared sometimes on crutches, struggling to carry an object such as a briefcase, asking a young woman to help him carry the item to his car.

In short, this tale from Apuleius contains several significant elements that we might expect in a story based on knowledge of real-life serial killings. This includes an area near a major roadway where unsolved mutilation murders occur, decidedly nonheroic victims unfamiliar with the local area, and a report by a witness (similar to the witness reports of Ted Bundy's methods). The story provides a good example of how serial murders can become folktales. Serial killers are much easier to deal with psychologically if they are transformed, metaphorically, into monsters, especially when elements of cannibalism might be involved. At a point in history when the people of Greece and Rome considered themselves to be living in civilized societies under local laws, it might have been considerably easier to believe in a monstrous creature rather than believing in humans eating humans.

Suspiciously Similar Mutilation Murders at Thespiae and Delphi

Many fictional stories about mutilation murders share a significant pattern: the location of the murders outside of a city or other settlement, often but not always on the roads linking one town to another. Apart from the roads, many serial killings from Greek and Roman myth and legend occur in or near natural settings untamed by culture, such as mountains, rocky cliffs, and caves. In classical literature, nonhuman monsters dwell outside of civilized, urban areas. Polyphemus, the Cyclops from the *Odyssey* who feasted on Odysseus's crewmen, lived in a cave, as did the anthropophagous giant Cacus, slain by Hercules. The Sphinx made her home on Mount Phicium outside of Thebes. Such remote locations make sense, because wilderness is

where "unordered" things such as monsters belong.[12] The abodes of monsters, situated outside urban areas, serve as symbols of the primitive, ani-
malistic, savage tendencies of such creatures.

But giant and hybrid monsters were not the only ones living outside of
settled areas. Some human murderers from classical literature also preferred
more remote and liminal locations. King Amycus used a cave as his lair.
Sciron waited for his victims on a cliff. The existence of stories about mutilation murders set in specific areas of the wilderness and attributed to local
monsters hints that such local legends arose from an awareness of real-life
serial mutilation murder, possibly even from original local events shrouded
in prehistory. Like the man-eating snake in Apuleius's *Metamorphoses*, some
of these "neighborhood" monsters may be stand-ins for or representatives
of humans who engaged in atrocious crimes. Two very similar narratives
from regions 75 miles (120 km) apart in central Greece suggest such a phenomenon. One story comes from Pausanias, who also wrote about the Hero
of Temesa (see chapter 9). In this case, he tells of a creature that wreaks
havoc near the town of Thespiae in Boeotia in a manner reminiscent of serial killing.

In Thespiae, the story goes, stood a bronze statue of Zeus the Savior.
When travelers, including Pausanias, inquired about this statue, the townspeople explained that at one time a giant serpent (*drakon*, "dragon") kept attacking their city. They did not mention where the dragon lived, but because
Thespiae rested at the foot of Mount Helicon, the geographical context and
the nature of serpents suggest that the creature lived in a cave or other underground dwelling. In any case, these attacks caused the townspeople to
appeal to Zeus, who told them how to save themselves. (Pausanias does not
specify the manner in which Zeus communicated with the townspeople,
but the usual method was an oracle.) The god instructed them to choose a
young man from the town once a year by lot and offer him up to the creature. The townspeople said that they did not remember the names of most
youths who perished in this way, but they remembered Cleostratus, who
survived because his lover Menestratus devised a trick to save him.

Menestratus, they said, made a special bronze breastplate for himself, at-
taching one fishhook, point turned outward and upward, to each of the armor's little segments. Donning this breastplate, he surrendered himself to
the monstrous serpent in Cleostratus's place, certain that once he did so he
would destroy himself but also the monster, because if the dragon swal-
lowed him, his breastplate would tear up the monster's insides. And that,
the townspeople say, is how Zeus acquired the epithet "Savior."[13]

Pausanias does not overtly state that Menestratus's plan worked, but
since the relieved inhabitants acknowledged Zeus's aid with this epithet, the

story certainly implies that Menestratus's actions saved Cleostratus and rid the town of the giant serpent. Possibly even Menestratus survived, by cutting his way out as protagonists in modern films often do, such as Agent K, who blasts his way out of a huge space bug in Barry Sonnenfeld's 1997 film *Men in Black*, or Fin Shepard, who uses a chainsaw to cut his way out of a gigantic shark in Anthony Ferrante's (hilariously campy) 2013 made-for-TV movie *Sharknado*. Other classical myths provide precedents for Menestratus to have made such an escape. In one version of the story about the Greek hero Perseus, because he wished to rescue the princess Andromeda from a sea monster, he allowed himself to be devoured in her place and killed the creature by destroying its liver and escaping from its insides. Similarly, Heracles rescued the princess Hesione from a sea monster at Troy by entering its mouth and killing it from the inside.[14] But if Menestratus had survived his encounter with the dragon of Thespiae, the story probably would have recorded that significant detail, as the Perseus and Heracles stories did. It seems likely that Menestratus perished. Otherwise, he might have been an even greater local hero, with the story's focus on him rather than on Zeus and the monster.

As Pausanias tells it, the townspeople offer a sacrificial young man annually and the monster spares the town. In stories like this, with human lives exchanged for a town's safety, the sacrificial victims usually conform to a certain type: virginal maidens, for example (as with the Hero of Temesa), or, as in this case, young men. Their perceived purity (virgins) or the willingness of the town to surrender part of its future strength (young men) "cleanses" the town from its sins, that is, from whatever its inhabitants did to offend the gods in the first place. Often, the stories have a sexual subtext. In the story of the Sphinx, Hera sent the creature to punish Thebes for King Laius's rape of Chrysippus. Pausanias's local legend does not say why the creature targeted Thespiae, but the story does contain sexual elements. First, Cleostratus's life is saved when his lover Menestratus takes his place. The legend describes Menestratus as the *erastês*, the adult male in a pederastic relationship with an *ephêbos*, an adolescent boy. Relationships like this one, between an adult male and teenaged boy, were socially acceptable in ancient Greece and served as a form of mentoring, as long as the young man consented. The more significant sexual element in the story, though, is the less explicit one: all the victims offered to the monster were *ephêboi*. In terms of patterns resembling serial mutilation murder, this story presents not only a consistent victim type but also hints of a sexual nature to the attacks, a possibility compounded by the implicit imagery of the dragon devouring its prey.

Also, several inconsistencies in the story suggest more to the legend's background than Pausanias recorded for posterity. For example, Zeus demanded that *ephêboi* be offered to the dragon, but apparently neither Zeus nor the dragon cared that Menestratus was not, in fact, an *ephêbos*. Zeus gave no advice on or approval of Menestratus's actions, but the townspeople called Zeus "the Savior," presumably because he told them to sacrifice their young men and the sacrifices did prevent the dragon from continuing its rampages. Yet Menestratus, not Zeus, killed the creature. Although it is never possible, necessary, or wise to force explanations and provide interpretations for every aspect of a myth or legend—literal interpretation being beside the point—such details allow speculation about the stories' origins and about the possibility that they indicate a societal awareness of serial mutilation murder. And although ancient Greece teemed with stories of monsters and the heroes who vanquished them, the Thespiae story so closely overlaps with a similar tale from neighboring Delphi that the two stories may have influenced each other, allowing for the inconsistencies as well as for the possibility that serial mutilation murder had occurred at some point in the region and had metamorphosed into local legend.

Delphi, not many miles from Thespiae, was plagued by a mysterious monster. As told by the second-century CE Greek author Antoninus Liberalis, the story goes like this:

> At the foothills of Mount Parnassus, toward the south, lies another, smaller mountain called Criphis, near the town of Crisa. In Mount Criphis there was—and still is—a gigantic cavern, in which dwelled a huge and unnatural creature. Some called it "Lamia," but others named it "Sybaris." Every single day this monster roamed far and wide, seizing livestock from the fields but also targeting people.
>
> After this went on for a while, the people of Delphi simply considered relocating to another area entirely, and consulted the Oracle as to where they should go. The god Apollo indicated that they would be saved from the creature's predation if they stayed but would be willing to leave by the cave one young man [*kouros*], chosen from among the citizens. The people followed the god's instructions and selected Alkyoneus, son of Diomos and Meganeira. He was their only son, and exceedingly handsome as well as pure of character. The town priests put a crown upon Alkyoneus's head and led him away to the cave of Sybaris.
>
> But by some chance, possibly divine, Eurybatos, son of Euphemos, a young man [*neos*] noble of mind, passing by on his way south, happened upon Alkyoneus as the boy was being led to his doom. Eurybatos, overcome by passion and inquiring as to the reason for the priestly procession,

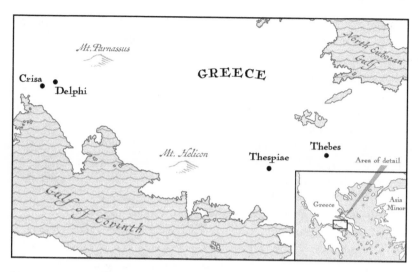

Map showing the proximity of Delphi and Thespiae. Note also the location of Thebes, home to the Sphinx. Map by Michele Angel.

thought it unconscionable not to aid Alkyoneus to the best of his ability rather than allow him to perish so piteously. Stripping the wreaths from the boy and placing them on his own head, he bade the priests lead him forward in place of Alkyoneus.

When the priests led Eurybatos to the cave, he rushed in, seized Sybaris, pulled her from her hiding place out into the open, and hurled her headlong down the cliff. As she fell, she struck her head upon the base of Mount Criphis. Grievously wounded, she disappeared from the world of men. But from the rock she had struck a fountain arose, and the people who lived nearby called it "Sybaris" in memory of the brave deed of Eurybatos. (Antoninus Liberalis, *Metamorphoses* 8)

A striking number of parallel details connect the Delphi and Thespiae stories. First, a monstrous creature lurking in the nearby mountains devastates the town and its surrounding regions, but most notably kills people indiscriminately, terrorizing the population. The monsters are both serpentine, as made explicit by the term *drakon* in the Thespiae version and implicit in the name "Lamia" in the second, *lamiae* often being described in classical literature as female creatures having serpentine features, such as a snaky tail in place of legs. In both stories the desperate townspeople consult an oracle, and the god instructs them to offer a young man as a sacrifice to appease the monster. In each case, a man in love with the intended sacrificial victim confronts the monster in the boy's stead and succeeds in killing the creature, saving his beloved. One main difference between the stories is evident in the length of time each town suffers. Whereas Thespiae sacrificed *ephêboi* for years before Menestratus stepped in, Delphi had to offer only one young man, who survived thanks to the intervention of a passing stranger. In the Thespiae story, the nature of the creature's initial attack on the town remains unclear; the phrasing "devastating the city"[15] could refer to physically destroying buildings and crops, to slaughtering livestock, to murdering townsfolk, or to all of the above. In the Delphi version, the monster specifically kills both livestock and people.

Again, none of this is intended to suggest that any story about a mythological monster mutilating people and requiring sacrifices must of necessity be based on a specific real-life incident, whether of wolf packs attacking livestock or of serial mutilation murder. There exist hundreds of stories, not only from classical antiquity but from many cultures and time periods around the world, in which people offer young men or women from their community as sacrifices to appease a monster threatening the local population. But it is certainly worth pointing out the patterns present in many of these local monster legends that happen to parallel the patterns in real-life cases. The two localized incidents described above include serial mutilation murder, the Thespiae version offers a common type of victim and a regular interval between killings, and both stories contain sexual subtext. Such tales may recall a time when people practiced human sacrifice, but, given the lack of sacrificial language in these stories and the scanty evidence for human sacrifice in ancient Greece and Rome,[16] the possibility exists that some local legends reflect cultural knowledge or recognition of the phenomenon now called serial killing—in other words, that, at the very least, a real phenomenon of horrific violence underpins various mythologized accounts.

CHAPTER 11

Serial Slaying of Suitors and Spouses

Because he had been away for twenty years and no one had brought any news of him, the people of Ithaca assumed that their king, Odysseus, had died at Troy sometime during the ten-year Trojan War. Unbeknownst to them, he had survived the war but had spent another ten years sailing around the Mediterranean trying to return to his island kingdom, enduring more than one storm that sent his fleet off course and encountering various monstrous creatures—the Cyclopes, Laestrygonians, and Scylla and Charybdis, among them—that made survival extremely difficult. While he was gone, the young men of the next generation, who had been too young to go off to the war when it started, grew up to woo Odysseus's apparent widow. But they did so with extraordinary rudeness. They took over Odysseus's palace, making themselves at home, eating his food and drinking his wine, mistreating his servants, mocking his son, Telemachus, and harassing his long-suffering wife, Penelope, who had never given up hope that Odysseus might someday return. And when he did return, Odysseus famously slaughtered those 108 unwelcome and aggressive suitors (see image on page 50). This massacre, carried out with the help of the goddess Athena, did not go unnoticed. The suitors' families sought revenge and would have killed Odysseus had Athena not intervened (see chapter 4). By modern standards, this well-known case of suitor-slaying from classical myth presents Odysseus as a mass murderer. But, once again, applying modern standards ignores the historical context. According to the ancient Greek ethos, Penelope's suitors earned their deaths for a number of traditional offenses, including an egregious violation of the guest-host relationship (*xenia*) so crucial to Greek culture, and their failure to solve the "riddle" posed to them as suitors: stringing Odysseus's bow.

Yet Odysseus is hardly the only character from Greek myth—or world

myth, for that matter—to kill unwanted suitors. Many international folktales employ similar motifs in similar tales, such as a suitor compelled to
perform tasks to win a bride, or beat his potential father-in-law in a chariot race. In many such folktales, the losing suitors simply depart in disappointment and disgrace. But in some contests between a maiden's father
and a suitor or between the maiden herself and a suitor, death is the penalty
for all who lose the race or fail at the assigned task. Apart from the story
of Penelope's unwanted suitors, slaughtered en masse, Greek myth also describes groups of women who kill their husbands in intentionally coordi-
nated mass murders; maidens and/or their fathers who arrange for suitors to
meet dismal fates one at a time; and, occasionally, husbands who kill a series
of wives. Such stories may have originated in a real practice resulting from
competition for the hands of eligible princesses,[1] but they also merit consideration in relation to serial killing, because they provide prototypes for the
modern "Black Widows" and "Bluebeards."

Although Odysseus's massacre of Penelope's suitors remains the most
well-known mass murder of unwanted spouses in Greek myth, two notable
myths present groups of women who organize synchronized killing of their
husbands. After the women on the Aegean island of Lemnos neglected to
worship Aphrodite, the goddess took vengeance by afflicting them with an
odor so foul that their husbands shunned them and took up with women
from nearby Thrace, on the mainland. The infuriated Lemnian women rose
up and killed all the males on the island. Similarly, the daughters of King
Danaus, forced to marry their cousins, killed these unwelcome spouses on
their wedding night. In some versions of the myth, Danaus himself instructed them to do so, agreeing that the girls should not be forced into
marriage. Psychologically, these women might be classified as "power seek-
ers," those who attempt to attain some kind of control or power in their personal lives because they feel that they have none.[2] The Lemnian women and
Danaides committed something in between mass murder and serial murder,
as each of them killed only her own husband as part of an organized plan
to eliminate all the husbands. But their stories remain relevant to a discussion of serial killing for two main reasons. First, such stories, along with the
myths of Medea, Clytemnestra, and others, reinforce the observation that
the Greeks had no qualms about imagining women as cold-blooded killers capable of coordinating complex murders. Second, Greek myth contains
several stories of women ridding themselves of unwanted suitors one by one
rather than en masse, a pattern reminiscent of serial murder. Also, such stories relate to the more modern-day concept of the "Black Widow," who kills

Robinet Testard,
*The Danaides Killing Their
Husbands* (ca. 1496).

her fiancé or husband, acquires a new one, then kills that one too, often repeating this pattern multiple times, with motivations running the gamut from desire for wealth to sheer enjoyment of murder.

Many folktales from around the world involve an organized, systematic, serial slaying of unwanted suitors, usually for failing either to solve a riddle or to meet another type of challenge posed to them. Typically, the killer is the father of the maiden being wooed, usually a king, who for various (and sometimes disturbingly Freudian) reasons does not want his daughter to marry. Occasionally the person instigating the killings is the maiden herself. Such stories involve various folktale motifs, such as "marriage tests" and a subset of these, "suitor tests."[3] The tests may be physical, such as footraces, chariot races, or archery contests. Alternatively, they may be intellectual, requiring the suitor to solve a riddle. The latter occurs in many Eastern folktales, where the eligible princess in question often asks suitors to solve a riddle rather than to meet a physical challenge—but nevertheless, while in pursuit of an answer to the riddle, the suitor may have to undergo physical hardships. In the centuries-old Persian story "What the Rose Did to the Cypress," a beautiful but proud and cruel princess forces all suitors for her hand to answer the title question, "What did the Rose do to the Cypress?" Those who fail to correctly answer forfeit their lives, and their severed heads decorate the battlements of the palace citadel. Giacomo Puccini's 1926 opera *Turandot*, based on a story from the twelfth-century epic Persian poem *Seven Portraits (Haft Peykar)*, tells of the Chinese princess Turandot who will only marry a suitor who can answer her three riddles. Those who fail lose their heads. The similar stories from ancient Greece, while occasionally including riddles, tend rather to emphasize the ancient Greek interest in athletics, with the suitors usually having to prove themselves through foot-races or chariot races.

To a modern audience, the suitors' deaths in the types of story described above may seem oddly and unnecessarily punitive. What crime did they commit by seeking the princesses' hands in marriage? Did they prove themselves completely unfit and unworthy of living by failing the suitor tests assigned to them? Are these just bizarrely Darwinian scenarios? Or did the suitors' failures constitute insults to the royal family? The questions arise because these suitors' deaths, on the surface, might seem like legitimate executions rather than serial murders. In most cases the suitors knew in advance that death would be the price of failure, so their own overconfidence plays a role in their deaths. But in many folktales employing the "suitor test" motif, the rules allow the losing suitors to depart in disappointment and disgrace, but alive. Execution is not a requirement. The kings in these stories do not exhibit other abuses of power, but the narrators frequently describe these kings and/or princesses with such adjectives as "cruel" or "pitiless" for promoting a contest in which suitors must die if they lose. Unlike, say, Roman gladiatorial contests put on for the entertainment of the people and featuring (for the most part) noncitizens, these suitor contests result in the deaths of many princes and the consequent devastation of their high-ranking families. The contests could reflect a desire to weaken the ruling families of neighboring cities and countries who might otherwise have challenged the king's power. But when suitors fail and meet their deaths in these cases, the royals' motives seem far more similar to those of serial killers than to those associated with necessary lawful executions or attempts to diminish neighboring powers. Many of these stories involve decapitation of the failed suitors and display of their heads on the palace walls as deterrents to overconfident young men, but also as trophies.

The Huntress Atalanta and Her Unwanted Suitors

Atalanta, a maiden from Arcadia in southern Greece, wanted nothing to do with men. One can hardly blame her. Atalanta's father wanted male heirs, so when his wife gave birth to a girl, he exposed the infant in the woods under the assumption that the child would die of hunger or thirst or animal attack. In ancient Greece and Rome, such exposure was a common method of trying to get rid of unwanted offspring, such as excess girl children (whose dowries could plunge a family into poverty) or a physically weak (and therefore useless) male infant. But in many myths and folktales, exposed children are often, instead, either found and raised by local shepherds or reared by "friendly" animals. Oedipus, for example, was rescued by a shepherd; Romulus and Remus were raised by a she-wolf. In Atalanta's case, a female bear nursed her until hunters found her and raised her as one of their own. In their company, the girl grew up a skilled huntress, renowned for being swift-footed. Able to track and shoot her prey, she easily defended herself from unwanted male advances; in one instance, when two centaurs tried to rape her, she shot and killed them with her bow and arrows. Her skill allowed her to participate in the famed Calydonian Boar hunt as the only female in the group. In most versions of the myth, she eventually reconciles with her father, who admires her "masculine" qualities. In some versions, he then wants her to marry and bear him grandsons; in others she asks his permission to remain a virgin. In versions of the latter scenario, the father and/or Atalanta devise a cruel scheme intended to deter all possible suitors: whoever bests Atalanta in a footrace will win her hand in marriage, but whoever loses must pay with his life.

One version from the second century CE presents the situation succinctly:

> When many suitors sought Atalanta's hand in marriage, her father established a contest, saying that whoever wished to marry her must first compete with her in a footrace, and that after a finish line was agreed upon, the suitor, unarmed, should flee while she pursued him with a spear. Her father further stipulated that if Atalanta overtook a suitor within the boundary of the racecourse, she should kill him and display his head in the stadium. After she had overcome and killed many suitors, she was finally defeated by Hippomenes. (Hyginus, *Fabulae* 185)

Atalanta's beauty attracted many lovestruck suitors who were oblivious to the danger and died in their attempt to win the contest. Quick-footed though they were, Atalanta was much swifter. Hippomenes won only because Aphrodite helped him. Pleased by his devotion to her, the goddess gave him three golden apples and instructions as to how to use them. During the footrace, whenever Atalanta began to pull ahead, Hippomenes dropped one of the golden apples, and the girl, attracted by the unusual and beautiful fruit, stopped to pick it up. This slowed her down considerably. She inevitably caught up, but as they were nearing the finish line neck and neck, Hippomenes tossed the third apple aside. When Atalanta veered off to retrieve it, the young man won the race and Atalanta's hand in marriage.

All versions of Atalanta's story quickly pass over what must have been the inevitable and gruesome result of the contest: a stadium decorated with the heads of the many failed suitors. And Atalanta's story concludes on an unhappy note: Hippomenes neglected to thank Aphrodite for her help, with the result that not long after the wedding the goddess compelled the couple to be seized with lust while on sacred ground (possibly the precinct of Artemis). The offended deity, disgusted that mortals had defiled a holy area, turned them into lions.

Creepily Overprotective Kings

Although Atalanta herself agreed with and, in many versions of the story, participated in the killing of her unsuccessful suitors, the lovely princesses Hippodameia and Marpessa had little say in their own fates. In a story dating back to at least the fifth century BCE, Hippodameia's father, Oenomaus, king of Pisa in southern Greece, received a prophecy that his son-in-law would kill him. Attempting to avoid this fate (not that trying to avoid fate ever worked out well in Greek myth), Oenomaus planned never to have a son-in-law in the first place. A master charioteer with horses "swifter than the North Wind,"[4] he challenged each of Hippodameia's suitors to a chariot race and declared that whoever beat him would receive the princess's hand in marriage. From all parts of Greece, suitor after hopeful suitor presented himself, but Oenomaus killed every one of them with a spear as he overtook them on the racecourse. He then cut off their heads and displayed them around the entrance to his palace, tossing the decapitated bodies in an unmarked mass grave. This was an especially cruel misdeed, given the importance of proper burial in ancient Greece. According to the myths, he killed at least twelve suitors and maybe as many as eighteen or more before finally losing a race.

Oenomaus met his fate at the hands of Pelops, a young man who traveled from Asia Minor to participate in the contest for Hippodameia, as

From left: Hippodameia, a maidservant, Pelops, Oenomaus, Myrtilos, and Aphrodite, with the decapitated heads of two suitors hanging on the wall. Line drawing of an Apulian red-figure vase attributed to the Varrese Painter, ca. 360–330 BCE.

fame of her beauty had spread far and wide. But when Pelops saw the human heads gruesomely nailed above the palace doors, ample evidence of the king's cruelty, he started to regret his decision. So Pelops approached Myrtilus, the king's charioteer, promising him half the kingdom if he would help defeat Oenomaus. Myrtilus agreed, and when he prepared the chariot he intentionally did not secure the wheel pins, leaving the wheels loose on the axle. In some versions of the story, Hippodameia herself, having fallen in love with Pelops, asked Myrtilus to help him. Either way, when Oenomaus whipped the horses, they raced so fast as to pull the weakened chariot to pieces. Myrtilus, at the front, was safe,[5] yet the wicked king was dragged and crushed to death, laying a curse on Myrtilus before succumbing to his injuries. Pelops won both the bride and kingdom but reneged on his promise to the charioteer, treacherously throwing him off a cliff into the sea and thus (unintentionally) fulfilling the king's curse. Some versions say Pelops did this because Myrtilus tried to rape Hippodameia. Whatever the version, before drowning, Myrtilus cursed Pelops and his descendants. Attempting to atone for his murder of Myrtilus, Pelops built a monument to Hippodameia's mutilated suitors and saw to it that they were buried properly. He also instituted an annual animal sacrifice in their honor. Pelops's attempts were only partially successful, because although he himself escaped misfortune, Myrtilus's curse fell upon Pelops's descendants, including his sons Atreus and Thyestes, who had a notoriously destructive sibling rivalry. After various slights on both sides, including Thyestes's committing adultery with Atreus's wife, Atreus killed Thyestes's sons and then fed them to his brother in a stew.

Oenomaus had a kindred spirit in King Evenus of Aetolia, a son of Ares and the mortal princess Demonice. Evenus wanted his daughter Marpessa to remain a virgin, so he challenged every one of her many suitors to a chariot race, promising her in marriage to any man who could beat him. But Evenus's preternaturally swift horses guaranteed that he won every race, after which he mercilessly cut off the heads of Marpessa's failed suitors and affixed them to the walls of his palace. Evenus finally met his match in Prince Idas, yet another son of Poseidon, who provided Idas's chariot with winged horses. Evenus had no choice but to allow the race, but even his famously swift horses could not catch up with Idas's chariot. Out of despair, Evenus drowned himself in the local river.

"Black Widows" Are Deadlier Than Spiders

Named after the venomous female spider that devours its own mate, the criminological category of "Black Widow" refers to women who murder a whole string of partners along with anyone else they perceive as an obstacle to their own happiness. This includes burdensome children, interfering in-laws and other relatives and lovers, and even inconvenient acquaintances. Their essential traits include intelligence, the ability to manipulate others, excellent organizational skills, and patience. The Black Widow carries out her crimes over a long period of time and is rarely suspected of murder until the victim count has become significant or the unusual number of deaths among her relatives and acquaintances can no longer seriously be considered coincidental. She often begins to murder late in life, after age thirty, and so has the patience and maturity for planning.[6] Vronsky considers the Black Widow a type of profit-motivated female serial killer, perhaps the female equivalent of the male "hedonist comfort" serial killer.[7] The term "Black Widow" really refers more to her modus operandi—the seduction of males to render them helpless—than her signature or profile. These women may kill for different reasons. Money certainly remains consistently high on the list, but sometimes the motive is vengeance, or control, or even a manifestation of Munchausen syndrome by proxy. Although a diagnosis of Munchausen syndrome usually is given to a woman who murders her own child (or children) to gain sympathy as a bereaved mother, the syndrome has also been diagnosed in female serial killers who murder other intimate associates for the same reason, that is, to gain attention and sympathy, since these killers make the deaths appear to have been caused by illness.

Notorious modern examples of the Black Widow type include Mary

Ann Cotton (1832–1873), one of the worst serial killers in English history. She killed an estimated twenty-one people (probably more) over twelve years, including three husbands, ten or eleven children, five stepchildren, and at least one unwanted suitor, all via arsenic. Rumors about the suspicious ill-health of so many people around her finally resulted in police investigation and her arrest. She was hanged in 1873. Even more infamous was Belle Gunness (1859–?). Nicknamed "Lady Bluebeard," she may have poisoned her first husband. Her second husband died under dubious circumstances with a gaping head wound. Then, over the course of six years, a number of men answered classified matrimonial ads Belle put in newspapers throughout the midwestern United States, and they all vanished without a trace. When her farmhouse burned to the ground in 1908, authorities found in the cellar the remains of four people: three children and one adult. For some reason, they assumed the adult woman corpse to be that of Belle, despite its lack of a head, which made identification impossible—not to mention that the body was quite small to be the six-foot-tall Belle. Authorities also found a number of butchered corpses buried around the property, all mutilated, with their heads hacked off and arms and legs severed. If Belle indeed killed all these people, she remains unusual among female serial killers as one of the very few who, rather than poison, used an ax and butchered her victims' bodies.

Despite the occasional murderous female in Greek and Roman history and the existence of such an adept poisoner as Locusta of Gaul, the fact that these patriarchal societies generally kept close watch over their women, restricting their mobility and activities, meant that Greece and Rome produced very few Black Widow equivalents that we know of. Among them, though, we can perhaps count Valeria Messalina (ca. 17–48 CE). At age fifteen, Messalina entered the imperial Roman family through marriage to the emperor Claudius, and thus had a higher degree of personal freedom than most women of the time. Characterized in the literary sources as intelligent, cruel, excessively adulterous, and highly manipulative, she used her power over the smitten Claudius, at least thirty years her senior, to rid herself of any inconvenient courtiers by convincing the gullible emperor to have them executed. The Roman historian Tacitus (ca. 56–120 CE), although by no means an unbiased source, expressed the opinion of many contemporary authors when describing members of the imperial court as fearful about the high number of deaths carried out on Messalina's orders,[8] and frustrated by their inability to convince Claudius of his wife's true nature.

Messalina took one lover after another, but when she grew tired of them and wanted to prevent them from publicizing her lewd indiscretions, had

Georges-Antoine Rochegrosse, scene from *The Death of Messalina* (1916).

them accused and convicted of treason or embezzlement of state funds. This inevitably resulted in their executions. To take just one example, Messalina engaged in an adulterous affair with Gaius Iulius Polybius, one of Claudius's freedmen. It was not long before she wearied of his company, made false accusations against him, and had him killed. Over a seven-year period, before she was barely out of her teen years, Messalina had dozens of court officials murdered, including those who rejected her advances, by convincing Claudius that they were a threat to his power. When Gaius Appius Silanus offended Messalina by refusing to have sex with her (because he recognized her as a seriously depraved individual), she convinced Claudius to order his death. Similarly, when Marcus Vinicius, a respected man who had been awarded many state honors, refused to have sex with her, she was absolutely furious and had him poisoned. In short, she rewarded men who cooperated with her with various state honors and official positions, but those who did not gained her hatred, and she destroyed them in every way she could.[9] When the traumatized and terrified palace staff conspired to murder her, she preempted them, sending dozens more to their deaths, including the commander of the Praetorian Guard, Catonius Justus, who had intended to inform the emperor of Messalina's crimes.

The last straw finally came in 48 CE when Messalina bigamously married Silius, one of her lovers, while her husband Claudius was away on state business. Although Claudius was willing to overlook even this, his courtiers had had enough. They convinced the emperor to deal with her. She fearfully returned to the palace, recognizing her dangerous situation, "with no pity from anyone, because the utter vileness of her crimes was so overpowering."[10] When Claudius hesitated to enact the appropriate punishment, one high-ranking officer ordered Messalina's execution without the emperor's consent. Yet when news of his wife's death reached him during dinner, Claudius showed no reaction, instead having another cup of wine and finishing his meal at his usual pace.

"Bluebeards" in Ancient Folktales?

"Bluebeard," the male equivalent of the female Black Widow type, has become "a generic term for any man who murders a series of wives or fiancées."[11] The concept comes from an old folktale, the most well-known literary version of which dates to 1697. Charles Perrault, a French author who helped establish the fairy tale as its own genre, included "Bluebeard" in an eight-story collection titled *Histoires ou contes du temps passé, avec des moralités* (*Stories or Tales from Past Times, with Morals*). Alongside such folktales as "Little Red Riding Hood," "Puss in Boots," and "The Sleeping Beauty in the Wood," many of which Perrault may have drawn from oral tradition, "Bluebeard" stood out as being especially gruesome. The story still stands out today for presenting a prototypical serial killer.

The story's title character, an extremely wealthy man with many fine houses full of gold and silver, happened to have a blue beard. Women thought this so hideous that they ran from the sight of him. Yet because of his wealth and jovial manner, he managed to marry—and more than once. No one knew what happened to his first several wives. Toward the beginning of the story, he takes another new bride. One day, planning to be away on an extended hunting trip, he gives his young wife the keys to his household. She has free use of all of them, he says, except for one, which unlocks a little closet that Bluebeard forbids her to enter. She promises to obey, but after a while her curiosity gets the better of her and she opens the forbidden door. To her horror, she sees that the floor is sticky with clotted blood from the bodies of several dead women. It does not take her long to realize that these were Bluebeard's previous wives. Trembling with fear, she drops the key before recovering herself, picking up the key, and locking the door. Then she notices the key is stained with blood. No matter how hard she tries, she is unable to remove the stain. Upon his return, Bluebeard notices the bloodspotted key and realizes his wife has seen the contents of the forbidden closet. He decides to kill her just like the others, and is about to cut off her head when, by sheer luck, her brothers arrive and run Bluebeard through with their swords.

The moral Perrault chose to accompany the story says this: "Curiosity, in spite of its appeal, often leads to deep regret."[12] Not surprisingly, the tale elicits comparisons with the stories of Eve and Pandora, regarding what Marina Warner calls the "fatal effects of female curiosity," that is, the message that women may be punished for insubordination—even though the last wife escapes punishment and Bluebeard himself is killed. But Warner sees a number of more subtle themes in "Bluebeard" and similar tales, such as "The Robber Bridegroom" and "Mr. Fox," as well as in antecedents going back as far as the Roman story of Cupid and Psyche: "The story isn't warning against temptation and curiosity in marriage, but [is warning about] the practical consequences of marriage. In the time when childbirth was a main cause of death for women, mothers warned their daughters that marriage could be deadly since you could be killed by your husband with the simple act of becoming pregnant by him. In this way, the tale loses its sadistic killer and becomes a tale of normal life."[13] But the story of Bluebeard also presents a prototypical misogynistic serial killer.

The term "Bluebeard" most likely originated with Gilles de Rais, an infamous fifteenth-century serial killer—not of wives but of children. He was supposedly the original Bluebeard, a moniker derived from the blue-black color of his beard. A French aristocrat, de Rais had served admirably in the French army and was even a close friend of the martyr Joan of Arc. But after de Rais retired from military service, authorities accused him of killing hundreds of girls and boys. Witnesses, and de Rais himself in his own confession, said that he cut their bodies open. Perhaps not surprisingly given his remarkable confession, in 1440 he was found guilty and then hanged. Supposedly de Rais drew some of his inspiration from Suetonius's *Lives of the Caesars*, which included shocking and repulsive details about the degenerate tastes of emperors such as Caligula and Nero, though Suetonius almost certainly exaggerated such descriptions. Years after de Rais's execution, a popular folktale attached the nickname "Bluebeard" to the fictional Chevalier Raoul, whose seventh wife found the corpses of her six murdered predecessors in a room her husband forbade her to enter.

Was the Bluebeard type apparent in ancient folktales? Classicist and fairy-tale scholar Graham Anderson has examined possible prototypes for the Bluebeard folktale in early Greek myths, and suggests that the serial

Bluebeard giving his wife the keys and a warning. By Gustave Doré, for an 1862 edition of Perrault's tales.

wife-killer can be traced back to King Minos of Crete. According to a number of myths, many women who had sex with Minos died in excruciating pain. Anderson also suggests that Minos's labyrinth on Crete prefigures the "secret chamber" so common to later European versions of the Bluebeard story. But Anderson also admits that in the mythological tradition "there is no single simple narrative thread, and no single source that preserves the tale intact."[14] When pieced together, the story relates that Minos took a great many mistresses. His wife, Pasiphae, angered and humiliated, arranged for a spell to be cast on him that was deadly for all the women he had sex with: it caused him to ejaculate venomous scorpions and snakes that fatally stung and bit the women. Minos was eventually cured of his unusual sexual problem, and the rationalizing mythographer Palaephatus suggests that Minos simply "suffered genital pain"—most likely meaning, in other words, that Minos had a sexually transmitted disease that caused his sexual partners to grow ill and die from the infection.[15] The myths add to Minos's characterization as a prototypical serial killer by noting his ritual sacrifice of seven young Athenian men and women to the Minotaur every nine years.

Although Minos provides an interesting and very early mythological example relating to serial wife-killing, the historical cases of Calpurnius Bestia and Nonius Asprenus, and possibly that of Oppianicus, indicate a more definite awareness that accusing a man of serial wife-killing for profit could be rhetorically effective (see chapter 6). And variant folktales containing the "serial wife-killer" appear in the centuries between ancient Greek myth and Perrault's iconic telling of "Bluebeard." One early serial wife-killer appears in the sixth-century CE French story of Conomor, an early ruler of Brittany. Known for his cruelty, Conomor murdered three wives before marrying a fourth, Tréphine. She initially refused to marry him because of his villainous reputation, but agreed to the match when he threatened to invade her father's lands. One day, while Conomor was away, Tréphine found a secret room in his castle containing the remains of his three previous wives, whose ghosts appeared to her and warned that Conomor, fearful of a prophecy that his own son would kill him, intended to murder her if she became pregnant. Tréphine did indeed become pregnant by him, but escaped the castle and gave birth in the nearby forest, hiding her infant son, Trémeur, before Conomor caught up with her and cut off her head. The tale says that Conomor eventually found and decapitated his son as well, despite Tréphine's efforts to keep him safe. Both Tréphine and Trémeur ended up being venerated as saints, and one main version of the legend asserts that Conomor's evil ways resulted in his being doomed to roam the earth as a werewolf who devoured travelers,[16] thus providing another example of the connection between werewolves and serial killers (see chapter 9).

Another early example of the Bluebeard serial-killer type is King Shahryar from *The Thousand Nights and a Night* (aka *The Arabian Nights*), a collection of Near Eastern and Asian tales from the eighth through thirteenth centuries CE. The character Scheherazade tells a number of tales about serial slaying of spouses, being in a precariously similar situation herself. In the frame story, the Persian king Shahryar marries a virgin every day but has her beheaded the very next morning, furious that his first wife cheated on him. After he executed his first wife, "he sware himself by a binding oath that whatever wife he married he would abate her maidenhood at night and slay her next morning to make sure of his honour; 'For,' said he, 'there never was nor is there one chaste woman upon the face of the earth.'" He did this for three years, "marrying a maiden every night and killing her the next morning, till folk raised an outcry against him and cursed him, praying Al-

Statue of the decapitated Saint Trémeur from a chapel in Cléden-Cap-Sizun, France, sixteenth to seventeenth century.

lah utterly to destroy him and his rule."[17] He killed one thousand women in this manner before Scheherazade came along and distracted him with her storytelling. The narrative overtly describes Shahryar as a pitiless monarch who abuses his power, oppressing and horrifying his helpless subjects. The subtext suggests an anger-retaliatory killer, one who intentionally rapes and murders his victims because he is driven by a need for vengeance against a female who offended him.

What the Stories Have in Common

Aside from showing an awareness of the real-life phenomenon we know as serial murder, the stories presented in this chapter clearly reflect anxieties about rites of passage, such as marriage and childbirth. Fathers have difficulty letting daughters go, mothers warn daughters about the dangers of pregnancy and childbearing, young women fear loveless arranged marriages and domestic abuse, and men feel insecurity and resentment when rejected by women. Perhaps not surprisingly, such universal concerns also provide the motivation for many real-life serial murders. Resentment, especially against women, has ranked very high among the motivations for many serial killers, who are often prompted by feelings of inadequacy and an exaggerated need to exert their masculinity. As discussed in chapter 3, Joseph Ture raped and killed several women in the 1970s, driven by the belief that he was superior to them and that they should acknowledge his superiority and yield to him.

Perhaps the most notorious real-life Bluebeard is Henri Désiré Landru (1869–1922), who wooed, married, and killed his female victims, apparently in pursuit of money, such as an inheritance or a payout from a life insurance policy. Between 1914 and 1919, Landru allegedly killed ten women (and one of their sons) in his native Paris after attaining their financial assets. He burned their bodies in his stove, leaving no physical evidence. But police proved that he had ties with all of the missing women, and Landru stood trial on eleven counts of murder. Convicted on all counts, he was executed by guillotine in 1922. In his for-profit serial killing of women, Landru hearkens back to Statius Albius Oppianicus, one of our examples from ancient Rome.

CHAPTER 12

Witches and Other Child-Murderers

In Tom Rob Smith's critically praised crime novel *Child 44*, set in the So-viet Union of 1953, children start turning up dead with identical wounds on their bodies. Smith describes how, in the mid–twentieth century, local peo-ple still ascribed such deaths to wild animals and even to the supernatural:

> Though the newspapers made no mention of these crimes, the incidents of murdered children had entered the public domain in the form of whis-pers and rumor. So far the militia in their closed localities had refused to see each murder as anything other than an isolated occurrence. But peo-ple outside of the militia, unburdened by any theory regarding the nature of crime, had begun to thread together these deaths. Unofficial explanations had begun to circulate. Nesterov had heard it stated that there was a wild beast murdering children in the forests around Shakhty. Different places had conjured different beasts, and supernatural explanations of one kind or another were being repeated all across the oblast. . . . One village had been sure it was a vengeful forest spirit, the inhabitants performing elaborate cer-emonies in an attempt to mollify this demon. (Smith, *Child 44*, 316)

Agent Leo Demidov eventually realizes that a child-murderer is behind the deaths. Smith took as his inspiration the real-life case of Andrei Chikatilo, a native of Ukraine convicted in 1992 of killing fifty-three children and young women. Unlike many serial killers, Chikatilo started late in life. He did not commit his first murder until he was in his forties, when he strangled, raped, and killed a nine-year-old girl. Over the next several years he killed dozens of young women and children, both boys and girls. The murders exhibited excessive brutality. Aside from having been raped and stabbed, many of the victims' bodies were mutilated. Some had their tongues bitten off, or were disemboweled, or were missing organs, and all of this evidence pointed toward cannibalism. Chikatilo, who acquired the nicknames "The Rostov Ripper," "The Butcher of Rostov," and "The Red Ripper," later admitted to "nibbling" on internal organs.[1]

As Smith's story suggests and as John Douglas has theorized, historical and literary sources describe supernatural creatures that prey on both adults and children—and in some cases only children—even when in reality a human being is behind the murders. Folktales provide an especially rich source for this sort of story. Take, for example, the Grimms' tale of Hansel and Gretel. In this story, children who were abandoned and lost in the forest stumble across the home of a witch who was in the habit of fattening them up before roasting and eating them—until Gretel gets the better of the witch by shoving her into the oven. Similar stories circulated in classical antiquity. Various legends describe witches and other creatures that specifically target infants and children. Real-life epitaphs (inscriptions on tombstones) bestow legitimacy onto such stories by attributing children's deaths to witches. These creatures are all female (which is unusual) and they all attack at night (which is not). They drink blood, providing a link to the modern conception of vampires. Some stories about these creatures may have been intended to account for the sudden, unexplained deaths of infants in the cradle—an ancient explanation for SIDS (Sudden Infant Death Syndrome), in other words—or deaths from childhood disease. The infant mortality rate was extremely high in antiquity and early modern Europe, and stories like these might have helped explain and somewhat mitigate the parents' losses. Parents might feel less to blame if uncontrollable supernatural forces could be held responsible for their children's deaths. Nursemaids and nannies also told such stories to children to induce them to behave (or the monsters would get them!). But many ancient stories about children taken by witches and other malevolent creatures describe bodily mutilation and other unexpected characteristics, suggesting that the stories may have reflected a concern with the real-life disappearances, deaths, and mutilations of children that, by all evidence, occurred in antiquity just as in modern times.

In reality, most killers in antiquity as in modern times have been male. The presence in Greek and Roman literature of so many female creatures that kill children reflects a strong, documented, and possibly misogynistic belief that childless women envied those who could and did bear children, and that these barren women consequently wished to snatch others' children for their own nefarious purposes. There may also have been an underlying belief that men were unlikely to kill their own heirs. Nearly all the child victims in these stories are male, probably because the Greeks and Romans considered male children so much more important than females that their deaths received proportionally more attention.

Witches

In some countries around the world people continue to believe in witches and magic, including the belief that witches kill babies and young children and use their body parts in spells. People believe in witches because witches still exist, even if the "magic" they perform cannot in reality be proven to work. Note, for example, this news report from Uganda from May 2017 with the headline "In This Nation, Children's Body Parts Are Sacrificed for Witchcraft":

> It's been a year since Cynthia Misanya found the dismembered body of her 10-year-old daughter, Jane, in a pit under an outhouse. The girl had gone to fetch water in a nearby swamp when she was abducted, strangled, and dismembered. Body parts were recovered miles away.[2]

The girl was missing nearly every part of her body. Police arrested a local businessman who confessed to having sacrificed Jane in a witchcraft ritual designed to bring good fortune to his failing business. Ugandan authorities estimate that dozens of children are sacrificed each year for similar reasons: there are witch doctors and true believers "willing to kill and offer body parts to dark spirits to get rich, heal diseases, mitigate misfortunes, forestall impending events," and even to help their favored political candidates win elections. These so-called witch doctors especially prize children's hearts and genitalia.[3] September of the same year saw several more child sacrifices, apparently intended to end a serious drought afflicting the country. Similar child sacrifices still occur across the globe thanks to the persistence of folk beliefs.

This belief in witches murdering children to use their body parts in spells goes back thousands of years. The efficacy of such spells is beside the question; these stories, including the one from Uganda, clearly describe serial child-murder. The motivation simply differs from what we might expect. Some of the usual reasons for serial killings, such as intense misogyny or desire for an inheritance, apply far less frequently in cases of child-murder, and desire for domination or sexual gratification may lie behind some of the child serial murders not attributable to belief in the mystical uses of children's body parts. Previous chapters have already introduced several stories from antiquity about child-killing, such as those about the monstrous serpents at Delphi and Thespiae demanding child victims and about Medea killing her own children. Medea was a witch, but she killed her children to spite her husband, Jason, not to use their body parts in her magic rituals. (And Medea's victims were not limited to children.) Other child-killing witches from antiquity specifically wanted internal organs of innocents for magic spells. The extent to which the Greeks and Romans truly believed in witches and other magic-working creatures can never be known, but much evidence survives to indicate that when people died under mysterious conditions, their relatives often blamed supernatural forces. For example, when Germanicus, the popular and virtuous nephew of the emperor Tiberius, fell ill and died under ambiguous circumstances at the relatively young age of thirty-three, people believed one of his political enemies had caused his death by placing curses and other evil magical items in his house (in addition to poisoning him). According to Tacitus,

> Hidden under the floor and in the walls were found the remains of desecrated human bodies, incantations and spells and the name of Germanicus inscribed on lead tablets, half-burnt ashy clumps smeared with gore, and other cursed objects through which, people say, souls of the living are dedicated to the infernal deities. (*Annales* 2.69)

Thousands of curse tablets from Greek and Roman times have survived, as have amulets intended to counteract the evil eye and bring good luck. Curse tablets like the one Tacitus describes as having been found in Germanicus's room were made from thin sheets of lead, inscribed with the curse and then rolled up and pierced with a nail before being deposited in a well or cemetery (where they might reach the infernal deities), or under the floorboards in a wall cavity (where they might more directly influence the cursed person).

These and other similar material objects, such as allegedly magical figurines in miniature coffins, demonstrate a widespread popular belief that unseen spirits and deities could influence everyday life. Nor was this belief limited to unseen entities, as the Greeks and Romans told many stories about witches, described as powerful females with evil intent, who could call down curses and mix potions to achieve their sinister goals. Witches might, for example, work their spells on adults, cursing women they perceived as rivals in love or cursing men who rejected them, demonstrating

Example of a lead curse tablet from Roman Britain, first to fourth centuries CE. This one curses a woman named Tretia Maria, wishing her ill health. The Latin inscription, illegible in some places, reads in part: Tretia(m) Maria(m) defico et illeus vita(m) et me(n)tem et memoriam [e]t iocinera pulmones interm{x}ix{i} ta fata cogitata memoriam sci no(n) possitt loqui (quae) sicreta (si(n)t neque . . . (Translation: "I curse Tretia Maria and her life and mind and memory and liver and lungs mixed up together, and her words, thoughts, and memory; thus may she be unable to speak what things are concealed, nor be able . . ." [illegible].)

that it was not only men who might seek vengeance after being scorned by the opposite sex. Apuleius tells a story about a witch who turned one cheating lover into a beaver, an animal believed to chew off its own genitals.[4] But quite a few classical stories about witches describe them as specifically targeting children. People believed then as now that body parts from pure and innocent children could be highly effective in witches' spells, so witches engaged in the serial murder of infants and young boys and girls.

As with descriptions of the Greek *lamia* (see chapter 10), many of the Greek and Roman stories about witches preying on children may have reflected what people believed to be envy on the part of childless women— either young women who were barren, or old women no longer able to bear children. Both groups were looked down upon as unable to fulfill a female's primary role in ancient society. Although the witches described in Greek literature ran the gamut from young to old, and some (such as Medea) had children, the majority of Roman witches were elderly, by implication never had children of their own, and showed no hesitation about murdering multiple children to use their tender body parts in potions and magical rituals. Some stories from antiquity indisputably describe the serial murder of children rather than individual cases. One witch in particular gained a reputation for slaughtering infants. The first-century CE Roman poet Lucan describes the crone Erictho as ripping unborn children from the womb to sacrifice them on burning altars, and as making this appeal to the infernal deities: "If any infant, whose head and entrails I placed upon these dishes for you / Would have lived (had I not killed it), grant my prayer."[5] Erictho would slash open the bellies of living pregnant women—or of pregnant women whom she first murders, or who die during this process—to tear out the fetuses. Lucan also implies that she was a child-snatcher. Erictho uses the dead fetuses and infants (or at least their entrails) in necromantic ceremonies, rituals to call upon the dead to prophesy the future. Lucan uses common (male) perceptions about older women to inform his portrait of Erictho as a dried-up old hag, who, far past her childbearing years, has no moral qualms about being up to her wrists in the blood of ripped-open wombs.

This alleged envy of mothers helps to explain another activity attributed to these crone-witches: taking a human child and replacing it with a changeling. Many medieval stories describe creatures such as fairies stealing human children and replacing them with fairy children, termed "changelings" because the fairies "exchanged" them for the human children. (Later tradition attributed shape-shifting abilities to these fairy replacements.) The motivations varied: fairies, trolls, and other creatures might steal human children because of their beauty or hearty constitutions and replace them with weak imposters. Petronius, a Roman author of the first century CE, gives us one early variation on the changeling tale. A young boy has died, and family and friends have gathered around the grieving mother:

> When his bereaved mother began to wail and most of us fell into despondency, suddenly the witches started up. The howling was such that you would have thought a dog was chasing a rabbit. We had with us at the time a man from Cappadocia, tall, very courageous, and so strong that he could have lifted an angry bull. Well, this man boldly drew his sword and rushed out the door, making an apotropaic gesture with his left hand, and he struck one of the witches right in the chest. We heard a groaning, but

didn't see the women. The brave fellow returned to us and threw himself down on the couch, whereupon we were shocked to see that his whole body was bruised as if beaten by whips. Evidently an evil hand had touched him. Shutting the door, we turned back to our mourning. But when the boy's mother embraced his corpse, she touched and saw instead a little bundle of straw! It had no heart, no innards, nothing at all. Clearly the witches had rushed away with the boy and put a straw manikin in his place. (*Satyrica* 63)

Here the witches have not taken a living child to raise as their own. They have instead taken a child's corpse, most likely to use his body parts in magic spells, as reflected in the straw doll's lack of innards. The story does not specifically say that the witches caused the human child's death in the first place, but Petronius's vagueness on this point allows for that possibility. There is also no overt evidence of serial child-murder; only the witches' behavior, including their swifter-than-the-eye-can-see body switching, suggests that they steal children's bodies (living or dead) as a matter of course. Folklorists who study changelings theorize that the "swapped child" theme may reflect the devastation felt by parents when their children turn out to have a deformity or disability.[6] In Petronius's story, however, the child-swapping seems more closely related to the sort of ritual child sacrifices carried out by witches, especially given the other interactions between witches and children in Roman literature.

Another such interaction appears in the work of the first-century BCE Roman poet Horace. A group of four witches—Canidia, Sagana, Veia, and Folia, possibly the closest thing to a witches' coven in Latin literature—steal a boy (*puer*) away from his parents, strip him, and bury him in the ground up to his chin. They plan to starve him to death, first torturing him by leaving food right in front of his face so that he will die staring at it. Finally, when his marrow and liver have shriveled up, they will extract both to use as ingredients in a love potion.[7] Clearly, long before witches in medieval literature cooked and ate babies, and two thousand years before a Ugandan businessman sacrificed Cynthia Misanya's young daughter in the belief that the girl's body parts would bring him good fortune, the ancient Romans believed such actions to be typical of witches.

Female Child-Snatching Monsters

Literary witches such as Canidia and Erictho were not simply old hags. Horace, Lucan, and other Roman writers describe witches as having sharp, claw-like fingernails, rotting teeth, wildly unkempt hair, and other physical characteristics designed to evoke feelings of disgust.[8] These, along with the witches' predilection for killing children, elicit comparisons to child-killing spirits of Roman folklore, such as the *striges*, malevolent witchy spirits resembling owls who suckled babies with their poisonous milk and drank children's blood. *Striges* and other female child-snatching monsters in classical antiquity trace their mythological ancestry to Near Eastern demons, such as Lilith, the Semitic demoness known for killing newborns. The Greek spirits Lamia, Empousa, Gello, and Mormo stole and ate other women's babies out of envy. Like witches, these creatures helped explain the unexpected deaths of children at home but, as in Smith's *Child 44*, were most likely also used to provide a supernatural explanation for the serial murder of children, given the descriptions of bodily mutilation in the stories.

The Roman poet Ovid (43 BCE–ca. 18 CE) describes the *strix* as a greedy bird-like creature with a large head, protruding eyes, a raptor's beak, grey feathers, and hooked claws. In brief, the *strix* sounds like a monstrous owl, albeit one with malevolent supernatural powers. Ovid says that the *striges* fly around at night and target children with absent or inattentive nursemaids. Snatching children from their cradles, the loathsome creatures rend the infants' bodies, pecking at the milky guts with their beaks and sating their thirsty throats with warm blood. According to legend, the *striges* are either born as these horrible bird creatures or turned into them by magic spells. Ovid provides a folk etymology explaining that the name *strix* comes from the verb *stridere*, "to shriek," because the creatures emit terrifying shrieks at night,[9] and the howling witches in Petronius's story of the changeling also reflect this characterization. In Latin, *strix* means both "owl" and "witch," even coming close to meaning what we think of as a vampire, in the sense of an evil spirit-creature that drinks human blood. In Ovid's story, a *strix* attacks a five-day-old infant in its cradle, but he is saved just in time by his nursemaid, who comes running at his cries. Most of the time, however, the *striges* seem to acquire their prey. Ovid introduces these creatures by saying that they "defile children's bodies, snatched from their cradles,"[10] which implies that it was not uncommon for children to go missing from their nurseries only to have their mutilated corpses discovered later elsewhere.

Similarly, the first-century CE Roman poet Statius describes a female monster (*monstrum*) that glides into bedrooms at night, snatches newborns, and gorges on them:

> It had the face
> and breast of a maiden, but from the top of its head,
> right from between its brows, always hissing, rose

a serpent. This abomination, slithering around at night.
sneakily slipping into bedrooms, ripped newborns from
the bosoms of their nursemaids, and with bloody maws
feasted upon them, greatly sated by the country's grief.
(Statius, *Thebaid* 1.596–604)

In this case, a brave youth named Coroebus convinces the community to
stop the monster. He gathers a group of young warriors and they hunt her
down. They find her on her way back from another household, just about to
pass through the city gates with the bodies of two small children hanging
at her sides, her curved claws already in their vitals, her iron nails digging at
their hearts, her belly covered with gore. Coroebus buries his sword in her
heart, killing her, and the townspeople rejoice through their tears.

Statius's story shares elements with the local legends of monstrous man-
eating snakes at Delphi and Thespiae. In all of them, a serpentine creature preys on young people, the town lives in grief and fear, and one man
is principally responsible for saving the town by killing the creature. But
the two local legends differ from Statius's story in having teenage boys being offered up by the townspeople as sacrifices to keep the monsters at bay,
whereas the creature Statius describes steals and mutilates infants (in addition to eating them) while the people remain terrified and largely helpless.
In this way, Statius's story lends itself well to the observations of Tom Rob
Smith and John Douglas, namely, that people tended to attribute the unexplained deaths of multiple children in localized areas over a period of time
to supernatural creatures rather than recognizing them for what they were,
serial murders.

The creature Statius describes, a physical combination of human female
and serpent, may have been a version of what the Greeks and Romans called
a *lamia*. In ancient Greek folklore, *lamia* was a name given to a kind of
daimon, an entity that was neither human nor god, one that was considered
a "spirit" of sorts but that also could manifest physically. The *lamia* may be
mythologically related to the very similar Near Eastern demon character, Lilith, that was believed to kill infants. The ancient Greek literary references
to Lamia lack detail until the late Hellenistic period, when she began to figure in a story eventually known as the "Libyan Myth," a tale that became
increasingly elaborate throughout the Roman era. In one of the story's old-
est versions, from first-century BCE author Diodorus Siculus, a cave in Libya
was the birthplace of (the allegedly original) Lamia, an exceptionally beautiful queen. When all her children died, she was so devastated by the misfortune that she began to envy women who had children, and as a result of
her envy she ordered the execution of all newborn babies in her realm. Dio-

dorus says that because of her cruel spirit her once-beautiful face gradually took on a bestial aspect, and even in Diodorus's own time her name was used to frighten children into behaving properly. But during the Roman Empire, Lamia gradually changed in the literature from an infant-killing spirit to a sexual monster that seduced and devoured young men, and her snaky characteristics became more prominent. Both the early and later branches of the Lamia story allow for various interpretations. As with the *striges*, the early Lamia type provides a supernatural explanation for the untimely deaths of infants and children, an explanation that may reflect deaths from childhood diseases and from abduction-murder cases. The later Lamia type, in contrast, opens itself up to even broader meanings, because the *lamiae* can, on the one hand, represent seductive women who distract men from pursuing philosophy and other prudent studies, while on the other they can fit into the pattern of irrational explanations for rational events, such as serial murder. Greek and Roman folktales include other creatures similar to the Lamia, such as the aforementioned Empousa, Gello, and Mormo, all malevolent spirit-beings believed to be responsible for the deaths of infants, feeding off their blood.

Material Evidence

Although the stories about witches, *striges*, *lamiae*, and other child-killing creatures discussed above are fiction, they have a basis in real-life fears. Children went missing in the ancient world just as they do now, and were sometimes found dead and mutilated. As Fritz Graf puts it, "Murder, of course, was a reality in antiquity, and sometimes its victims were young."[11] As it happens, we have more than fictional stories to show that people attributed inexplicable children's deaths to supernatural forces. We also have material evidence, mainly in the form of inscriptions on grave markers. One tombstone from about 20–30 CE, commemorating a child believed to have been killed by witches, bears a Latin inscription translated as follows:

> Iucundus, the slave of Livia the wife of Drusus Caesar, son of Gryphus and Vitalis. As I grew towards my fourth year I was seized and killed, when I had the potential to be sweet for my mother and father. I was snatched by a witch's hand [*saga manus*], ever cruel so long as it remains on the earth and does harm with its craft. Parents, guard your children well, lest grief of this magnitude should implant itself in your breast.[12]

Another epitaph says that a boy of three was "snatched away by poison" (*veneno ereptus*), and Graf, who has done an in-depth study of such inscriptions, notes

MYTHO-HISTORICAL MASS MURDER OF INFANTS

In Diodorus's story of the creature's origins, Lamia was originally a barren queen who was so envious of childbearing women that she ordered the execution of all newborn babies in her realm. This is hardly the only or even the most well-known tale from antiquity of mass slaying of infants. More familiar to modern audiences may be the story of Moses and the ten plagues of Egypt, or Herod's Massacre of the Innocents. In the Old Testament, Moses repeatedly asks Pharaoh to free the enslaved Israelites. Upon Pharaoh's refusal, God sends a series of plagues upon the Egyptians, who then suffered through water turned to blood, frogs, lice, flies, a pestilence that killed their livestock, boils, hail, locusts, and darkness. Moses warns that the tenth and worst plague will be the death of all the firstborn children in Egypt, but Pharaoh does not heed him. So the Lord smites all the firstborn, including the firstborn of Pharaoh and even the firstborn of the cattle (Exodus 7:16–12:29). In the New Testament, wise men from the East tell Herod, king of the Roman province of Judaea, that a king of the Jews was born in Bethlehem and would be worshipped far and wide. Displeased at the thought of this rival, Herod orders the execution of all boys ages two and under in the region encompassing the city of Bethlehem (Matthew 2:1–8). Could any of these stories be based on fact? Possibly. A childhood disease could have wiped out a large percentage of children in a given area. In the case of Egypt, scientists have tried to find plausible explanations for the ten plagues. For example, they postulate a blooming of red algae for the first plague, water turning to blood. The last plague, the killing of the firstborns, could have been caused by certain airborne toxins especially deadly to infants and children. But of the three stories, the Massacre of the Innocents may be the most likely to be based on truth. Herod, like some of the other kings, tyrants, and emperors discussed throughout this book, had already proven himself willing to murder anyone who crossed him. His victims included three of his own sons (whom he feared were trying to kill him and take the throne). He had also planned to have all the Jewish leaders in Judaea executed upon his own death, so that the Jews (who hated him) would have something to mourn rather than something to celebrate. In short, Herod, if more an abusive monarch than a serial killer, was certainly the type to order a massacre of newborns. The fact that there were probably only a dozen or so male children under the age of two in the small town of Bethlehem and environs at the specific time in question adds to the possibility. On the other hand, the story appears in no other Gospel than Matthew, nor does it appear in the accounts of Josephus, whose first-century CE *Antiquities of the Jews* provides the most extensive and nearly contemporary history of Judaea and Herod's life.

Mugshot of Albert Fish, upon conviction for grand larceny, 1903.

that without more details the circumstances of death are ambivalent, but that in the overall context the epitaph probably means to say that the boy died as a result of witchcraft rather than from the effects of poison.[13]

A number of other children's tombstones from Greece and Rome bear inscriptions similarly attributing such unexpected, untimely deaths to poison or to some "undefined secret evil action that we usually call, in a somewhat imprecise term, witchcraft or sorcery," because what other explanation could grieving parents find to adequately explain the death of a young son or daughter? And many of these inscriptions contain invocations imploring a deity to take revenge on the unknown attacker. This indicates that whoever composed the inscription suspected "foul play by some unnamed person," though Graf explains that because the epitaphs express only the subjective perspective of those left behind to mourn the deceased, we cannot always know whether the inscription refers to "open murder" or to an ailment the Greeks and Romans attributed to sorcery.[14] These epitaphs, understandably, do not provide specifics such as whether the child's body was mutilated, though some of the ones referring to poison say that the deceased suffered a long illness before death.

Less clear, especially in the cases where the children died at home, is the witch's motivation. What reason would a witch have for causing a child's death but not extracting any body parts, a scenario that does not occur in any of the major literary witch tableaux? Was there an underlying suspicion on the part of grieving parents that they had been somehow cursed? It is difficult to tell. Given that families might have needed a scapegoat to blame for untimely deaths, we need not expect them to have a rational explanation for what they believed to be a supernatural event. Rather, it is enough to recognize that serial child-murder occurred in antiquity just as it does today. And whereas many instances are blamed on sorcery, others have far more mundane causes. One particularly appalling case of modern-day serial child-murder (if any can be described as more appalling than others) was that of Albert Fish (1870–1936), a grandfatherly figure whose innocuous exterior hid a voracious appetite for child rape, murder, and cannibalism. His family had a history of mental illness, which in his case may have been exacerbated by continued physical abuse during his years in an orphanage. He confessed to three murders (and was suspected of five others). In 1935 he was tried, convicted, found guilty, and executed in the electric chair.

Two of the most notorious child-killers of the twentieth century were Ian Brady and Myra Hindley, who between 1963 and 1965 in Manchester, England, sexually assaulted and then brutally murdered five children ages ten to seventeen. Authorities discovered three of the victims in graves dug on Saddleworth Moor (which lent its name to these "Moors Murders") and found another victim's body at Brady's house. The fourth victim was never found. Both Brady and his girlfriend Hindley were sentenced to life in prison, eventually dying there. Still also in the public's awareness are the Atlanta child-murders of 1979–1981, which remain notoriously unsolved: at least twenty-four boys and girls between the ages of seven and fourteen were murdered, most of them strangled. Less known, but bearing more resemblance to the child-killers of classical antiquity, is Luis Garavito, who preyed on the children of Bogotá, Colombia, during the 1990s. Abused and tortured by his father and later by a pedophile, Garavito kidnapped, killed, and mutilated hundreds of children, mostly boys ages six to sixteen. He removed various body parts and dumped the corpses at different sites around the city, targeting mainly poor, orphaned, and/or homeless children whom no one would miss. But physical evidence eventually tied him to several crime scenes. He was unable to articulate a reason for his compulsion to kill and mutilate, other than claiming to have been drunk while executing these crimes.

Garavito currently ranks as one of the worst serial killers in all of recorded history. It may surprise people to learn that Garavito and many other serial killers with exceedingly high numbers of victims are not from the United States or Western Europe, since one main misconception about serial murder is that it is mainly a Western problem brought about by the decadence of our overindulgent society. In fact, serial murder has clearly occurred all over the world (except, so far, in sparsely populated Antarctica). And, as this and other chapters have aimed to demonstrate, serial murder has a much longer history than most people know. Both of these aspects of serial killing—its global nature and its long-standing history—provide the topic of the next and final chapter.

CHAPTER 13

Serial Murder Then and Now, There and Here

I have aimed to demonstrate that serial killing has a much longer history than most people realize, a history going back at least as far as the Greece and Rome of two and three thousand years ago. Previously, when pressed to name the first serial killer, many people would probably point to London's Jack the Ripper, often credited as the "modern-day father of serial murder," as Amanda Howard puts it. But in her historical survey, Howard argues that such crimes must go back much further, and suggests that the world's first documented serial killer lived in pre-Buddhist China. Liu Pengli, a member of the Han royal family, ruled Jidong in 144 BCE. During his reign, he frequently pillaged towns in his own kingdom, accompanied by a gang of slaves. According to Chinese historian Sima Qian (ca. 145 to ca. 86 BCE), Liu Pengli committed at least a hundred murders merely for sport, leaving his subjects so terrified that they stayed in their homes at night. Pengli was eventually put on trial for his crimes. The courts demanded his execution, but the emperor, his cousin, merely exiled him. Given that he held an office of significant power, we might ask the same question already posed about Nero and others: Can Pengli legitimately be called a serial killer, as opposed to a cruel and abusive despot whose position gave free rein to his vicious instincts? Unlike most serial killers, Pengli did not commit his crimes in secrecy and did not follow any patterns in choosing his victims or in his methods of killing. Pillaging puts him and his slave accomplices more in line with groups of raiders, such as pirate gangs or highway robbers. But whereas those groups plundered primarily for profit, Pengli committed unrestrained murder apparently just because he could. Howard therefore quite reasonably points to Pengli as a prototype for serial killers, noting that Pengli "set a precedent for many royal murderers who have littered history with the blood of their own subjects."[1]

Pengli committed his murderous rampages in the second century BCE. But, as we have seen, Greek and Roman history that predates Pengli by centuries records many rulers, ambitious politicians, and highway bandits whose homicidal behavior rivals or surpasses his. Along with Howard, other authors who study the history of serial crime list Locusta of Gaul among the notorious historical serial killers of the past three thousand years, placing her alongside Agrippina, sister of the Roman emperor Caligula and mother of the future emperor Nero. Both women were also noteworthy for being among the few egregious female multiple murderers of history.

But these authors neglect many other Greek and Roman examples presented in this book, some of them from much earlier than the first century CE. Many histories of serial murder skip antiquity entirely and jump directly to the story of Ethne the Dread, a "cannibal killer" who lived in fifth-century CE Ireland. Although they usually refer to Ethne herself as the killer, the story as told in the medieval Irish narrative *The Expulsion of the Déisi* (eighth century CE) relates that it was actually her father and mother, the rulers of their tribe, who killed young boys and fed them to her so that she might fulfill her prophesied destiny of leading their clan to greatness. Ethne's parents believed that she would grow up strong if she fed on the flesh of boys, so they first made all the families of their clan provide Ethne with any boys they bore after the first two, and then, having used up the supply from their own clan, raided neighboring villages for more boys. In this respect, Ethne's story resembles those about mass murders of children, such as Herod's slaughter of the infants of Bethlehem (see chapter 12). No account records the number of victims, but Ethne apparently fulfilled the prophecy: when the king of Munster proposed marriage, she demanded for her bride-price enough land for all of her mother's kindred, allowing the clan to spread.

Perhaps a better example of an early serial killer outside of classical antiquity comes from fifth-century CE Yemen, known at the time as the Himyarite Kingdom. A wealthy man called Zu Shenatir, who lived in the seaport city of Aden, lured an unknown number of young boys into his home, offering them food and money. There he raped them, before killing them by throwing them out an upstairs window. His horrendous deeds seem to have been known to the people (throwing victims out of your window is not an especially subtle method of murder), and they abhorred him, but because of his wealth they remained frustratingly unable to take any action against him. Finally, Shenatir himself was stabbed to death by one of his intended victims, who had unexpectedly decided to fight back.

Written history says little more about serial murders until the fifteenth century, when another type of serial killer gained unwanted publicity. At this time in Scotland a story began to spread about Sawney Beane, head of a large cannibal clan. Accounts vary, but the main versions have him active during the reign of King James IV (1488–1513). Sawney and his common-law wife, who were averse to "honest employment," as the anonymous treatise describes it, fled society to live in a cave on the Galloway coast.[2] They started a family that grew to several dozen over a few decades, thanks to incestuous inbreeding. The clan robbed and murdered anyone they could get their hands on, took the bodies back to their cave, pickled the mangled limbs, and ate them. The larger the family grew, the bolder they became, and at times did not even hesitate to attack groups of five or six grown men traveling together.

These activities continued for at least twenty-five years, because the cave the Beane clan inhabited was so remote that it was not easily found, and people had grown sufficiently afraid of the area that hardly anyone was actively seeking the Beane home. The family was finally caught when one of their male victims escaped and described his experience to the authorities. The king himself then sent a small army to search for the cave. Upon finding it at last, the men were dismayed to see an array of human limbs hung up in rows "like dried beef." They also found piles of money, watches, rings, swords, pistols, and clothes taken from the victims. The entire family was arrested and executed. The exact number of their victims was never known, but the legend claims that it was upward of one thousand.[3] The story of Sawney Beane may or may not have any basis in fact, but it has come up in association with true crimes such as those committed by the Manson "family" in the 1960s, and seems to have been a primary influence on fiction such as Jack Ketcham's novel *Off Season* and its sequel *Offspring*, about a cannibalistic, inbred clan living in remote seaside caves in Maine, preying on unsuspecting residents of the surrounding area. Sawney Beane and his cannibal clan also inspired Wes Craven's 1977 film *The Hills Have Eyes* (and its sequels and remakes), about an extended family of cannibals living in the California desert.

Awareness of Serial Killing Spreads: Notorious Cases

The above stories, in addition to the many accounts from ancient Greece and Rome discussed throughout this book, represent the few accounts of serial murder (or something very much like it) known before the invention of the printing press and its spread across the globe made news of unusual events, including serial murders, easier to disseminate. There is really no way to tell how many serial murders went unrecorded hundreds and thousands of years ago, when transmission of news was nearly nonexistent and when people cared about the poorer classes even less than they do now. But from the fifteenth century on, in Europe at least, historical records—however unreliable or exaggerated—contain increasingly frequent accounts of serial killings. In late sixteenth-century Germany, for example, Nicklaus Stüller was executed by hanging after being found guilty of cutting open (and thereby killing) three pregnant women. In France, around the same time, a man named Gilles Garnier earned himself the nickname of "The Werewolf of Dole" after confessing to stalking, murdering, and cannibalizing several children.

Serial killers are not always men, as we have seen. Locusta, Agrippina, and Ethne (or at least her mother) provide early examples of women prone to multiple murders, as is Sawney Beane's wife, though her infamy pales in comparison to that of her husband (particularly given that the sources do not give her name). Another prominent example of a female serial killer comes from the sixteenth century. Lucretia Borgia (1480–1519) supposedly poisoned her enemies with a powder she kept in a ring on her finger, although that rumor has not been substantiated. Probably the most notorious female serial murderess of all time was Countess Elizabeth Báthory of the Kingdom of Hungary (1560–1614), who allegedly tortured and killed hundreds of young women over the course of ten years, supposedly because she believed that bathing in their blood would preserve her youthful complexion. Countess Báthory was able to get away with the murders for such a long time because she chose as her victims mere peasant girls, sometimes lured to the castle with the promise of employment, sometimes kidnapped outright by the countess's henchmen. Báthory was arrested in 1610, because after apparently exhausting the supply of local peasant girls she had resorted to killing the daughters of various nobles, causing the authorities to finally take notice. Her astounding story resulted in hundreds of characters in literature, on stage, and eventually in film and video games being based on "The Blood Countess," as she became known. In her lust for blood, Countess Báthory differed from many female serial killers throughout history, most of whom (such as Locusta, Agrippina, and Lucretia Borgia) preferred poison to bloodletting and most of whom were motivated by greed rather than a desire for eternal youth. But her story bears similarities to those of Roman witches, such as Canidia and Sagana, who used the internal organs of children in love potions.

Many other similar cases were recorded in seventeenth-century England. Because of the difficulty of proof, poisoning remained popular into the eighteenth century. In 1719 Naples, Italy, a woman known to history mainly by her nickname, "La Tofania," was executed after having confessed (under torture) to six hundred murders. She supposedly made her own arsenic-based potion, which she used on at least one of her own male relatives. But she mainly supplied the poison to other women who were interested in getting rid of the annoying men in their own lives. Her case bears a resemblance to that of the Roman matrons (see chapter 5). Still, the more lurid cases, involving gore rather than poison, gained the most attention. The most famous serial killer of the eighteenth century was also fictional: Sweeney Todd, "The Demon Barber of Fleet Street," who actually first appeared in a nineteenth-century, serially published story called *The String of Pearls*. But the story, about a barber who murders some of his clients (who are then baked into meat pies by his neighbor, Mrs. Lovett), was set in 1785 London. The tale of Sweeney Todd became so popular in Victorian England that people eventually came to believe it must have had a historical basis. The story was made even more famous by the 1979 musical (lyrics by Stephen Sondheim, originally starring Angela Lansbury and Len Cariou), and several film versions (such as Tim Burton's 2007 take on the story, starring Johnny Depp, Helena Bonham Carter, and Alan Rickman). Even today at least half a dozen companies offer walking tours of Sweeney Todd's London. A bit farther south, in the town of Canterbury, a pizza restaurant called Sweeney Todd's, coincidentally(?) located at 8 Butchery Lane, thrived during the 1980s and 1990s, although it was perhaps best not to inquire what sort of meat they used as a pie topping.[4]

The nineteenth century saw several particularly notorious sets of serial murders in Great Britain and the United States. The criminal duo of William Burke and William Hare became infamous in 1828 for a series of crimes that shocked the city of Edinburgh, Scotland. Both Irish immigrants, Burke and Hare initially made their living from the quite dubious (i.e., illegal) practice of grave-robbing, selling the corpses to anatomy schools for dissection practice. Such corpses were otherwise in short supply, as the only bodies legally available for anatomy students were those of executed criminals, and demand exceeded availability. The two body snatchers, or "resurrectionists," as they preferred to be called, decided that murder was much easier than digging up dead bodies, so they proceeded to suffocate a number of residents from the boardinghouse run by Hare, followed by a number of local beggars, prostitutes, and other victims who would, they assumed, hardly be missed. In all, they killed at least fifteen people before being caught. Hare confessed, and testified against Burke, who was executed by hanging.

But the most well-known case of the century in Britain, and possibly still the most famous case of serial murder in all of recorded history, was that of Jack the Ripper. He terrorized the slums of London in 1888 with a series of murders of prostitutes in the eastern sections of the city that were frequented by pickpockets, muggers, and other desperate sorts. True crime writer Martin Fido has called Jack the Ripper "a mythic figure comparable with Frankenstein's monster and Dracula," both because of the excessively grisly nature of the crimes and because authorities never caught the murderer.[5] But unlike those fictional characters, and unlike Sweeney Todd, the person nicknamed "Jack the Ripper" was a real killer, even if his true identity has never been discovered. He seems to have given the nickname to himself, if the "Dear Boss" letter with this moniker, sent to the local police and newspapers, was penned by the real murderer and not, as authorities quietly suspected, by a local journalist stirring things up. Jack was responsible for at least five murders that became known as the "Whitechapel Murders," even though two of the known victims were found not in Whitechapel parish but in neighboring Spitalfields. Most of the victims were horribly mutilated, the last with her abdomen emptied of its viscera, which were carefully arranged around her body.

Also in the nineteenth century, a number of infamous serial killings occurred in the United States. Two of these stand out. The first was the case of the "Bloody Benders" of Kansas, who killed travelers staying at their roadside inn; to this day, no one knows what became of the Bender family (see chapter 2). The second case was a series of murders occurring over the 1880s and '90s (overlapping with Jack the Ripper in London), eventually discovered to have been perpetrated by H. H. Holmes, whose real name was Herman Mudgett. Holmes confessed to 27 murders, was suspected of nearly 200, and was ultimately convicted and sentenced to death for just one, that of a business associate. He received much attention for being recognized (incorrectly) as the first official serial killer caught and executed in the United States. Possibly even more attention was paid to the astoundingly complicated "murder house" he claimed to have constructed for himself. "The Castle," as he referred to it, allegedly had room after room connected by secret passageways, hidden staircases, false walls, and, perhaps most disturbingly, gas chambers and a room equipped for dissections. These details about the so-called murder castle may in reality have been complete fabrications by the newspapers,[6] exhibiting a level of sordid exaggeration akin to that in

Excerpt from page 2 of the illustrated confession of H. H. Holmes, from New York newspaper *The Journal*, 1896.

the stories Tacitus and Suetonius wrote about Caligula and Nero. Holmes was finally caught when trying to perpetrate an insurance scam. His story became known to a wider audience with the publication of Erik Larson's *Devil in the White City* (2003), which told how Holmes prowled the 1893 Chicago World's Fair in search of his victims.

Serial Killing: A Global Phenomenon

So far, the main examples here have come from Western Europe and the United States, largely because more complete and extensive written records exist for these areas than for other parts of the world. But more recent work on serial killings has turned up many examples from other countries. Australia, for example, has seen a number of serial killers, including British-born John Glover, the "Granny Killer," who bludgeoned and strangled to death six elderly women in Sydney between 1988 and 1991, taking the small amounts of money they had in their handbags. Many countries in Africa have seen an increase in serial murder over the last several decades; more than a dozen serial killers have been caught just in South Africa in the last twenty years, including Moses Sithole, who raped and strangled nearly forty women in 1994–1995 after luring them into nearby fields with a promise of employment, so desperately needed by many families.

The former Soviet Union, also most likely as a result of expanded journalistic freedom, has reported more serial killings in the last three decades. Newton comments, "Prior to the advent of glasnost in 1987 (and the Soviet Union's collapse four years later), Communist censors and police worked in tandem to suppress reports of 'decadent Western-type crime' in what was supposed to be a socialist Utopia."[7] Whatever the reason, at least half a dozen serial murderers have been identified in Russia since the late 1980s, including child-murderer Andrei Chikatilo. China, too, has had a hidden history of serial killing that only recently came to light, again probably because of the slight loosening of journalistic restrictions in the post-Mao era. A similar incremental easing of other restrictions may also be a factor contributing to an increase in crime and crime reporting in China. As *Time* magazine put it in 2003,

> When China was under the ultra-rigid control of Chairman Mao—with every adult reporting to a work unit or a nosy neighborhood committee— people could barely get away with bicycle theft. That overly restrained but safe China is now long gone. Big Brother isn't watching so carefully anymore (unless you're a political dissident) and tens of millions of Chinese are on the move, wandering to different parts of the country in search of jobs. Society is all shook up, and anonymity is now possible for the first time. . . . One of the darker results is a phenomenon once thought to exist only in the decadent West. "We've reached the age of serial killing in China," says Wang Dazhong, a famed criminal investigator who trains cops at the Chinese People's Security University in Beijing.[8]

In contrast to *Time*'s assessment, some criminologists and psychologists, including Helen Morrison, suspect that serial murders did occur in China, if not in such numbers, but that they were not reported to the police, or that, if reported, officials kept the reports quiet so that journalists never heard about them.[9] China has seen a succession of serial murders in the last few decades, including the case of Yang Xinhai. He killed nearly seventy people between 1999 and 2003, mostly farmers and their families. Finally caught, he was executed by firing squad in 2004.

Other countries in Asia have also produced serial killers, if not quite so many. Japan has reported at least a dozen during the last century, nearly all of whom targeted young women (in contrast to Tsutomu Miyazaki, who strangled little girls; see chapter 8). India and Southeast Asia have identified several serial killers during the same period. In Pakistan, a strange case came to light in 1999. Javed Iqbal, a chemical engineer whose crimes might otherwise have gone unpunished, sent a letter to authorities confessing to the sexual abuse and murder of one hundred boys, some of whose remains were found dissolving in a vat of acid in Iqbal's small suburban home. He had even kept a detailed diary of his murderous activities. In court, Iqbal boasted about how easy it had been to kill the boys, saying that he could have killed hundreds more had he wished, but that his goal had been just one hundred, and, having met that goal, he now desired to be punished.

In Latin America, Mexico has seen nearly a dozen separate cases of serial murder in the last half century, especially in the northern state of Chihuahua in the area known as Ciudad Juárez, the site of a series of unsolved rapes and murders of female workers—perhaps as many as four hundred feminicides since 1993. The drug trade may be responsible for some of these crimes, but the nature of the mutilations and the similarities among the victims has had authorities considering serial murder rather than gang violence. A number of suspects have been identified over the years, but in most of the cases police have made no definitive convictions. Colombia, Ecuador, Peru, and Venezuela have all had their share of serial killers, such as Bogotá child-killer Luis Garavito.

The list of serial killers around the globe contains hundreds of names—and those are just the ones authorities know about. Choose any country and chances are that country has produced several serial killers during its history, many of whom have yet to be identified and caught. In general, the numbers of killings seem proportional to the presence of media reporting and openness of journalism in these countries. Part of the point of this brief survey is to provide a reminder that serial killing is not and never has been confined to Western Europe and the United States. At the same time, because of the freedom of the press in many Western societies, people tend to hear about more such cases from these areas of the world. And while this book has focused on prototypical serial murders from ancient Greece and Rome, we should note that modern Greece and Italy have also produced serial killers. One of the most notorious is the "Monster of Florence," who has never been identified. Over the course of many years (1960s–1980s), this killer claimed more than a dozen victims in the idyllic countryside around Florence, Italy. The first victims, both male and female, were simply shot, but eventually the Monster began mutilating his female victims, cutting out their genitals and breasts. The details of this case appear in Douglas Preston and Mario Spezi's 2008 book *The Monster of Florence*.

What It All Means

Although no crime scene evidence, eyewitness accounts, or firsthand interviews with killers survive from the Greece and Rome of two and three thousand years ago, information from ancient sources very strongly indicates that the Greeks and Romans showed an awareness of what we call "serial murder," that it occasionally occurred in their cities and countrysides, and that it was a phenomenon distinct from one-off killings resulting from disputes within families, among business associates, or between political rivals. The killers in the stories presented here, whether described as inhuman monsters or as monstrous humans, exhibited many characteristics familiar to us from modern criminological analyses of serial murder. They could seem like friendly neighbors whom one would never suspect of heinous mutilation murders. They had victim preferences and consistent methods. Some of them took trophies from their victims. Some had murder kits. Many sources for our stories are historical while others are fictional, but they all still indicate that this type of killing was known in the Western world three thousand years before Jack the Ripper.

Cultural contexts also play a role in influencing the type and method of serial murder, and certain types of criminal become memorable because "they seem to embody the darkest impulses and obsessions of their day—all that is most reprehensible about any given age. As much as any hero or celebrity, they personify the spirit of the time—what the Germans call the zeitgeist."[10] H. H. Holmes appeared to be a debonair ladies' man, throwing money around to show them a good time. But after luring dozens of young women to his "Castle," he allegedly killed and dismembered them in some of the most torturous, gruesome ways imaginable. His entire method epitomized the excesses of the Gilded Age, the late nineteenth-century era that saw rapid industrialization and consequent economic growth across large swaths of the United States. When the Lindbergh baby was kidnapped, in 1932, and later found dead, serial killer Albert Fish represented many parents' worst nightmare: a seemingly kindly old man who used his harmless appearance to lure children to his home, where he killed, cooked, and ate them. Ted Bundy embodied the danger of the carefree 1970s attitude toward hitchhiking and accepting rides from strangers.

Cultural developments mattered in antiquity, too, when the proliferation of roads between major cities across the Mediterranean was a dramatic enough change for ancient societies that many stories focused on serial highway murders. As long as roads remained the main conduit of transportation for those traveling by foot, horseback, or carriage, highway bandits were ubiquitous. When steam rail became a major method of transportation, railroads became both a new target for bandit gangs and "the preferred mode of transportation for roving psychopathic killers," such as Carl Panzram and "Railway Killer" Angel Maturino Resendez. The latter was a migrant worker from Mexico who hitched rides on freight cars and killed both men and women at one random destination after another during the 1990s.[11]

To reiterate, the aim of this book has been to emphasize that serial killing is not just a phenomenon affecting modern society. We are not suddenly producing more psychopaths, sociopaths, and other empathy-deficient murderers than ever before. Deviant behavior like serial killing has existed through the ages, and has had profound emotional effects on the societies that experience it. Serial killing simply has not always been described in terms easily recognizable to the modern world. Legends often have roots in real life; appalling actions can take on a mythical quality. I hope the Greek and Roman accounts presented in this book will take their proper place in the history of serial killing, not least because stories about serial killers from antiquity may provide useful analogues for their modern counterparts.

Acknowledgments

When I was growing up in the Los Angeles of the 1960s and '70s, two subjects dominated the news headlines: the Apollo moon landing and the Tate-LaBianca murders. The first was exciting and wondrous, the second shocking and horrifying. Both occurred in 1969—in July and August, respectively—and both continued to vie for prominence in the *Los Angeles Times*, as the Apollo lunar missions continued and the Manson family trials dragged on for months. Because they were local and ongoing, the Manson trials largely overshadowed the intermittent Apollo missions, and the *Times* was not above printing sensationalistic headlines such as "Savage Mystic Cult Blamed for 5 Tate Murders, 6 Others" (Dec. 2, 1969). Add to this the bizarre Patty Hearst kidnapping case, the Hillside Stranglers killings, and the Night Stalker murders of the 1980s—and throw in the Zodiac Killer murders in northern California around the same time—and it's no surprise that many of us in Los Angeles ended up fascinated by true crime, wondering why people would enact such terrible violence upon each other. Spree killing (such as in the Manson family case) and serial killing (as in the cases of the Hillside Stranglers, Night Stalker, and Zodiac) are really very rare, but the unusually horrific nature of the crimes imprints itself on people's imaginations in a way other crimes seldom do.

Despite the fact that information about all of these events was ingrained in my mind from elementary school on, it was not until 2007 that I suddenly realized how many of the myths and legends from classical antiquity and later periods attributed serial killer–like characteristics to some of their villains. Like many people, I had unquestioningly believed that serial murder was a relatively recent phenomenon, a modern problem arising from societal problems such as population increase, lack of mental health care, lenient criminal sentences, and the like. But upon rereading stories about various Greek heroes, it finally dawned on me that a number of their foes followed patterns: seeking out similar victims, killing them by similar methods, sometimes taking "trophies," and generally eluding justice for a very long time before being caught. Some of them were described in terms of the "friendly neighbor" cliché—as in "We never thought he could possibly do anything like that!" After discussing these stories with a few friends and colleagues, I found that the idea that serial killers existed in the ancient world had certainly occurred to other people but that the stories and theories about them had yet to be compiled in one place. And so this book was under way.

I am extremely grateful to a number of people for their encouragement and advice during the long process of getting these thoughts about serial killers in antiquity from page to press. Among the foremost are my agent, Jill Marsal, of Marsal Lyon Literary Agency in—where else?—California, who believed in this project, and Adrienne Mayor, who not only referred me to Jill in the first place but who also let me know I was not out of my mind for thinking that Procrustes sounded like a serial killer. This project also would never have seen the light of day without my writing partner, Meg Meiman, who helped motivate me by her mere presence and who read draft after repetitive draft, always with patience, and offered excellent advice. Similarly, Melissa Mueller provided incisive and extremely useful comments, while Craig Gibson brought the invaluable Libanius passage to my attention.

Immense thanks are due to Jim Burr and the University of Texas Press for taking a chance on another weird topic of mine, the first being ancient ghost stories (see *Haunted Greece and Rome: Ghost Stories from Classical Antiquity*)—about which, as with this project, most people were (at the time) highly skeptical. I am grateful to the press's several anonymous readers for taking the time to read through the manuscript and provide not only helpful suggestions but extra examples(!). Freelance copyeditor Scott Barker and especially senior manuscript editor Lynne Ferguson did wonderful work getting the final copy into shape. I am also grateful to my home institution, the University of Massachusetts Amherst, for research support over the years, and to Benjamin Powers, my one-time graduate student research assistant.

Closer to home, I'd like to thank the Sunderland Public Library for providing an ideal working environment—I was a fixture at one of their large tables for several summers—and also Jen, Dan, and the rest of the folks at Leo's Table in South Deerfield for providing both caffeine and sanity. Jim and Alex Miller supplied patience and hilarity during the seemingly never-ending process of getting this manuscript out the door. And, finally, I would like to thank my dad, Lewis Felton, a civil engineer, for always being supportive of my decision to study the humanities and for humorously fostering my fascination with the macabre.

Notes

Introduction

1. Douglas and Olshaker (1995:18). In 2017, their book was adapted into a TV series, *Mindhunter*, the popularity of which speaks to the ongoing fascination with serial murder.

2. Oakley (2008) takes a quick look at a few Roman emperors. Other accessible (nontechnical) books that discuss lack of empathy include Hare (1993) and Baron-Cohen (2011).

3. Thompson (1955–1958) motifs H300–99.

Chapter 1. Identifying Serial Killers Then and Now

1. Mob hits tend to involve guns, which of course can result in severe mutilation, especially when they are machine guns. But the bodily mutilations that often accompany serial killings are considerably different inasmuch as they tend to be more deliberate, elaborate, and hands-on. See below about the infrequency of gun use in serial killing. For more on general distinctions between mass murder and serial murder, see Bonn (2019). For mob "contract hit man" as serial killer, see Vronsky (2007:22).

2. For a brief overview of mass shootings in the United States in the 2010s, see Hockley (2019).

3. So much so that in the 1983 sequel *Psycho II*, the narrative absolved Anthony Perkins's Norman Bates of the original murders. 1986's *Psycho III*, with Anthony Perkins as star and director, continued to depict Norman as sympathetic but increasingly losing his barely recovered sanity.

4. See, for example, Schmid (2005) and Spitznagel (2018).

5. I am not unaware of the irony in my own current contribution to this ongoing popularity and in my counting on it for readership. On fascination with violence, see also Duclos (1998).

6. For example, Medea killing her children to spite Jason, when he announced he was forsaking her for a better match with the princess of Corinth. In 2016,

Brandi Worley killed her 7-year-old son and 3-year-old daughter after her husband filed for divorce; in 2011 Fiona Donnison smothered her three young children for revenge against her estranged husband. For other examples, see Resnick (2016), who also references Medea.

7. Fagan (2011:45).

8. For more on interpreting monsters in classical myths, see Felton (2012).

9. Palaephatus, *Peri Apiston* 4, in Stern (1996). Gibson (2012:8) also mentions the Theban Sphinx very briefly as a potential "invisible serial murderer," that is, a story that may have had its basis in serial murder. Cf. Hawes (2014:197–198 and 198n77).

10. Pausanias 9.26.2.

11. See, for example, discussion in Gloyn (2020), chapter 8.

12. On Caligula's disturbed mental state and possible personality disorder, see Sidwell (2010).

13. For a very basic discussion of nature versus nurture in relation to psychopathy, see Oakley (2008:54–58).

14. For example, Schechter (2003:123–125).

Chapter 2. Methods to the Madness

1. The earlier definition appears in Douglas et al. (2006:96–97, 461). At a 2005 FBI conference on serial murder, there was considerable support for reducing the number of murders needed to qualify as serial murder from three to two, a criterion adopted in the current FBI *Crime Classification Manual*, as cited here (*CCM-III*, 2013: 471).

2. See, for example, *CCM-III*, 2013:237 and 263.

3. Author Ann Rule, who considered Bundy a close friend, was stunned to learn that he was a serial killer. She wrote about the experience in *The Stranger beside Me* (1980), and went on to become a chronicler of true crime.

4. Vronsky (2004:327–328). Psychologists, criminologists, and law enforcement authorities disagree as to whether killing for profit and/or personal advancement is a characteristic of serial killers.

5. Vronsky (2004:43).

6. See Keppel (1997:2–7).

7. All translations of Libanius are by Gibson (2008). Craig Gibson also brought to my attention this passage from the Roman rhetorician Quintilian, 5.9.13: "The Areopagites, when they condemned a boy for tearing out the eyes of quails, seem to have made this judgment for no reason other than that such an action was a sign of an excessively malevolent mentality, one that would have become a danger to many, if the boy had reached adulthood" (my translation).

8. Herodotus, *Histories* 4.64–65.

9. Morrison and Goldberg (2004:272).

Chapter 3. Motives for Serial Murder across the Ages

1. Newton (2006:185).

2. Vronsky (2004:163).

3. *Singulari scelere et audacia* (*Pro Cluentio* 8.23); cf. 9.27, 10.29, 11.31.

4. Allely et al. (2014:288).

5. I thank George Kazantzidis for bringing this information to my attention. For details, see Thumiger (2017:265–272); see also Kazantzidis (2018:238–239).

6. Female serial killers, though rare, have shown motivations in line with various "types," including hedonist-lust, power-control, and power-assertive. As Vronsky notes (2007:65), it is the "mode of expression" of these motives that differs.

7. Vronsky (2004:205–206, 272–273).

8. Bloch (1993:228).

9. I am not the first to suggest this: cf. DiGerolamo (2018:22), and https://mariamilani.com/ancient_rome/emperor-neros-personality-profile.htm.

10. Suetonius, *Nero* 27–29.

11. *"Ventrem feri"* (Tacitus, *Annales* 14.8).

Chapter 4. Murderous Greek Roof-Tiles and Other Legal Problems

1. The Greek god Apollo, for example, had to do penance for killing the guardian serpent at Delphi, whom he named "Python"; he also did penance for killing the Cyclopes.

2. Both citations are from Vronsky (2004:43).

3. Coleman (1990:58).

4. Gagarin (2005:30).

5. Plastow (2020:1). For general discussion and two specific case studies, see Gagarin (2003).

6. For more details about the Athenian legal system—especially homicide law—see Loomis (1972), Allen (2002), and Phillips (2008).

7. In addition to Ares, a number of other mythological characters—humans rather than deities—were tried at the Areopagus, including Daedalus, Cephalus, and, most notably, Orestes. See Harding (2008:33–34 and 205–207), who notes that according to Aeschylus's *Eumenides* the trial of Orestes (rather than that of Ares) becomes the founding myth of the Areopagus, and the name is explained by the story of when the Amazons invaded Attica in the time of Theseus, camped on the hill, and sacrificed to Ares there.

8. The term also encompassed political massacres (Gagarin 2005:129n49). The related verbs, *sphagiazo* and *sphagizomai*, mean "to slay a sacrificial [animal] victim." See also Carawan (1998) and McDevitt (1970:504–505).

9. Although Greece was under Roman rule at this time, certain aspects of the Greek legal system still applied.

10. Gibson (2008:141–143).

11. Libanius, *Progymnasmata* 1.2, in Gibson (2008:145).

12. In the last three lines of this passage there seems to be an intentional rhetorical increase in the strength of the Greek words used for "kill." *Apólluto* is a general word for "destroy" or "kill"; *diephtheireto* is also a general term for "kill" or "perish" but with an intimation of more brutality; and *apesphatteto* often specifically refers to throat-slitting. Libanius 1.7-9, in Gibson (2008: 147–149).

13. Libanius 1.12, in Gibson (2008:149).

14. Libanius 1.10, in Gibson (2008: 147–149).

15. Libanius 1.24–25, in Gibson (2008:153–155).

16. Libanius 1.14, in Gibson (2008:147–149).

Chapter 5. Murder and the Advantages of Roman Citizenship

1. Gaughan (2010:9–11). That is, the punishment for killing *dolo sciens*, a technical phrase for "with murderous intent," differed from killing *imprudens*, a term indicating lack of forethought or intent. See also Bauman (1996:9).

2. Gaughan (2010:xv).

3. Gaughan (2010:30). The word *murder* came to English through Germanic languages, and shares an early (Proto-Indo-European) root *mer-* ("to harm, to die") with Latin *mors* ("death").

4. Gaughan (2010:5). As Gaughan explains (xv), this lack of homicide law was most likely because of the nature of political power in Rome. The right to kill was embedded in two key definitions of power. The first was *patria potestas*, the power possessed by a Roman father over his children, which included the *vitae necisque potestas*, "the power of life and death." The second was magisterial *imperium*, "the power to command," which included the power to kill Roman citizens.

5. Gaughan (2010:70–1). Investigation concerning a homicide would have been *de homine occiso* ("concerning a person having been killed"), rather than *de re atroci magnaque* ("concerning an atrocious and weighty matter").

6. Harris (2009:365). In 2019, Atlanta officials decided to retest various materials from the murders, in an attempt to see whether updated methods might absolve or confirm Williams as the killer.

7. Yam (2014).

8. This and the rest of the account are paraphrased from Livy 8.18.

9. Gaughan (2010:79). Moreover, accidental poisoning resulting from trying to mix a benign potion was not all that unusual; see the cases discussed in Ogden (2009:104–107).

10. Aside from Newton, see also https://listverse.com/2017/06/21/top-10-horri fying-serial-killers-in-early-history and https://en.wikipedia.org/wiki/List_of_se rial_killers_before_1900.

11. Other examples of groups include the cannibalistic Sawney Beane clan of fifteenth- or sixteenth-century Scotland, while examples of partners include Americans Charlie Starkweather and Caril Ann Fugate (1958), British "Moors Murderer" Ian Brady and Myra Hindley (1963–1965), Americans Kenneth Bianchi and Angelo Buono (aka the "Hillside Stranglers," 1977–1978), Canadian couple Paul Bernardo and Karla Homolka (1990–1992), and the Russian "Cannibal Couple" Dmitry Baksheev and his wife, Natalia Baksheeva, who in 2017 were arrested on suspicion of killing and eating several dozen victims. See Newton (2006:437–454; "Appendix B: Team Killers") for further examples. There are also close examples from Greek myth, such as the Danaides and the Lemnian women, who worked in organized groups to murder their husbands. On these, see chapter 11.

12. As Gaughan notes (2010:78 and 162n28), the Roman government was constantly on the watch for conspiracies against the state. The threat to social order must have seemed particularly great because the plague was so widespread.

13. An interesting case, but one that lacks enough detail to be described either as mass or serial murder, occurred in 184 BCE. Livy (39.41), drawing on the works of Valerius Antias, a slightly earlier historiographer, tells how one Roman official, Quintus Naevius, was assigned to investigate charges of poisoning (*quaestiones veneficii*) in Sardinia, the province under his jurisdiction. Naevius was reported to have sentenced more than two thousand people on this charge. But that is all Livy says. We do not know who the victims or the accused were, whether they were of high or low status, or what the evidence of poisoning was. We can only surmise that a high number of suspicious deaths caused the Roman government to take notice, probably concerned about the possibility of a large-scale conspiracy.

14. This was very close to an unsettling event known as the "Bacchanalian Affair," an alleged conspiracy against the Roman government. The Senate, afraid of losing power, passed an infamous decree in 186 BCE forbidding certain rituals celebrating the worship of Bacchus, in an attempt to prevent crowds of people (mainly women) from gathering and getting out of control.

15. Livy 40.37.

16. Livy 40.43. Mayor (2003:126–127) points out that Livy and other Roman historians refer to the malicious transmission of plagues without giving specifics, but that Greek historian Dio Cassius (second to third centuries CE) provides details about two allegedly man-made epidemics. The first, which occurred before Dio's time, took place in 90–91 CE under the reign of Emperor Domitian. Dio says, "During this time certain persons infected needles with poison and went around pricking anyone they wanted to. And many of those infected in this way never even understood what was causing their deaths. But, too, many of those responsible were denounced and punished" (*Epitome* 67.11.6). The second man-made plague occurred in Dio's lifetime, in approximately 189 CE during the reign of Commodus: "A plague occurred, the greatest of any I know about, for two thousand people often died in Rome over the course of a single day. But many also died, not just in the City but throughout almost the entire empire, at the hands of evildoers. For they smeared tiny needles with certain poisons and, for payment, used them to infect other people" (*Epitome* 73.14.3–4).

17. Gaughan (2010:82).

18. Gaughan (2010:72).

19. Newton (2006:185), in disagreement.

20. See, for example, Mayor (2010:111).

21. Gaughan (2010:126). Proscriptions were used intermittently after Sulla, most infamously in 43 BCE by the Second Triumvirate (Octavian, Lepidus, and Mark Antony), one of whose victims was Cicero.

22. As in the case of the bandit known as "Corocotta" (a name that might mean "hyena"). See Braund (1980) and Fuhrmann (2012:155–156).

Chapter 6. The Popularity of Serial Poisoning

1. On the suitor's comment and Odysseus's own acquaintance with Ephyra, see Mayor (2003:56–58); for details about the incident at Cirrha, see Mayor (2003: 100–106).

2. Ogden (2009:103–104).

3. On the types of poison and motives, see Kaufman (1932:157–158); on the preference for poison by women, Cilliers and Retief (2000:90).

4. Horace, *Satire* 2.1.56.

5. Tacitus, *Annales* 2.69–75 and 3.7. See also Cilliers and Retief (2000:90).

6. Versions of the story appear in Ovid, *Metamorphoses* 7.406–419, and Pliny the Elder, *Natural History* (*NH*) 27.2. The word "aconite" may derive from the Greek *akon*, "dart," since the tips of darts were poisoned for effectiveness; or it may derive from the Greek *akonae*, the rocky ground where the plant was believed to grow. Pliny himself remained unsure of the origin of the plant's name, connecting it with the port of Aconae (*NH* 6.4), with the rocky ground where the plant grew (*NH* 27.10), and with *akone* ("whetstone") "because it had the same power to cause rapid death as whetstones had to give an edge to an iron blade" (*NH* 27.2).

7. Pliny the Elder, *NH* 27.2.

8. Syme (1986:315).

9. Newton (2006:116).

10. Mayor (2010:215).

11. Mayor (2010:2).

12. Ramsland (2005:5).

13. *Venenariorum indice* (Suetonius, *Nero* 33.2).

14. Tacitus, *Annales* 12.66.

15. *Nuper veneficii damnata et diu inter instrumenta regni habita* (Tacitus, *Annales* 12.66).

16. Tacitus, *Annales* 13.15–16.

17. Suetonius, *Nero* 47.1–2.

18. Dio, *Historia Romana* 64b.3.4.1.

19. The incorrect version appears in Ramsland (2005:8), who accepted it uncritically from Michael Newton's first edition of *The Encyclopedia of Serial Killers*. The story does not appear in his second edition, but, unfortunately, appeared here, among other places: http://www.cracked.com/article_20751_6-true-stories-from -history-creepier-than-any-horror-movie_p2.html (accessed August 14, 2019).

20. An example of this false rumor about Carpophorus appears in Karl Smallwood, "10 Cruel and Unusual Facts about the Colosseum's Animal Fights," January 15, 2014, http://listverse.com/2014/01/15/10-cruel-and-unusual-facts-about-ani mals-in-the-roman-colosseum. The author of this piece does not cite his sources, and incorrectly places Carpophorus in Apuleius's story about Lucius. A detailed correction about Lucretia and the giraffe also appears in a discussion in Sudipto Karmakar, "Was Locusta Really Raped to Death by a Giraffe?," Quora, September 13, 2015, https://www.quora.com/Was-Locusta-really-raped-to-death-by-a-giraffe.

21. Cilliers and Retief (2000:89). Cf. Juvenal, *Satires* 6.133 and 602–643; 7.169; and 14.250–255, all of which also exhibit a high degree of misogyny in their descriptions of female poisoners.

22. *Antidotis praemunitam* (Suetonius, *Nero* 34.2).

23. Cilliers and Retief (2000:96–98). On Mithradates, see Mayor (2010).

24. The "Five Good Emperors" and their reigns: Nerva, 96–98; Trajan, 98–117; Hadrian, 117–138; Antoninus Pius, 138–161; and Marcus Aurelius, 161–180.

25. On the decline, see Cilliers and Retief (2000:98–99). But Aelianus Spartia-

nus (ca. 300 CE) reports in his *Life of Hadrian* a rumor that Hadrian killed his own wife with poison.

Chapter 7. Heracles and the Headhunters

1. Much of the information here on bandits in the ancient Roman world is based on Grünewald (2004) and van Hoof (1988).

2. Livy 1.4.

3. See Carucci (2017:181–183), and on the dangers of roads across the ancient world, see Felton (2019).

4. For discussion of Heracles's semidivine nature and possible basis in history, see Philips (1978).

5. See Hurwit (2006).

6. Pausanias 6.21.3.

7. Pindar, *Isthmian* 4.3.

8. The anatomical details come from Philostratus, *Imagines* 2.21.

9. Amitay (2014:1). He goes on to discuss other versions and interpretations of the Heracles–Antaeus myth.

10. On the possibility of there actually having been a giant skeleton in this location, see Mayor (2000: 121–126).

11. Vronsky (2004:315).

12. Apollodorus, *Bibliotheca* 2.5.11. See also McPhee (2006:45), and for detailed discussion of the literary sources for the Bousiris story, see Livingstone (2001:78–85).

13. Herodotus 2.45.1–2.

14. Asheri et al. (2007:270). Cf. Bowden (2005:3) and McPhee (2006:46).

15. Plutarch, *Parallela minora* 315b.

16. According to Plutarch, *Theseus* 11.1–2.

17. Scholia on Pindar's *Olympian* 10.19.

18. Diodorus Siculus, *Bibliotheca Historica* 4.31.6.

19. Padilla (1998:23).

20. On the Ofnet finds, see Orschiedt (2005:67–70); on Roquepertuse, see Armit (2012:129, 147). The lintel, a horizontal support, shares its root with the Latin *limen*, "threshold," whence "liminal."

21. On the Celts, see Armit (2012:20–27); on headhunting in the ancient world more generally, see Armit (2012:37–39); on the Romans, see Armit (2012:40); on the London finds, see Black (2014). Skull collecting was not confined to Europe and the Near East, but has occurred all over the world. For examples, see Wade (2018) on the recent find of an Aztec skull display from Tenochtitlan, Mexico, dating to the fifteenth century CE.

22. Archaeologists have found some evidence that might indicate human sacrifice in the Thrace of nearly 3,000 years ago (Miller 2015). See also Herodotus 5.5, where he describes Thracians sacrificing wives as part of the burial ritual for their dead husbands.

23. Mueller (2018:80). The Greek *skula* is unrelated to the English "skull."

24. Armit (2012:37–40, 102, 118). He observes that a similar concept existed in Iron Age southern France, and that the metaphorical relationship between the ac-

tion of the sickle, harvesting crops, and that of the sword, swiping off heads, "occurs quite widely in the ancient world" (118). See also Felton (1998).

25. Rebecca Lämmle came to a similar conclusion in her 2013 study of Heracles in Greek satyr plays.

26. Use of the bow and arrow to hunt dates back to at least the Paleolithic period if not earlier, and hunters still use them today. Burkert (1985:209) suggests that the core myth of Heracles may have developed as early as the Paleolithic. Swords developed during the Bronze Age. On Heracles's weapons, see, e.g., Padilla (1998:30–33) and Brommer (1986:65–67). The latter points out that not until the seventh century BCE does Heracles appear using the bow as a weapon, and both discuss the depictions of Heracles in hoplite gear. For Heracles as a civilizing force, see, e.g., Stafford (2012:23) and Padilla (1998:22).

27. The quotes and general information here about ancient Greek roads are from Bernard Alkire, Michigan Technological University, personal correspondence.

Chapter 8. Theseus and the Highway Killers

1. Paraphrase translation from Plutarch, *Theseus* 6.4–5.

2. Plutarch, *Theseus* 6.3. On *kakourgoi* (sing. *kakourgos*), see chapter 4.

3. Schechter and Everitt (2006:52–53). But antecedents of Lombroso's theory can be found at least as early as Chaucer's use of physiognomy to delineate character. See Cohen (1996:9–10) on the example of Thomas More's description of Richard III, the king's deformed body a reflection of his deviant morality.

4. An urban legend circulating for many years claimed that Myers's mask was based on actor William Shatner's face, specifically a "Captain Kirk death mask." The legend seems to have been verified as fact: see Startrek.com staff (2016).

5. Compare also Gollum (originally Sméagol), from both the book and film versions of *The Lord of the Rings*, and Voldemort (originally Tom Riddle) from the *Harry Potter* series. Both characters grow more physically hideous as they become more depraved.

6. Pausanias 2.1.4.

7. Plutarch, *Theseus* 8.2.

8. Pausanias 1.37.3.

9. Plutarch, *Theseus* 10.1.

10. Ward (1970:102).

11. Ward (1970:102) suggests that this part of the story originated from the presence of a turtle-shaped rock. This sort of natural etiology may seem like a stretch, but is not unusual. Another example appears in the *Antiquities of the Jews* by the Romano-Jewish historian Flavius Josephus (first century CE). Writing in Greek, he recounts the fate of Lot's wife, who disobeyed God's order not to look back at the destruction of Sodom as she and her family fled. "She was turned into a pillar of salt," Josephus says. "I examined it myself, and it's still there" (1.11.4). There are indeed salt formations situated in the region that may have given rise to this part of the story, which also appears in Genesis 19. There, it is the angels who warn Lot and his family not to look back, but the outcome is the same.

12. Vronsky (2004:196).

13. Vronsky (2004:206–207).

14. Probably a stretch for most of us, but not for director Sam Raimi and his infamous tree-rape scene in *The Evil Dead* (1981), a scene unfortunately little changed in Fede Alvarez's 2013 remake.

15. Conrad (2006:30).

16. Simpson (2000:97); Williams (1996:255).

17. Plutarch, *Theseus* 6.4. According to classical Athenian law, it was legal to kill a robber who waylaid you on a road.

18. Ward (1970:5–6).

19. Strand (2012:1–4).

20. Morrison and Goldberg (2004:201).

Chapter 9. From Murderous Contests to Olympic Sports

1. Miller (2004:115).

2. The Greek king Agamemnon's sacrifice of his daughter, Iphigenia, to appease the goddess Artemis provides another point of comparison.

3. Hughes (1991:78)

4. The story summary presented in these paragraphs is based on the main literary version of Amycus's story, that of Valerius Flaccus, *Argonautica* 4.99ff., esp. 181–185. Amycus's story appears with some variation but fewer details in Apollonius Rhodes, *Argonautica*, book 2; Apollodorus, *Bibliotheca* 1.9.20; and Hyginus *Fabulae* 17. Gantz (1996:349) also cites evidence for Amycus from artistic tradition dating back to the fifth century BCE.

5. Vronsky (2004:196).

6. As exemplified by Jason's speech to Medea in Euripides's *Medea* (431 BCE), lines 522–541.

7. Set in the (mythological) chronological period after the fall of Troy, Vergil's *Aeneid* contains another example of a brutal king characterized as "primitive" in part by his despicable treatment of corpses. The Etruscan king Mezentius, more than once referred to as a "despiser of the gods" (*contemptor divum*, e.g., 7.648), was infamous for his arrogance and cruelty. Vergil says Mezentius committed "unspeakable murders" (*infandas caedes*, 8.483) and describes how the tyrant "joined the bodies of dead men to those of the living as a form of torture (*mortua . . . iungebat corpora vivis . . . tormenti genus*, 8.485–87), placing them face to face until the live victims died a lingering death from exposure to the putrid decaying flesh. The horrified Etruscan citizens finally staged a coup, and Mezentius fled to a neighboring region. Aeneas later kills Mezentius, in a duel that emphasizes the victory of the "civilized" over the "primitive," as in the stories about Heracles and Theseus.

8. Nagy (2013:109).

9. ATU tale type 300, "The Dragon-Slayer" (Uther 2004).

10. Currie (2002:25–26).

11. The story of the Hero of Temesa is a particularly difficult one, requiring some explanation. Motifs of rape and homicide appear surprisingly often in relation to a city's founding, and may metaphorically express the incorporation of nature (female) with culture (male) or the conquest of one by the other. See Brelich (1958) and Dougherty (1993:66–7), and compare the murder of Remus by Romulus and the rape of the Sabine women in connection with the founding of Rome. The Hero may

thus have been a *ktistês* figure, *ktistês* being the ancient Greek term used to describe founders of cities. One problem with this interpretation is that usually when the founder of a Greek colony or city is a murderer, he has been exiled from his hometown for his crime and has undergone ritual purification before the founding. This has not occurred in the case of the Hero of Temesa. Lack of purification after rape is also an issue; see Parker (1996: 185), and note Pausanias 8.5.12, in which Aristocrates, after raping a maiden in the sanctuary of Artemis in Arcadia, is stoned to death by the locals. See Dougherty (1993), chap. 2, on the "murderer-founder analogy."

12. Miller (2004:160–165). For such cults devoted to women, see Larson (1995).

13. Odysseus seemed to make a habit of this, having initially sailed away from Circe's island without noticing that his crewman Elpenor had gotten drunk, fallen off Circe's roof, broken his neck, and was lying on the ground unburied. Elpenor had to point this out to Odysseus when Odysseus visited Hades (*Odyssey* 11.51–79).

14. For details of this serial killer "learning curve," see Vronsky (2004:291, 202). Pausanias does not specifically say that the *daimon* kills the young women, but his text strongly implies this. Scholars have debated the meaning of "wife" in the text. The girls may in reality simply have had a year of temple service before their marriage, but in that case, why would they need "saving"? An earlier source for this story, the poet Callimachus (third century BCE), says that the maidens were deflowered and returned to their parents the next morning, suggesting some sort of prenuptial ritual involving the temple priests (fr. 99a, *Dieg.* IV.5-17, see Harder 2012, 1:279). But then why didn't Pausanias, while mentioning the rape of a local girl, also mention the ritual deflowering? And Pausanias does not use the language usually associated with sacrifice, or for that matter even with ritual, which suggests that the story as he heard it did not have its roots in intentional, conscious, community sacrificial custom. Visintin, interpreting the Hero as one of the "restless dead" (*biaiothanatos*), believes he is a revenant and that the rite performed for the Hero at Temesa was one of human sacrifice, "marriage to Death," rather than ritual defloration, as discussed in Currie (2002:27).

15. For a good introduction to the Zodiac Killer, see Robert Graysmith, *Zodiac* (2007). In 2004, criminologist Richard Walter agreed to look at the Zodiac case. He analyzed all four of the crime scenes and developed a profile based on Zodiac's behavior at those scenes. Walter believes that Zodiac was not a "powerless nobody" as previous law enforcement officials had thought. Rather, Walter believes that Zodiac was a "power-assertive" killer. This type of perpetrator is one who deals from a position of power and whose crimes are committed to increase his feelings of power, not to compensate for feelings of powerlessness, as suggested by other profilers. What he desires is power that is limited only by the bounds of his own imagination. In short, Walter believes that the reason the Zodiac Killer was never apprehended is that he was the exact opposite of the type of person the police and profilers were seeking for forty years.

16. Vronsky (2004:203).

17. That's either 700-plus human sacrifices or 700-plus maidens required to do temple service of a sort that they feared, and from which they wished to be rescued (as opposed to, say, being chosen as the Pythia of Apollo, or as a Vestal Virgin at Rome, positions that were considered great honors). For the wife-killing angle, see also discussion of the "Bluebeard" type, chapter 11.

18. The Greek geographer Strabo, presenting a shorter variant on this story, says the sailor's name is Polites (6.1.5). Harder (2012, 2:754–6), when comparing the versions of Pausanias and Strabo with that of Callimachus, notes details not found in Callimachus and says that Pausanias makes clear "it was the hero's [*sic*] ghost which was terrorizing the people of Temesa." Both Pausanias and Strabo say that the Hero was angry because he was murdered by the people of Temesa, but Pausanias adds that the killing by stoning was the people's revenge for the Hero's first having violated a local girl, whereas Strabo suggests a treacherous murder without explaining its cause. Both mention that the Delphic Oracle ordered the people of Temesa to appease the Hero. In Pausanias, Euthymus arrives without a specific motive; in Strabo, his action is related to Locrian supremacy over Temesa. Pausanias adds the romantic detail of Euthymus marrying the Hero's last intended victim and how the Hero disappeared into the sea. The accounts of Pausanias and Strabo suggest that in their time the story of the Hero of Temesa had become well known and that there were different traditions concerning the details.

19. Stoning was a common but not always fatal method of punishment. See the story of Cleomedes at Pausanias 6.9.6–8, and cf. 8.5.12 for rape in a temple punished by stoning (because the sanctity of the temple was violated).

20. For more discussion, see Woodward (1979). See also chapter 9 in Duclos (1998: 133–143).

21. Herodotus 4.105. For a detailed discussion of werewolves in antiquity, see Ogden (2021).

22. Pliny the Elder, *NH* 8.80–81.

23. Petronius, *Satyrica* 61–62.

24. Pausanias 6.6.9.

25. Ramage (1868:149).

26. Crossan (2011).

Chapter 10. Serial Murders in Local Legends

1. According to the Scholiast on Euripides, *Phoen.* 26, the fifth-century BCE poet Corinna said that "Oedipus himself killed not only the Sphinx but also the Teumessian fox" (fr. 672). She could simply mean that Oedipus *caused* the Sphinx's death, but the wording strongly suggests that he himself slew her. The Teumessian fox, a gigantic creature, was sent by the gods to kill the children of Thebes in revenge for an unspecified slight. The main version of the fox's story says that it could never be caught, and that Zeus turned it to stone. Corinna seems to present alternate versions of the Oedipus and Teumessian fox myths, in which Oedipus used weapons to kill both creatures.

2. Palaephatus 4, in Stern (1996); Pausanias 9.26.2–3.

3. Sophocles, *Oedipus Tyrannus* 292.

4. Noted by Dawe (2006) in his commentary on line 292, to which he compares *Odyssey* 13.123: when the Phaeacians deposit the sleeping Odysseus on Ithaca, they hide the gifts they want to leave for him off the path "lest some wayfarer [*tis hodi-taôn anthropôn*], before Odysseus wakes up, come upon them and plunder them."

5. "Deserted area," *deserta regione* (Apuleius, *Metamorphoses* 8.21); *an nulli scitis quo loco consederitis* (8.19), or, more literally, "do you not know in what place you have

settled?" (that is, sat down to rest). The time of day, though not specified, is likely around noon; since the travelers reach the next village by night, they have probably stopped here for a midday meal, given how much time elapses between this rest stop and their later arrival in the village. In Greek and Roman literature (as often elsewhere), noon is a time of day when odd events are more likely to happen. Noon is considered a "liminal" or "threshold" time of day, neither morning nor afternoon. Like midnight (neither night nor morning), such times of day are open for supernatural occurrences. See Felton (2019).

6. Apuleius, Metamorphoses 8.21.

7. Scobie (1977:340).

8. Apuleius, *Metamorphoses* 6.14.

9. On this episode from the story of Cupid and Psyche, see Felton (2013).

10. Harris (1988:99–100).

11. Bowman (1999).

12. Bremmer (1997:3).

13. Pausanias 9.26.7–8.

14. See Ogden (2013:170, 153).

15. *Lumainomenou tên polin* (Pausanias 9.26.7).

16. Hughes (1991:78).

Chapter 11. Serial Slaying of Suitors and Spouses

1. On several of the stories here presented as reflecting a historical process, see Gresseth (1974), who also analyzes a number of folktale motifs in the stories.

2. Vronsky (2007:26). In most versions of these two myths, Hypsipyle, queen of the Lemnian women, secretly spares her elderly father, and one of the Danaides spares her husband, having fallen in love with him.

3. Thompson (1955-1958) motifs H300–499.

4. Hyginus, *Fabulae* 84.

5. On this and other odd aspects of the story as well as on this folktale type in general, see Hansen (2000).

6. Schechter (2003:35).

7. Vronsky (2007:181).

8. Tacitus, *Annales* 11.28.

9. The story appears in Dio 60.

10. Tacitus, *Annales* 11.32.

11. Newton (2006:22–23).

12. For the entirety of Perrault's version, including the moral, see his "Blue Beard," https://www.pitt.edu/~dash/perrault03.html.

13. Warner (1994:244). Among other things, the bloodstained key becomes a phallic symbol related to lost virginity. Regarding the Pandora comparison, we must note that the original Greek story says nothing about curiosity being Pandora's flaw. Rather, Zeus sends her to Earth as a punishment to men in revenge for Prometheus's giving man the benefit of fire against Zeus's will. In that context, it seems that Pandora was intended to open her *pithos* and let evils loose on mankind. See Hesiod, *Works and Days*, lines 54–105. Eve, for her part, was not so much curious as disobedient, allowing herself to be persuaded by the Serpent.

14. Anderson (2000:98–99); see also Barzilai (2009:4), who explores precedents for Bluebeard in midrashic tradition.

15. Palaephatus 2 in Stern (1996).

16. For details of the Conomor story, see Dash (2015). Conomor's being cursed to roam the Earth as a werewolf recalls the ancient story of King Lycaon. Told by both Greeks and Romans, the main version appears in Ovid's *Metamorphoses* (1.163–239): Lycaon tried to feed human flesh to the god Jupiter (Zeus), who punished this impious savagery by turning Lycaon into a wolf.

17. Burton (1885:14).

Chapter 12. Witches and Other Child-Murderers

1. Newton (2006:40–41). Chikatilo was executed in 1994.

2. Onyulo (2017).

3. Onyulo (2017). In a separate phenomenon, women and especially children in various countries are being accused and executed as witches.

4. Apuleius, *Metamorphoses* 1.9. Needless to say, the ancient observation about beavers chewing off their genitals was incorrect (Kitchell 2014:14–15).

5. Lucan, *Pharsalia* 6.710–11. The actions of some of these literary witches and child-snatching monsters are reflected in real-life examples, such as the case of Lisa Montgomery, who in 2004 strangled an eight-months-pregnant Bobbie Jo Stinnett and cut out the baby, then pretended it was her own. She was executed by the U.S. federal government in January 2021.

6. See Eberly (1997), who suspects that medical conditions such as dwarfism and progeria greatly influenced stories of changelings. Other diseases and disabilities, including Down syndrome and autism, have also been suggested as influencing such stories, especially with the greater incidence of such conditions in male children possibly reflected in the prevalence of boys in the folktales.

7. Horace, *Epode* 5.37–38. The liver was believed to be the seat of passion, and would be especially potent in this case as the boy would die intensely desiring food.

8. See Felton (2016).

9. Ovid, *Fasti* 6. 131–143.

10. *Vitiant cunis corpora rapta suis* (Ovid, *Fasti* 6.136).

11. Graf (2007:142).

12. Translation of *CIL* VI.19747 from Ogden (2009:119).

13. Graf (2007:141).

14. Graf (2007: 139, 141).

Chapter 13. Serial Murder Then and Now, There and Here

1. Howard (2010:55).

2. *The History of Sawney Beane and His Family* (1800?).

3. *The History of Sawney Beane and His Family.*

4. In 2004 the Moorish restaurant Café Mauresque took over the site and as of this writing was still there.

5. Fido (1987:3).

6. Little (2020). Cf. Schechter (1994).

7. Newton (2006:96).

8. See Forney (2003).

9. Morrison and Goldberg (2004:238).

10. Quotes and subsequent discussion about the "zeitgeist" from Schechter and Everitt (2006:335–337).

11. Schechter and Everitt (2006:247–248).

Bibliography

Allely, C. S., H. Minnis, L. Thompson, P. Wilson, and C. Gillberg. 2014. "Neuro-developmental and Psychosocial Risk Factors in Serial Killers and Mass Murderers." *Aggression and Violent Behavior* 19 (3): 288–301.

Allen, D. 2002. *The World of Prometheus: The Politics of Punishing in Democratic Athens*. Princeton, NJ: Princeton University Press.

Amitay, O. 2014. "*Vagantibus Graecia fabulis*: The North African wanderings of Antaios and Herakles." *Mediterranean Historical Review* 29 (1): 1–28.

Anderson, G. 2000. *Fairytale in the Ancient World*. Abingdon: Routledge.

Armit, I. 2012. *Headhunting and the Body in Iron Age Europe*. Cambridge: Cambridge University Press.

Asheri, D., A. B. Lloyd, and A. Corcella. 2007. *A Commentary on Herodotus Books I-IV*, edited by O. Murray and A. Moreno; translated by B. Graziosi, M. Rosetti, C. Dus, and V. Cazzato. Oxford: Oxford University Press.

Baron-Cohen, S. 2011. *The Science of Evil: On Empathy and the Origins of Cruelty*. New York: Basic Books.

Barzilai, S. 2009. *Tales of Bluebeard and His Wives from Late Antiquity to Postmodern Times*. New York: Routledge.

Bauman, R. A. 1996. *Crime and Punishment in Ancient Rome*. London: Routledge.

Black, J. 2014. "Gruesome Evidence of Ancient Roman Head Hunters in London." *Ancient Origins* online, January 16. https://www.ancient-origins.net/news -history-archaeology/gruesome-evidence-ancient-roman-head-hunters-london -001225.

Bloch, R. 1993. *Once around the Bloch: An Unauthorized Autobiography*. New York: Tor Books.

Bonn, S. 2019. "Serial Murder versus Mass Murder: Two Very Different Types of Crime." *Psychology Today*, January 7. https://www.psychologytoday.com/us/blog /wicked-deeds/201901/serial-murder-versus-mass-murder.

Bowman, D. 1999. "Profiler." Salon, July 8. http://www.salon.com/1999/07/08/profiler.

Braund, D. C. 1980. "Corocottas: Bandit and Hyena." *Liverpool Classical Monthly* 5(1): 13–14.

Brelich, A. 1958. *Gli eroi greci: Un problema storico-religioso*. Rome: Edizioni dell'Ateneo.

Bremmer, J. 1997. "Monsters en fabeldieren in de Griekse cultuur." *Mededelingen-blad Vereniging van Vrienden Allard Pierson Museum* 68:2–5.

Brommer, F. 1986. *Heracles: The Twelve Labors of the Hero in Ancient Art and Literature*, translated by S. J. Schwarz. New Rochelle, NY: Aristide D. Caratzas.

Burkert, W. (1977) 1985. *Greek Religion: Archaic and Classical*. Translated by J. Raffan. Malden, MA: Blackwell Publishing.

Burton, R. F., trans. 1885. *The Book of the Thousand Nights and a Night*. Vol. 1. Printed by the Burton Club for private subscribers only.

Carawan, E. 1998. *Rhetoric and the Law of Draco*. Oxford: Clarendon Press.

Carucci, M. 2017. "The Dangers of Female Mobility in Roman Imperial Times." In *The Impact of Mobility and Migration in the Roman Empire*, edited by E. Lo Cascio and L. E. Tacoma, 173–190. Leiden: Brill.

Cilliers, L., and F. P. Retief. 2000. "Poisons, Poisoning and the Drug Trade in Ancient Rome." *Akroterion* 45:88–100.

Cohen, J. J. 1996. *Monster Theory: Reading Culture*. Minneapolis: University of Minnesota Press.

Coleman, K. M. 1990. "Fatal Charades: Roman Executions Staged as Mythological Enactments." *The Journal of Roman Studies* 80:44–73.

Conrad, M. T. 2006. *The Philosophy of Film Noir*. Lexington: University Press of Kentucky.

Crossan, R. 2011. "In the Footsteps of the Mafia in Italy." *The Guardian*, February 25. https://www.theguardian.com/travel/2011/feb/26/aspromonte-national-park-calabria-italy.

Currie, B. 2002. "Euthymos of Locri: A Case Study in Heroization in the Classical Period." *Journal of Hellenic Studies* 122:24–44.

Dash, M. 2015. "The Breton Bluebeard." A Blast from the Past, December 28. https://mikedashhistory.com/2015/12/28/the-breton-bluebeard.

Dawe, R. D. 2006. *Sophocles Oedipus Rex*. Rev. ed. Cambridge: Cambridge University Press.

DiGerolamo, T. 2018. *F*ck You, I'm Italian: Why We Italians Are Awesome*. Berkeley, CA: Ulysses Press.

Dougherty, C. 1993. *The Poetics of Colonization: From City to Text in Archaic Greece*. New York: Oxford University Press.

Douglas, J., A. W. Burgess, A. G. Burgess, and R. K. Ressler, eds. 2006. *FBI Crime Classification Manual: A Standard System for Investigating and Classifying Violent Crime*. 2nd ed. (*CCM-II*). San Francisco: Jossey-Bass.

———. 2013. *FBI Crime Classification Manual: A Standard System for Investigating and Classifying Violent Crime*. 3rd ed. (*CCM-III*). Hoboken, NJ: John Wiley & Sons, Inc.

Douglas, J., and M. Olshaker. 1995. *Mind Hunter: Inside the FBI's Elite Serial Crime Unit*. New York: Pocket Books.

Duclos, D. 1998. *The Werewolf Complex: America's Fascination with Violence*. Translated by A. Pingree. Oxford: Berg.

Eberly, S. S. 1997. "Faeries and the Folklore of Disability: Changelings, Hybrids, and the Solitary Fairy." In *The Good People: New Fairylore Essays*, edited by P. Narváez, 227–250. Lexington: University of Kentucky Press.

Fagan, G. G. 2011. *The Lure of the Arena: Social Psychology and the Crowd at the Roman Games*. Cambridge: Cambridge University Press.

Felton, D. 1998. "The Motif of 'Enigmatic Counsel' in Greek and Roman Texts." *Phoenix* 52 (1–2): 42–54.

———. 2012. "Rejecting and Embracing the Monstrous in Ancient Greece and Rome." In *The Ashgate Research Companion to Monsters and the Monstrous*, edited by A. S. Mittman and P. J. Dendle, 103–131. Farnham: Ashgate Press.

———. 2013. "Apuleius' Cupid Considered as a Lamia (*Metamorphoses* 5.17–18)." *Illinois Classical Studies* 38:229–244.

———. 2016. "Witches, Disgust, and Anti-Abortion Propaganda in Imperial Rome." In *The Ancient Emotion of Disgust*, edited by D. Spatharas and D. Lateiner, 198–202, Oxford: Oxford University Press.

———. 2019. "Monsters and Fear of Highway Travel in Ancient Greece and Rome." In *Monster Anthropology: Ethnographic Explorations of Transforming Social Worlds through Monsters*, edited by Y. Musharbash and G. H. Presterudstuen, 29–44. Abingdon: Bloomington Academic.

Fido, M. 1987. *The Crimes, Detection, and Death of Jack the Ripper*. London: Orion Books.

Forney, M. 2003. "Blood in the Streets." Time.com, January 27. https://murderpedia.org/male.G/g/guocheng-duan.htm.

Fuhrmann, C. J. 2012. *Policing the Roman Empire: Soldiers, Administration, and Public Order*. Oxford: Oxford University Press.

Gagarin, M. 2003. "Athenian Homicide Law: Case Studies." In *Athenian Law in Its Democratic Context*, edited by A. Lanni. Republished in C. W. Blackwell, ed., *Dêmos: Classical Athenian Democracy*. The Stoa Consortium, http://www.stoa.org/demos.

———. 2005. "The Unity of Greek Law." In *The Cambridge Companion to Ancient Greek Law*, edited by M. Gagarin and D. Cohen, 29–40. Cambridge: Cambridge University Press.

Gantz, T. 1996. *Early Greek Myth: A Guide to Literary and Artistic Sources*. 2 vols. Baltimore: The Johns Hopkins University Press.

Gaughan, J. E. 2010. *Murder Was Not a Crime: Homicide and Power in the Roman Republic*. Austin: University of Texas Press.

Gibson, C. 2008. *Libanius's Progymnasmata: Model Exercises in Greek Prose Composition and Rhetoric*. Atlanta: Society of Biblical Literature.

Gibson, D. C. 2012. *Legends, Monsters, or Serial Murderers? The Real Story behind an Ancient Crime*. Santa Barbara, CA: ABC-CLIO.

Gloyn, L. 2020. *Tracking Classical Monsters in Popular Culture*. London: Bloomsbury Academic.

Graf, F. 2007. "Untimely Death, Witchcraft, and Divine Vengeance: A Reasoned Epigraphical Catalog." *Zeitschrift für Papyrologie und Epigraphik* 162:139–150.

Graysmith, R. 2007. *Zodiac*. New York: Berkley Books.

Gresseth, G. 1974. "Ancient Greek Folktales: Courting Types." *Texas Studies in Literature and Language* 15 (5): 903–913.

Grünewald, T. 2004. *Bandits in the Roman Empire: Myth and Reality*, translated by J. Drinkwater. London: Routledge.

Hansen, W. F. 2000. "The Winning of Hippodameia." *Transactions of the American Philological Society* 130:19–40.

Harder, A. 2012. *Callimachus* Aetia: *Introduction, Text, Translation, and Commentary*. 2 vols. Oxford: Oxford University Press.

Harding, P., ed. and trans. 2008. *The Story of Athens: The Fragments of the Local Chronicles of Attika*. New York: Routledge.

Hare, R. D. 1993. *Without Conscience: The Disturbing World of the Psychopaths among Us*. New York: The Guilford Press.

Harris, Thomas. 1988. *The Silence of the Lambs*. New York: St. Martin's Press.

Harris, Trudier. 2009. *The Scary Mason–Dixon Line: African American Writers and the South*. Baton Rouge: Louisiana State University Press.

Hawes, G. 2014. *Rationalizing Myth in Antiquity*. Oxford: Oxford University Press.

The History of Sawney Beane and His Family. [1800?] [London?]: Printed for the Company of Running Stationers. Electronic resource. Reproduction of the original from the Bodleian Library (Oxford). Farmington Hills, MI: Thomson Gale, 2003.

Hockley, N. 2019. "The Real Legacy of the Last Decade Will Be Mass Shootings." *InStyle*, December 13. https://www.instyle.com/news/mass-shootings-2010s-decade-legacy.

Howard, A. 2010. "Serial Killers as Practical Moral Skeptics: A Historical Survey with Interviews." In *Serial Killers: Philosophy for Everyone*, edited by S. Waller, 53–65. Chichester: Wiley-Blackwell.

Hughes, D. D. 1991. *Human Sacrifice in Ancient Greece*. London: Routledge.

Hurwit, J. M. 2006. "Lizards, Lions, and the Uncanny in Early Greek Art." *Hesperia* 75 (1): 121–136.

Kaufman, D. B. 1932. "Poisons and Poisoning among the Romans." *Classical Philology* 27 (2): 156–167.

Kazantzidis, G. 2018. "Haunted Minds, Haunted Places: Topographies of Insanity in Greek and Roman Paradoxography." In *Landscapes of Dread in Classical Antiquity: Negative Emotion in Natural and Constructed Spaces*, edited by D. Felton, 226–258. London and New York: Routledge.

Keppel, R. 1997. *Signature Killers*. New York: Pocket Books.

Kitchell, K. F., Jr. 2014. *Animals in the Ancient World from A to Z*. London: Routledge.

Lämmle, R. 2013. *Poetik des Satyrspiels*. Heidelberg: Universitätsverlag Winter.

Larson, E. 2003. *The Devil in the White City: Murder, Magic, and Madness at the Fair That Changed America*. New York: Crown Publishers.

Little, B. 2020. "Did Serial Killer H. H. Holmes Really Build a 'Murder Castle'?" *History*, January 23. https://www.history.com/news/murder-castle-h-h-holmes-chicago.

Livingstone, N. 2001. *A Commentary on Isocrates's Bousiris*. *Mnemosyne*, Suppl. 223. Leiden: Brill.

Loomis, W. T. 1972. "The Nature of Premeditation in Athenian Homicide Law." *Journal of Hellenic Studies* 92:86–95.

Mayor, A. 2000. *The First Fossil Hunters: Paleontology in Greek and Roman Times*. Princeton, NJ: Princeton University Press.

———. 2003. *Greek Fire, Poison Arrows, and Scorpion Bombs: Biological and Chemical Warfare in the Ancient World*. Woodstock, NY: Overlook Duckworth.

————. 2010. *The Poison King: The Life and Legend of Mithradates, Rome's Deadliest Enemy*. Princeton, NJ: Princeton University Press.

McDevitt, A. S. 1970. "Andocides 1, 78 and the Decree of Patroclides." *Hermes* 98 (4): 503–505.

McPhee, I. 2006. "Herakles and Bousiris by the Telos Painter." *Antike Kunst* 49:43–56.

Meehan, B. 1994. "Son of Cain or Son of Sam: The Monster as Serial Killer in *Beowulf*." *Connecticut Review* 16 (2): 1–7.

Miller, M. 2015. "Bulgarian Archaeologists Find Evidence of 2,700-Year-Old Thracian Child Sacrifice." *Ancient Origins* online, April 19. https://www.ancient-origins.net/news-history-archaeology/bulgarian-archaeologists-find-evidence-sacrifice-thracian-child-020304.

Miller, S. G. 2004. *Ancient Greek Athletics*. New Haven, CT: Yale University Press.

Morrison, H., and H. Goldberg. 2004. *My Life among the Serial Killers: Inside the Minds of the World's Most Notorious Murderers*. New York: HarperCollins.

Mueller, M. 2018. "Dreamscape and Dread in Euripides's *Iphigenia among the Taurians*." In *Landscapes of Dread in Classical Antiquity: Negative Emotion in Natural and Constructed Spaces*, edited by D. Felton, 77–94. London: Routledge.

Nagy, G. 2013. *The Ancient Greek Hero in 24 Hours*. Cambridge, MA: The Belknap Press of Harvard University Press.

Newton, M. 2006. *The Encyclopedia of Serial Killers*. 2nd ed. New York: Checkmark Books.

Oakley, B. 2008. *Evil Genes: Why Rome Fell, Hitler Rose, Enron Failed, and My Sister Stole My Mother's Boyfriend*. Amherst, NY: Prometheus Books.

Ogden, D. 2009. *Magic, Witchcraft, and Ghosts in the Greek and Roman Worlds*. 2nd ed. Oxford: Oxford University Press.

————. 2013. *Dragons, Serpents, and Slayers in the Classical and Early Christian Worlds: A Sourcebook*. Oxford: Oxford University Press.

————. 2021. *The Werewolf in the Ancient World*. Oxford: Oxford University Press.

Onyulo, T. 2017. "In This Nation, Children's Body Parts Are Sacrificed for Witchcraft." *USA Today* online, May 1. https://www.usatoday.com/story/news/world/2017/05/01/uganda-human-children-sacrifice/100741148/.

Orschiedt, J. 2005. "The Head Burials from Ofnet Cave: An Example of Warlike Conflict in the Mesolithic." In *Warfare, Violence and Slavery in Prehistory: Proceedings of a Prehistoric Society Conference at Sheffield University*, edited by M. P. Pearson and I. J. N. Thorpe, 67–73. BAR International Series 1374. Oxford: The Basingstoke Press by Archaeopress.

Padilla, M. W. 1998. *The Myths of Herakles in Ancient Greece: Survey and Profile*. Lanham, MD: University Press of America.

Parker, R. 1996. *Miasma: Pollution and Purification in Early Greek Religion*. Oxford: Clarendon Press.

Philips, F. C. 1978. "Heracles." *The Classical World* 71 (7): 431–440.

Phillips, D. D. 2008. *Avengers of Blood: Homicide in Athenian Law and Custom from Draco to Demosthenes*. Stuttgart: Franz Steiner Verlag.

Plastow, C. 2020. *Homicide in the Attic Orators: Rhetoric, Ideology, and Context*. Abingdon: Routledge.

Ramage, C. T. 1868. *The Nooks and By-ways of Italy: Wanderings in Search of Its Ancient Remains and Modern Superstitions*. Liverpool: Edward Howell.

Ramsland, K. 2005. *The Human Predator: A Historical Chronicle of Serial Murder and Forensic Investigation*. New York: Berkley Books.

Resnick, P. J. 2016. "Filicide in the United States." *Indian Journal of Psychiatry* 58 (Suppl. 2): S203–S209. https://www.ncbi.nlm.nih.gov/pmc/articles/PMC5282617/.

Rule, A. 1980. *The Stranger beside Me*. New York: Norton.

Schechter, H. 1994. *Depraved: The Shocking True Story of America's First Serial Killer*. New York: Pocket Books.

———. 2003. *The Serial Killer Files*. New York: Ballantine Books.

Schechter, H., and D. Everitt. 2006. *The A to Z Encyclopedia of Serial Killers*. New York: Pocket Books.

Schmid, D. 2005. *Natural Born Celebrities: Serial Killers in American Culture*. Chicago: University of Chicago Press.

Scobie, A. 1977. "An Ancient Greek Drakos-Tale in Apuleius' *Metamorphoses* VIII, 19–21." *Journal of American Folklore* 90 (357):339–343.

Sidwell, B. 2010. "Gaius Caligula's Mental Illness." *Classical World* 103 (2): 183–206.

Simpson, P. 2000. *Psycho Paths: Tracking the Serial Killer through Contemporary American Film and Fiction*. Carbondale: Southern Illinois University Press.

Smith, T. R. 2008. *Child 44*. New York: Grand Central Publishing.

Spitznagel, E. 2018. "Inside the Creepy Underground World of Serial Killer Art, Where Manson Means Money." *Observer*, October 29. https://observer.com /2018/10/serial-killer-art-lucrative-charles-manson-richard-ramirez/.

Stafford, E. 2012. *Herakles*. London: Routledge.

Startrek.com staff. 2016. "Michael Meyers' Halloween Mask WAS Shatner's Face." StarTrek.com, October 31. http://www.startrek.com/article/michael-myers-hal loween-mask-was-shatners-face.

Stern, J., trans. and comm. 1996. *Palaephatus Peri Apistôn: On Unbelievable Tales*. Wauconda, IL: Bolchazy-Carducci.

Strand, G. 2012. *Killer on the Road: Violence and the American Interstate*. Austin: University of Texas Press.

Syme, R. 1986. *The Augustan Aristocracy*. Oxford: Clarendon Press.

Thompson, S. 1955–1958. *Motif-Index of Folk-Literature*. Bloomington: Indiana University Press.

Thumiger, C. 2017. *A History of the Mind and Mental Health in Classical Greek Medical Thought*. Cambridge: Cambridge University Press.

Uther, H.-J. 2004. *The Types of International Folktales: A Classification and Bibliography, Based on the System of Antii Aarne and Stith Thompson*. 3 vols. FF Communications No. 284. Helsinki: Academia Scientiarum Fennica.

Van Hoof, A. J. L. 1988. "Ancient Robbers: Reflections behind the Facts." *Ancient Society* 19:105–124.

Vronsky, P. 2004. *Serial Killers: The Method and Madness of Monsters*. New York: Berkley Books.

———. 2007. *Female Serial Killers: How and Why Women Become Monsters*. New York: Berkley Books.

Wade, L. 2018. "Feeding the Gods: Hundreds of Skulls Reveal Massive Scale of Human Sacrifice in Aztec Capital." *Science* online, June 21. https://www .sciencemag.org/news/2018/06/feeding-gods-hundreds-skulls-reveal-massive -scale-human-sacrifice-aztec-capital.

Ward, A. G. 1970. *The Quest for Theseus*. New York: Praeger.

Warner, M. 1994. *From the Beast to the Blonde: On Fairy Tales and Their Tellers*. New York: Farrar, Straus and Giroux.

Williams, T. 1996. *Hearths of Darkness: The Family in the American Horror Film*. Madison, NJ: Fairleigh Dickinson University Press.

Woodward, I. 1979. *The Werewolf Delusion*. New York: Paddington Press.

Yam, A. 2014. "Nick Broomfield's 'Tales of the Grim Sleeper' Says the LAPD Ignored a Serial Killer Because His Victims Were Poor and Nonwhite." IndieWire, November 11. https://www.indiewire.com/2014/11/nick-broomfields-tales-of-the -grim-sleeper-says-the-lapd-ignored-a-serial-killer-because-his-victims-were -poor-and-nonwhite-125476/.

Image Credits

p. vi   Photo by Marie-La Nguyen. Wilimedia Commons, https://commons
         .wikimedia.org/wiki/File:Theseus_Minotaur_BM_Vase_E84_n3.jpg.

p. 17   Wikimedia Commons, https://commons.wikimedia.org/wiki/File
         :Corrado_Giaquinto_-_Medea,_1750s.jpg.

p. 30   Photo by K. M. Sullivan. Wikimedia Commons, https://commons
         .wikimedia.org/wiki/File:FH000036.jpg.

p. 41   Wikimedia Commons, https://commons.wikimedia.org/wiki/File
         :Collier-Clytemnestra_after_the_murder.jpg.

p. 44   Wikimedia Commons, https://commons.wikimedia.org/wiki/File:Nerón
         _ante_el_cadáver_de_su_madre,_Agripina_la_Menor_(Museo_del
         _Prado).jpg.

p. 50   Wikimedia Commons, https://commons.wikimedia.org/wiki/File
         :Thomas_Degeorge_Ulysse.jpg.

p. 62   Map illustration by Michele Angel. Used with permission.

p. 68   Wikimedia Commons, https://commons.wikimedia.org/wiki/File
         :Unidentified_Sicarius,_female.jpg.

p. 74   Wikimedia Commons, https://commons.wikimedia.org/wiki/File
         :Johann_Köler_-_Hercules_Removes_Cerberus_from_the_Gates_of
         _Hell,_1855.jpg.

p. 78   Wikimedia Commons, https://commons.wikimedia.org/wiki/File
         :Woodcut_illustration_of_Agrippina_Minor,_Nero_and_Claudius
         _-_Penn_Provenance_Project.jpg.

p. 80   Wikimedia Commons, https://commons.wikimedia.org/wiki/File
         :Sylvestre_Locuste_essaye_le_poison(2).jpg.

p. 91   Wikimedia Commons, https://upload.wikimedia.org/wikipedia
         /commons/8/8d/Herakles_Bousiris_Staatliche_Antikensammlungen
         _2428.jpg.

p. 96   Photo by Robert Valette, 2008. Wikimedia Commons, https://upload
         .wikimedia.org/wikipedia/commons/thumb/c/c2/Roquepertuse_Portique
         .jpg/1280px-Roquepertuse_Portique.jpg.

p. 103   Map illustration by Michele Angel. Used with permission.

Index